T0305307

Personnel Economics in Sports

NEW HORIZONS IN THE ECONOMICS OF SPORT

Series Editors: Wladimir Andreff, *Department of Economics, University of Paris 1 Panthéon Sorbonne, France* and Marc Lavoie, *Department of Economics, University of Ottawa, Canada*

For decades, the economics of sport was regarded as a hobby for a handful of professional economists who were primarily involved in other areas of research. In recent years, however, the significance of the sports economy as a percentage of GDP has expanded dramatically. This has coincided with an equivalent rise in the volume of economic literature devoted to the study of sport.

This series provides a vehicle for deeper analyses of the demand for sport, cost–benefit analysis of sport, sporting governance, the economics of professional sports and leagues, individual sports, trade in the sporting goods industry, media coverage, sponsoring and numerous related issues. It contributes to the further development of sports economics by welcoming new approaches and highlighting original research in both established and newly emerging sporting activities. The series publishes the best theoretical and empirical work from well-established researchers and academics, as well as from talented newcomers in the field.

Titles in the series include:

The Econometrics of Sport
Edited by Plácido Rodríguez, Stefan Késenne and Jaume García

Public Policy and Professional Sports
International and Australian Experiences
John K. Wilson and Richard Pomfret

The Economics of Competitive Sports
Edited by Plácido Rodríguez, Stefan Késenne and Ruud Koning

Disequilibrium Sports Economics
Competitive Imbalance and Budget Constraints
Edited by Wladimir Andreff

Sport Through the Lens of Economic History
Edited by John K. Wilson and Richard Pomfret

The Economics of Sports Betting
Edited by Plácido Rodríguez, Brad R. Humphreys and Robert Simmons

Sports Economics Uncut
Brian Goff

Personnel Economics in Sports
Edited by Neil Longley

Personnel Economics in Sports

Edited by

Neil Longley

Full Professor, Isenberg School of Management, University of Massachusetts Amherst, USA

NEW HORIZONS IN THE ECONOMICS OF SPORT

Edward Elgar
PUBLISHING

Cheltenham, UK • Northampton, MA, USA

Published by
Edward Elgar Publishing Limited
The Lypiatts
15 Lansdown Road
Cheltenham
Glos GL50 2JA
UK

Edward Elgar Publishing, Inc.
William Pratt House
9 Dewey Court
Northampton
Massachusetts 01060
USA

A catalogue record for this book
is available from the British Library

Library of Congress Control Number: 2018944730

This book is available electronically in the **Elgar**online
Economics subject collection
DOI 10.4337/9781786430915

ISBN 978 1 78643 090 8 (cased)
ISBN 978 1 78643 091 5 (eBook)

Typeset by Servis Filmsetting Ltd, Stockport, Cheshire
Printed and bound by CPI Group (UK) Ltd, Croydon, CR0 4YY

Contents

List of figures   vii
List of contributors   viii
Preface   ix

1. An introduction to personnel economics and its application
    to sport   1
    Neil Longley

PART I: RECRUITING AND HUMAN CAPITAL
           DEVELOPMENT

2. The failed promise of the draft in the NFL and NBA   26
    David Berri

3. The golden generation: the personnel economics of youth
    recruitment in European professional soccer   47
    Joachim Prinz and Daniel Weimar

PART II: PAY, PERFORMANCE, AND INCENTIVES

4. Determining the drivers of player valuation and compensation
    in professional sport: traditional economic approaches and
    emerging advances   73
    Christian Deutscher

5. Multi-period contracts as risk management in professional
    sports   88
    Joel Maxcy

PART III: TEAMWORK, AND THE IMPACTS OF
           MANAGEMENT

6. Impacts of co-worker heterogeneity on team performance   112
    Robert Simmons

7. Pay dispersion and productivity in sports   136
    Leo Kahane

8. Magicians, scapegoats and firefighters: the peculiar role of head
    coaches in professional soccer   168
    Bernd Frick

Index   185

Figures

3.1 Expenses for youth recruitment in the first and second
     Bundesliga   52
3.2 Distribution of soccer players by month of birth   62
3.3 Distribution of births per month in Germany   63
3.4 Relative age net effects as the difference in percentage points
     between general birth rates and representation among soccer
     players   64
7.1 Kernel density graphs of team payrolls pre-lockout
     (2001–2002 to 2003–2004) and post-lockout (2005–2006 to
     2007–2008) (millions of 2007 dollars)   154
7.2 Box-plots for within-team salary standard deviation, pre-
     lockout (2001–2002 to 2003–2004) and post-lockout
     (2005–2006 to 2007–2008)   155
8.1 Points per game realized by dismissed coaches (0), substitute
     coaches (1) and permanent coaches (2) in the German
     Bundesliga, 1997/1998 to 2016/2017   170
8.2 Realized versus predicted points   172
8.3 Points differential and dismissals   172

Contributors

David Berri is Professor of Economics at Southern Utah University, USA.

Christian Deutscher is Professor of Sport Economics at the University of Bielefeld, Germany.

Bernd Frick is Professor of Organizational Economics at Paderborn University, Germany and is Professor of Sport Economics at Seeburg Castle University, Austria.

Leo Kahane is the Michael A. Ruane Distinguished Chair in Economics at Providence College, USA.

Neil Longley is a Full Professor in the Isenberg School of Management at the University of Massachusetts Amherst, USA.

Joel Maxcy is Professor of Sport Management and Director of the Center for Sport Management at Drexel University, USA.

Joachim Prinz is a Professor in the Mercator School of Management at the University of Duisburg-Essen, Germany.

Robert Simmons is Professor of Economics at the Lancaster University Management School, UK.

Daniel Weimar is a Lecturer in the Mercator School of Management at the University of Duisburg-Essen, Germany.

Preface

This book examines personnel economics within the context of the sport industry.

The field of personnel economics studies the intra-firm relationship between the employer and employee. It examines all aspects of the relationship, right from the initial hiring of the employee, through to the employee's eventual departure from the organization, and everything in between.

Lazear and Oyer (2012) identify the five primary aspects of the employment relationship that comprise the field of personnel economics: matching firms with workers (often known as recruiting and selection), incentives, compensation, skill development, and the organization of work. They note that, while personnel economics is a sub-field of labor economics, there are many topics in labor economics that are not part of personnel economics. Any topics that pertain to the overall market-wide interaction of firms and workers – for example, estimating an earnings function that shows the return to certain skills – are outside the choice set of a firm's managers, and are hence not within the realm of personnel economics. In personnel economics, the focus is on the firm, and how economics can be used to help managers make better personnel decisions.

In essence, personnel economics is a field that applies microeconomic theory to topics normally found within the human resource management (HRM) literature. Personnel economics differs from the HRM literature in that the former takes a 'rational actor' approach to the topic – from the economist's perspective, the traditional HRM literature suffers from the lack of an explicit and rigorous theory of human behavior, and hence is of limited value in consistently explaining and predicting organizational outcomes. In personnel economics, both employers and employees are assumed to be rational, self-interested, utility maximizers, whose interests are not always congruent. Much of the theory in personnel economics is rooted in such core themes as asymmetric information, the principal-agent relationship, monitoring, and optimal contract design.

The origins of personnel economics can be traced back to the early 1900s – a time when the fields of HRM and economics were rooted largely in the same foundations (Kaufman, 2000). By the 1930s, however, the two disciplines began to take very different intellectual paths, and it was not until the late 1980s that a reintegration began to occur – a reintegration driven almost exclusively by the seminal works of Stanford University economist Edward Lazear. Lazear's contributions are so extensive that he is often viewed as the single-handed founder of the modern field of personnel economics. In the 30 years that have passed since Lazear's earliest works in the area, the field of personnel economics has grown immensely, evidenced, in part, by the fact that it now has its own JEL code (M5).

Because of the field's focus on intra-organizational relationships, most researchers have been economists from business schools, rather than economics departments. Much of the research has been theoretical rather than empirical – largely due to data availability issues. Empirical work in the area requires researchers to have access to internal, firm-level data, and is thus dependent on firms voluntarily opening their personnel records. Further complications arise because detailed firm-level data on employees is, by its nature, proprietary and confidential, and is therefore not generally accessible for replication and verification by others. In his various writings, Lazear has often noted the difficulty in empirically testing theories within personnel economics (see, for example, Lazear, 1999).

This is where the professional sport industry plays a role. The employer-employee relationship in professional sport is much more visible and transparent than in almost any other industry. As a result, the researcher has information on a host of demographic variables pertaining to individual employees (i.e. players), such as their age, race, national origin, tenure with the organization, previous experience and training, etc. In addition, the researcher knows what each employee gets paid, who their co-workers (i.e. teammates) are, who their managers/coaches are, etc. Equally critically, the performance/productivity of pro athletes can be more objectively measured than in most other occupations. This array of data not only allows the researcher to test the relationship between critical personnel economics variables, like, say, pay and performance, but also enables the researcher to control for a wide range of other factors that may impact the relationship.

Not only can sports be a means to inform the personnel economics literature, the reverse is also true – the personnel economics literature can provide insight into better understanding the sport industry, which has become a focus unto itself for some economists. The field of sports economics has grown immensely in recent decades, in part because of sport's broad popular appeal, but also because its industry structure – essentially a bilateral monopoly – is not found in most other industries.

While there have been many journal articles written by sports economists that would fall within the topic area (personnel economics in sport), there is an overall absence in the literature of any attempt to pull this body of knowledge together into a more unified theme. These journal articles, by their very nature, have been 'stand-alones', and, in most cases, the authors never explicitly identify that their work falls within the broader field of personnel economics. This book will attempt to show that these individual works, when looked at more broadly, all deal with the employment relationship in a firm. As such, the book presents the important research findings in a more systematic, structured, and unified way, and shows that sports economics can inform all facets of the employment relationship – from recruiting and selection, to pay and performance, to work team design.

The book is organized into eight chapters. In Chapter 1, Neil Longley first provides a basic overview of the broad field of personnel economics, examining some of its key research questions and approaches. He then discusses how this broader field can be applied specifically to professional sport, particularly focusing on the peculiar institutional mechanisms in sport that potentially impact this application. Chapter 1 serves as both a background and a contextual foundation for the chapters that follow.

The remaining chapters are organized around the functional areas of personnel economics. Part I (Chapters 2 and 3) deals with recruiting, Part II (Chapters 4 and 5) with pay, performance, and incentives, and Part III (Chapters 6 through 8) with the organization of work, which includes the functioning of work teams and also the roles and impacts of management.

In Part I, the two chapters on recruiting illustrate the fundamentally different institutional structures found in North American pro leagues versus European soccer – in North America, the entry point for players into the pro leagues is through the draft system, whereas in Europe, individual clubs recruit players at a very young age and develop them through their own training academies.

The North American system is discussed in Chapter 2, written by David Berri. He focuses on the player drafts in the National Football League (NFL) and the National Basketball Association (NBA), and argues that the collective track-record of teams is not particularly strong in being able to identify which players will ultimately be the most productive at the pro level – in other words, the draft-position at which a player is selected is not always a reliable indicator of his future success as a pro. With the NFL, Berri focuses on quarterbacks, and attributes the results to the general inability of a player's college performance to predict his performance as a pro. In the NBA, he argues that the reason for the lack of predictability in the draft is not so much that college performance is unrelated to a player's pro performance – in fact, some college statistics are correlated with productivity as a pro – but more due to the fact that NBA teams tend to make systematic errors in evaluating the information presented to them.

They tend to overvalue, for example, both a player's scoring in college, and the number of wins of the team for which he played. In other words, the factors that drive a player's draft position are not necessarily the same factors that drive that player's contribution to team wins at the NBA level.

Chapter 3, written by Joachim Prinz and Daniel Weimar, continues with the recruitment theme. Prinz and Weimar focus on the youth training academy system in German soccer. They note that the academy system acts not only as a long-term screening function (i.e. a long-term probation), but also has a training and development purpose whereby teams impart both general soccer-related skills to youth as well as club-specific skills, knowledge, and attitudes. From a recruiting perspective, the training academies allow the clubs to gain private information about players, helping the club to ultimately determine the quality of the club-player match. Prinz and Weimar report that only 2 to 5 percent of youth players in an academy ever go on to enter professional soccer, so, from the club's perspective, the return on investment from these players must be sufficient to cover the costs associated with the other 95 to 98 percent who do not make it to the pro level. They also detail several impediments to effectively identifying the best youth players, including the continued long-term persistence of the so-called 'relative age effect'.

Taken together, Chapters 2 and 3 illustrate how difficult it is to forecast future performance in sport, whether it be a North American-style draft system or the academy system of European soccer. This difficulty occurs even when worker (i.e. player) performance is much more easily measured in the sport industry than it is in non-sport industries. As much as human resource professionals may like to be believe that they can consistently identify 'stars' well in advance, the evidence suggests otherwise. This brings into question the amount of resources that firms – whether they be sport or non-sport – should be devoting to such forecasting.

Part II of the book – containing Chapters 4 and 5 – examines the relationship between pay, performance, and incentives. These are, by far, the most studied topics in personnel economics. In Chapter 4, Christian Deutscher provides an overview of the literature studying player performance and salaries. He argues that the 'traditional' approaches tended to view the drivers of salary for a player as falling into one of four broad categories – experience, performance, talent, and popularity. However, he notes that using just these traditional drivers is deficient, in that, collectively, they usually fail to explain 30 to 40 percent of the variation in salaries. He then discusses new advances in the literature that attempt to better incorporate into salary models factors like non-cognitive skills and work habits, and explains how researchers are now examining such player-characteristics as leadership skills, performance under pressure, and performance volatility to determine which, if any, of these factors may impact salary. Deutscher also notes how traditional measures are being enhanced by technological advances that better capture on-field performance, and by new metrics that attempt to summarize a variety of, sometimes disparate, player-performance outcomes into a single comprehensive statistic, such as wins-above-replacement (WAR).

In Chapter 5, Joel Maxcy examines issues related to contract-length in sport. He notes that the literature has focused both on identifying the rationales for multi-period contracts, and on measuring the impacts of such contracts on players' incentives to shirk. Maxcy is particularly interested in the observed phenomena in baseball where players on long-term contracts also receive a salary premium – a result that is counter to the standard hypothesis that workers on long-term contracts transfer their performance risk to clubs, and hence should be willing to accept a salary penalty for such transference. Maxcy discusses a possible reason for this empirical finding – high-skilled free agents are difficult to replace, and teams may be willing to enter long-term contracts to protect against future increases in the market price for these players' services. In his empirical work, Maxcy finds that both player performance and free agent status (as opposed to players that are only arbitration-eligible) independently increase the probability of a player receiving a long-term contract.

Part III includes Chapters 6, 7, and 8, and examines the economics of workplace interactions, including building effective work teams, and assessing the role and importance of management. Robert Simmons authors Chapter 6, and his focus is co-worker heterogeneity. He examines the extent to which workers impact each other's productivity. Simmons reviews some of the key literature examining the impact on team performance of factors such as (i) potential productivity spillovers across teammates, (ii) heterogeneous abilities among teammates, and (iii) cultural diversity within a team. In addition to these, he notes how pay dispersion within a team may also be important to team performance, and highlights some of the key literature in that area.

In Chapter 7, Leo Kahane more comprehensively examines this pay dispersion issue first raised by Simmons in Chapter 6. Kahane contrasts the two competing theories related to pay dispersion – the tournament model versus the fairness model. In Kahane's empirical work, he examines pay dispersion in the National Hockey League in the three seasons just prior to, and the three seasons just after, the 2004–05 season-long work stoppage that ultimately resulted in a collective bargaining agreement that drastically compressed salaries in the league. His empirical results lend strong support for the fairness model, meaning that lower within-team pay disparities result in, all else equal, higher team performance.

Chapter 8, written by Bernd Frick, examines the impacts of coaches on team performance. Frick focuses on soccer, and analyzes the impact of head coach dismissals on the subsequent performance of the team. He examines some of the methodological difficulties in studying such a question, and highlights some of the important research in the area. He notes that, while the specific results vary widely across papers, there seems to be no strongly consistent evidence that coaching changes fundamentally improve team performance.

Taken together, the chapters in this book are intended to provide the reader with a sense of the types of sport-related work being done within each of the broad functional areas of personnel economics. Each chapter contains a thorough literature review that, while not exhaustive, provides the reader with a sense of the breadth and depth of the work being done in the area, and can help inform the various ways in the which the literature can move forward, both in a sport and non-sport context.

Neil Longley

REFERENCES

Kaufman, Bruce (2000) 'Personnel/human resource management: its roots as applied economics', *History of Political Economy*, **32** (Suppl 1), 227–256.

Lazear, Edward (1999) 'Globalisation and the market for team-mates', *Economic Journal*, **109**, C15–C40.

Lazear, Edward and Paul Oyer (2012) 'Personnel economics', in Robert Gibbons and John Roberts (eds), *The Handbook of Organizational Economics*, Princeton, NJ: Princeton University Press, pp. 479–519.

1. An introduction to personnel economics and its application to sport

Neil Longley

1.1 A BASIC PRIMER ON THE APPROACHES OF PERSONNEL ECONOMICS

In order to provide a framework for studying personnel economics within the specific context of sport, it is important to first understand the approaches used in the broader (i.e. non-sport) field of personnel economics. With this base, one can then better appreciate how the concepts can be applied to sport, and how the institutional peculiarities of the sport industry sometimes complicate these applications.

The personnel economics literature has now become vast, so the overview provided here provides more of a high-level primer on the basic conceptual approaches in the field, rather than a detailed and exhaustive examination of specific topics and issues.[1]

Recruiting

The recruiting process involves the firm conducting a search to fill a vacant position – by its nature, it is the first step in the employer-employee relationship. The process involves the firm first generating a pool of applicants, and then using various screening mechanisms to select the best candidate from that pool. The goal of the firm is to hire the most productive employee, relative to the costs of finding that employee.

Since screening is costly, a key choice variable for the firm is to decide the amount of screening it will undertake for any given job. This decision will be driven by a number of factors. First, the nature of the job will matter. For example, lower-skilled jobs will tend to have more routine and structured tasks, so the potential variability in performance across employees will often be relatively small. In this case, one employee will be almost as productive as any other, and firms may not expend many resources on the recruitment process. However, as one moves up the job hierarchy in an organization, jobs inherently become more complex, multi-dimensional, and less well-defined. With these jobs, subtle, difficult to measure differences across applicants may ultimately result in large performance differences. This greater dispersion in potential performance – compared to the situation with lower-skilled jobs – forces firms to adopt more intensive hiring processes so as to identify those who are most capable.

The firm's production technology – in the sense of how various jobs in the organization interact with each other – also impacts the search. In the most basic case, a worker's productivity is predetermined and set, and is independent of that individual's co-workers. While applicants may differ in productivity, that productivity is unrelated to where an applicant works. Thus, there is no firm-specific matching, in the sense that one candidate would be a better 'fit' for that particular organization than would another. Instead, the search merely involves the organization identifying the candidate(s) with the highest potential productivity.

A more complex scenario is where a candidate's productivity is a function of the organization for which they work – i.e. the candidate's value is higher to one organization than to another. The search task then becomes more than simply identifying the most productive applicant, and instead becomes more about determining whether the candidate is the best 'match'; Oyer and Schaefer (2010) term this 'match-specific productivity'. Match-specific productivity results from complementarities between the candidate and the organization – either complementarities between the candidate's skills and the skills of existing employees, or complementarities between the candidate's skills and the production processes of the organization. The hiring decision is now much more complicated, in that a firm must not only seek to determine the candidate's individual attributes/ quality, but must now also estimate how well that candidate will interact with the firm's existing workers. In situations where the screening process fails to identify an effective employer-employee match, the result is often employee turnover. Such turnover is potentially costly to the organization, not only because it requires a new search, but because training costs incurred for the departed employee are not recoverable.

At the operational level, recruiting is essentially an exercise in forecasting – it seeks to predict the future job performance of applicants. For firms, an applicant's past performance is often one of the most critical screening mechanisms used to forecast future performance. However, information on a worker's past performance, particularly as it relates to the specific job in question, is often difficult to obtain. First, for younger workers, because they are relatively new to the labor market, little or no measures of past performance would even exist. Second, even when employees are experienced, their past performance is with another firm, and is often difficult for other employers to evaluate. Job-seekers also have an incentive to overstate their past performance, particularly where any new employer would have difficulty verifying such information.

Because the screening process is inherently characterized by bilateral asymmetric information – i.e. the candidate knows more about their own skills than does the prospective employer, and the employer has more information about the specifics of the job and the work environment than does the prospective employee – the parties will often attempt to 'signal' their worthiness and quality to the other. The concept of signaling was developed by Spence (1973). An employer may use its public reputation as a signal that it is a good place to work. For job-seekers, a signal is a credential that, while not directly related to the duties of a job, is intended to proxy those workers' productivity. In most labor markets, education is perhaps the most common signal. Factors like education are considered 'signals', in that they do not necessarily measure attributes directly related to the job in question, but rather are proxies for other qualities that are presumed to be related to job performance. For a signal to be effective as a separating mechanism, high-quality candidates must be able to obtain the signal at a lower cost than low-quality candidates; for example, higher-aptitude individuals should be able to obtain a graduate degree at lower cost (in terms of effort) than lower-aptitude individuals. Signals tend to be most effective in situations where there is a limited amount of other information about the candidate; for example, with workers new to the labor force.

Firms can bring new employees into the organization in one of two basic ways. They can hire largely at the entry level, and eventually promote these individuals to fill higher positions in the organization. Or, for at least some higher-level positions, the firm can go outside and 'raid' workers from other firms.

When a firm hires/raids workers from other firms, it will do so only if the worker is more valuable to the raiding firm than to the individual's current employer. One possibility is that both firms (the raider and the current employer) assess the individual's future productivity similarly, but that the raider can convert this productivity into greater revenues, say due to firm size or market share. Another possibility is that the raider is more optimistic about the individual's future productivity than is the current employer – estimating future performance is an inexact science, particularly where job duties are complex, and where difficult-to-measure 'intangible' factors are critical factors to job success. Different firms may simply have different subjective assessments about the employee's potential.

However, raiding firms face the problems of both the 'winner's curse' and adverse selection. With the winner's curse, the raiding firm is, by definition, the firm in the marketplace that places the most optimistic estimate on the individual's future productivity, and hence may overpay for that person. With adverse selection, the raiding firms may disproportionately attract lower-productivity candidates, since these individuals' current employers will make less effort to retain them, relative to that firm's more productive employees.

As a supplement to pre-employment screening, employers can use an employee's 'probationary period' as an additional source of information – in essence, part of the screening occurs *after* the person is hired. This probationary information is particularly valuable because it is based on observing actual on-the-job performance; information that was clearly not available at the time of the hire. In these cases, a natural sorting occurs during the probationary period, where both employers and employees further evaluate the quality of the match. Thus, one would expect turnover to be higher for more recent hires than for those who have been with the organization for a longer period of time.

Furthermore, when firms require new employees to go through a probationary period, it facilitates a natural sorting and self-selection; it can discourage unproductive workers from applying, since they know they are likely to be 'discovered'. In conjunction with this, employers often pay probationary workers much less than those that have achieved permanent status; this low wage during probation may not be a problem for productive employees, since they can more than recoup this by earning higher wages after they have achieved permanency. However, for unproductive workers, i.e. those who are unlikely to make it past probation, this low wage is intended to discourage them from applying to the organization, and instead seek work with firms at which they are better suited (and, presumably, at which they will be paid more). In effect, then, the low probationary wage acts a screening mechanism, and serves to decrease adverse selection, a situation where workers self-select themselves into jobs for which they are unsuited. The key decision point for the employer is to set the probationary wage and the permanent wage at levels such that it encourages productive workers to apply and discourages unproductive workers from applying.

Because the exact future productivity of applicants is not known to the firm at the time of hiring, firms must make estimates of this productivity. Some applicants will inevitably present more 'risk' than others. For example, assume there are two candidates, A and B, and that both have an expected mean productivity of 100. Candidate A, however, is riskier, in that they have a higher standard deviation in productivity – assume they have a 50 percent chance of having a productivity of 150, and a 50 percent chance of having a productivity of 50. Candidate B, on the other hand, is a 'safe' choice, whose productivity is known with certainty to be 100. Lazear and Oyer (2012) argue that organizations may prefer the riskier candidate, in that they provide a greater option value to the firm – if the worker turns out to be a high performer, the organization is better-off than if they had hired the safe candidate, but if the worker turns out to be a low-performer then they are terminated and the organization does not bear the costs of this low performance.

This advantage to hiring riskier workers is lessened to the extent that organizations must engage in long-term employment contracts, and to the extent that termination and severance costs are incurred. This potential preference for riskier workers often translates into a preference for younger and/or inexperienced workers, since their future productivity is much more uncertain and difficult to predict compared to workers that have been in the labor force for many years – in effect, younger workers have a greater potential 'upside'. Risky workers who are younger are particularly valuable to the firm, since the firm can potentially benefit from the upside for a longer period of time, compared to workers who are closer to the end of their careers. The value to the firm of a risky worker is also a function of the length of time the firm can retain the employee at below-market costs. If, for example, workers that turn out to be high performers are quickly bid-away in the market, firms will be less able to capture the benefits of the worker's upside. This possibility is lessened where there is asymmetric information about the worker's abilities – i.e. the current employer is more aware of the high-quality of the worker than are other firms – and/or where the worker's productivity is heavily firm-specific, making the worker more valuable to the current employer than to other firms.

Training and Development

While the recruiting process is a means to evaluate a worker's potential productivity at the time of hiring, that productivity is not necessarily static or fixed, but can be enhanced after the worker enters the firm. In HR management terms, this process is known as training and development (T&D). Analyzing T&D decisions within firms involves applying human capital theory.

There are two types of training – general and firm-specific. General training provides the employee with skills that can be used with any employer. In contrast, firm-specific training only increases the worker's productivity with their current firm, not at any other firms. In reality, most training programs fall somewhere between the two extremes. General training might involve, for example, teaching employees to use basic computer software packages, like Excel or Word, the types of skills that they can use with a wide variety of employers. An example of firm-specific training would be where an employer teaches its employees to use accounting software that is uniquely customized to that particular organization. The skills learnt using this software would typically be non-transferable to another employer. An example of a somewhat less-tangible form of firm-specific training occurs when the firm educates its employees in the norms, values, and culture of the organization. This type of training is intended to increase the social cohesiveness of the workgroup, and convey a set of behavioral expectations on the employee.

The cost of acquiring general skills is paid for by the individual. If a firm were to pay, any employee that left the firm could fully transfer those skills to the new employer. Thus, there is no incentive for the firm to pay – its optimal choice is to wait for other firms to pay. However, all firms have this same incentive structure, so none will pay.

When firms provide workers with general training, it raises the workers' productivity across all organizations, not just with the firm providing the training. Since the firm providing the training cannot capture the benefits of providing such training, it will force the worker to pay for such training, either directly through compensating the firm, or, more typically, through reduced wages. This is one reason why younger (i.e. inexperienced) workers are paid less than their older counterparts – part of the young worker's total compensation is recaptured by the firm to cover training costs incurred on the worker's behalf. In essence, workers receive lower wages early in their career, i.e., while they are in their training period, so that they can receive higher wages later in their career.

Firm-specific training increases the worker's productivity at their current employer, but not with other employers. While the firm providing the training benefits from the increased productivity of the worker, the firm has an incentive to share some of these benefits (in the form of salary increases) of this increased productivity with the worker; otherwise the worker is indifferent between remaining with the current employer and moving to another employer. If the firm shares some of these benefits, the worker can earn more with the current employer than with other employers, and thus has an incentive to not move. However, the firm will not share all the benefits; otherwise, it would have no incentive to train workers. Thus, workers will be paid more than they could earn elsewhere, but less than their value to the firm.

With firm-specific training, where both the firm and worker share the benefits of increased productivity, both parties have an incentive to continue the employment relationship. Firms are better off because they are able to capture some of the benefits of the worker's increased productivity; correspondingly, workers have an incentive to remain with the firm because they can earn a higher wage with the current employer than with other employers. The manifestation of firm-specific training is reduced turnover – both the firm and the worker have an incentive to maintain the relationship. There is also a related age factor at work. Since younger workers have gained less firm-specific human capital than older workers, the former are more likely to switch jobs than the latter.

Of course, turnover can still occur amongst longer-tenured employees. This turnover reflects a decrease in the quality of the employer-employee match, to the point where one or the other party seeks to end the relationship. For example, changes in management, production processes, or co-worker groups might all lead an employee to seek a different position. Turnover can be costly to the organization, particularly for positions that require high amounts of firm-specific knowledge – whether it be knowledge of production processes, management structures, cultural norms, etc. This firm-specific knowledge is usually only developed over a considerable length of time, and, by definition, cannot simply be purchased in external labor markets, making it difficult for organizations to quickly and seamlessly replace a departed employee.

As workers get older, the amount of T&D that firms devote to them will decline. This occurs for two reasons. First, T&D exhibits diminishing returns – the more T&D a worker has, the lower the marginal gains from providing more training. Second, the older the employee, the fewer the number of years the firm will have to recapture its investment, and the less willing it will be to invest in T&D for the worker.

Empirically, the relative importance of general skills versus firm-specific skills can be ascertained by examining the salary returns to 'experience' versus 'tenure'; experience measures an individual's total length of time in the labor market, whereas tenure measures the individual's time with the firm. The greater the returns to tenure, relative to experience, the more important is firm-specific training relative to general training.

Incentives, Compensation, and Performance

Personnel economics models the employee-employer relationship as an agency problem. The firm's goal is to maximize worker output; this output, however, is based not only on the skills/abilities the worker possesses, but also on the worker's effort level. Since effort is costly to the worker, the worker may have a tendency to provide less effort than is optimal for the firm. In other words, workers have a tendency to shirk. One way the firm can enforce effort by the worker is to directly monitor and control the worker's behavior. Another way is to create a monetary incentive structure that aligns the interests of the worker with the interests of the firm.

In this regard, so-called piece-rate compensation schemes directly con-nect output with pay – the worker gets paid per unit of output they pro-duce. An example of such a scheme might be a sales job that is 100 percent commission-based. For piece-rate compensation to be most effective, a worker's output must be both measureable, and be largely independent of the efforts of co-workers. However, most jobs in today's modern economy do not meet this criteria – jobs, particularly those requiring higher skills, tend not to have easily measureable output; relatedly, the nature of work processes in many organizations requires employees to work as a team, meaning that one person's output, even if measureable, is a function of factors beyond simply that person's individual effort. As a result, most workers today are salaried, where their compensation is set in advance, and where it is independent of their current-period output – in other words, compensation is input-based, with the input being the worker's time.

The design of compensation structures can also be related to recruit-ing issues. For example, highly productive workers might be attracted to firms that utilize a piece-rate compensation scheme (where such high productivity is directly rewarded), whereas low-productivity workers may be attracted to firms that employ fixed-rate compensation schemes. Thus, piece-rate firms may be more productive, not necessarily because piece-rates encourage workers to give greater effort, but because piece-rate firms attract higher-quality workers.

When workers are on fixed-rate (i.e. input-based) pay schemes, different mechanisms must be used to discourage shirking. One such mechanism can be found in the overall pay structure of typical firms, where workers with more seniority get paid more. This positively sloped age-earnings profile can act as a motivator, both to younger workers and older workers. For younger workers, they have an incentive to reduce their shirking in the present, in hopes that they will retain their employment with the firm and enjoy advantages later in their career, where their pay will exceed their productivity. For older workers, they are already enjoying such benefits (of pay exceeding productivity), and thus have an incentive to minimize their shirking so as to be able to maintain these benefits.

Firms and workers will also sometimes enter into longer-term employ-ment contracts. These contracts will specify a predetermined level of compensation for a predetermined time period. They create a potential disconnect between the employee's productivity and what the employee gets paid. The contract sets compensation based on the worker's expected productivity over the life of the contract; however, this productivity may deviate from expectations, due not only to the effort put forth by the worker (i.e. the worker may shirk now that they have a long-term contract), but also because of luck, or because of macro factors beyond the worker's control. By providing a contract, the firm is essentially guaranteeing the worker a set payment regardless of productivity, and hence is reducing the worker's risk. In return, workers are likely to accept a salary penalty – i.e. they will agree to a compensation level that is lower than what they could expect to earn by continuously contracting on the spot market.

The Organization of Work: Work Teams and the Role of Management

Firms often seek to utilize work teams to accomplish production tasks. In designing and constructing these teams, the firm's goal is always to maximize team productivity. The specific nature of work teams differs greatly across organizations depending on the production technology of the firm in question. Sometimes, a work group may be referred to as a 'team', but in reality the individual workers will have very little interaction with each other. An example here might be a team of salespeople in a furniture store – each salesperson can perform their job with little to no interaction or support from co-workers. In this instance, the total production of the sales team will simply be additive across the various salespersons.

However, in more complex production technologies, the productivity of the team is dependent not only on the sum of the skills of the individual workers, but on how these workers interact with each other – the greater the complementarities across workers, the greater the team output. Firms will often try to mix workers – whether by age, experience, skills, nationality, cultures, etc. – to enhance the team's collection of capabilities. For example, older workers can help mentor and train younger workers – this is particularly important where the position relies heavily on firm-specific skills. Older workers are especially important in situations where their skill set remains current, and where factors like technological change do not quickly erode their productivity.

Also important to team production is the need to develop and maintain a cohesive work group. For example, workers in teams need to be able to effectively communicate with each other, and such communication can be affected by age differences, language differences, etc. Team members also need to have a sense of equity – i.e. the sense that all team members are contributing their share, and that team members are rewarded fairly. With the latter, one area that has been extensively studied is determining the effects on team production of relative pay inequality within the team. Two schools of thought have dominated the discussion – the so-called tournament model, and the fairness model. The tournament model, developed by Lazear and Rosen (1981), argues that large compensation differences within a work group – where a few workers at the top earn disproportionately high salaries for relatively small ability differences compared to their peers – encourages maximum effort in that it will incentivize 'rank-and-file' workers to achieve these heights. In contrast, the fairness model argues that large pay disparities, particularly when not supported by comparable ability differences, are detrimental to team cohesiveness and performance.

The roles and effectiveness of management is another area that has been of interest to personnel economists. Managers serve a number of potential roles in overseeing workers, ranging from the technical (overseeing workflow patterns, assigning workers to tasks, etc.) to the more interpersonal (motivator, coach/mentor), etc.

As Lazear et al. (2015) discuss, managers/leaders have the ability to impact the work performance of many other workers, so their impact can be multiplicative. The importance of leaders will vary across organizations and functional areas. In general, leaders will be more important in situations that are high-variance – that is, where the outcome will depend significantly on the decision made by the leader (Lazear, 2012). The best leaders are those that can utilize their judgment and experience to adopt the most effective course of action for their organization.

Empirically measuring the effectiveness of leaders can be difficult, because it generally requires detailed firm-level data. However, one common approach in the literature has been to examine the impacts of the sudden departure of CEOs due to their unexpected death. To the extent that such events impact the firm's stock price, it is taken as an indication of the extent to which the CEO's leadership impacted firm success.

1.2 THE UNIQUE CHARACTERISTICS OF THE EMPLOYMENT MARKET IN PROFESSIONAL SPORTS

The specifics of any particular employer-employee relationship are always a function of the market structures within which that relationship occurs. The sport industry in North America is particularly unique, in that the four major professional leagues (the 'Big 4') operate both as monopolists in the output market and monopsonists in the input market; leagues like the National Football League (NFL), for example, are the sole suppliers of elite-level professional football entertainment in the US, and are simultaneously the sole buyers of elite-level football talent.

While all of the Big 4 have been challenged by rival leagues at certain points in their histories, none of these rival leagues survived over the long term, and any competition in the output market was always temporary and fleeting, eventually reverting back to monopoly. In recent decades, the monopoly positions of the Big 4 now seem completely entrenched and impenetrable, with no legitimate rival league existing in US sports since the collapse of the United States Football League (USFL) in 1985. Without the threat of rival leagues, the established leagues have used their monopoly position to limit the supply of their output, particularly as it relates to ensuring that the number of franchises in the league is kept at an artificially low level.

This scarcity of franchises means that the number of jobs (i.e. roster spots) is also scarce, and leads to a tournament-style process in the labor market whereby large numbers of prospective employees compete to secure one of the relatively few positions in the major pro league. For example, the NBA employs only about 390 players (30 teams with 13 players each) in any given season, but thousands of players compete each year at the Division I college level and in European leagues. Competition is intense, as small differences in performance can result in large differences in compensation. For example, consider two basketball players of almost equal ability – one earns the final roster spot on a National Basketball Association (NBA) team and makes the NBA minimum salary of over $800,000 per year, while the other gets sent to the D-League, the NBA's developmental league, where salaries average about $25,000 per year.

This windfall payoff that goes to those reaching the elite level incentivizes aspiring professional players to invest heavily – both monetarily and in terms of time commitments – in the development of their (athletic) human capital. However, working counter to this incentive is the fact that the athletic skills needed to reach the elite levels of a sport are almost completely non-transferable outside of the sport sub-sector in which they play. For example, the unique set of skills needed to play quarterback in the NFL are not adaptable in any meaningful way to jobs outside of sport, nor, for that matter, are they even adaptable to other sports, like hockey or basketball. This non-transferability increases the risk of investing heavily in these skills, and introduces an all-or-nothing type of outcome – the player either reaches the elite-level league and earns the commensurate windfall payoffs, or does not, and hence gets no return on their investment of time and money.

The lack of transferability of athletic skills to other jobs, combined with the tournament-style system within sport labor markets, also means that those players that do reach the elite leagues in their sport will earn considerable economic rents – in other words, a player's next-best alternative to their job in the elite league will pay a much lower salary, usually by several orders of magnitude. In unregulated or non-unionized environments, employers (i.e. team owners) could potentially take advantage of such a situation in negotiations, knowing that players could take salary cuts and still earn much more than in alternative (non-sport) occupations.

A Brief History of the Employer-Employee Relationship in Sports

The unique nature of the sport labor market described above inherently puts players at a natural disadvantage when dealing with team owners. For players, the lack of transferability of their athletic skills to other types of employment, the potential economic rents they can earn in the sport industry, combined with the monopsony power of team owners, all serve to drastically reduce their bargaining power

In the early decades of professional sport in North America, owners used their superior bargaining position to unilaterally implement several institutional mechanisms to even further reduce the bargaining power of players. These mechanisms ensured that individual franchises within a league did not compete against each other for players. Two mechanisms were particularly important in this regard: (i) the player draft, for new players entering the league, and (ii) the reserve clause, for veteran players already established in the league.

With the draft, teams sequentially select from a group of prospective incoming (amateur) players; once a team selects a player, that team holds exclusive negotiating rights to that player. Draft systems take away from the player any ability to decide the team for which they will play. The NFL was the first of the Big 4 to implement a draft, in 1936; the NBA followed suit in 1947, with the National Hockey League (NHL) and Major League Baseball (MLB) implementing their drafts in 1963 and 1965, respectively.

While the draft system removed the bargaining power of incoming players, the bargaining power of established (i.e. veteran) players was removed by the so-called 'reserve clause'. The reserve clause was first employed in 1884, in baseball, and essentially bound players to their original teams, unless the team decided to trade or release the player. When a player's contract (typically, one year) expired, the reserve clause provided the player's team the right to unilaterally renew (usually with a small salary increase) that contract for another year. This gave a team perpetual control over the player, and prevented any voluntary player movement within a league. Versions of the reserve clause were ultimately adopted in basketball, hockey, and football.

Team owners took a very paternalistic approach to players, promoting the notion that owners and players were a family, and assuring players that they would be 'looked after' and that owners always had their best interests in mind. Simultaneously, owners never missed an opportunity to remind players that they were privileged to be able to play professional sports, and that they earned much higher incomes than most other Americans.

This one-sided employer-employee relationship ultimately provided the impetus for players to unionize. During the 1950s, all of the Big 4 leagues began to see their players become more vocal in their discontent and to begin to mobilize into collective action; by the mid-1960s, players' associations had formed in all four leagues. However, in that era the players' associations were 'company unions', in that they were largely controlled by the owners; the players' associations were a vehicle where players could air grievances, but within a framework where owners could still control and contain the discussion.

The relatively benign nature of players' associations changed abruptly in 1966 with the appointment of Marvin Miller as Executive Director of the Major League Baseball Players' Association (MLBPA). Miller adopted a much more confrontational approach to owners, ultimately resulting in the first-ever strike in US professional sport, when MLB players walked out for 13 days at the start of the 1972 season. As part of the settlement of that dispute, players gained improved pensions, and also the right to binding arbitration for salary disputes with owners – the latter gain seemed relatively modest at the time, but it would soon turn out to be the foundation for the most radical transformation of employer-employee relations in baseball history.

December 23, 1975: The Beginning of the Modern Era in Player-Owner Relations

On the advice of Marvin Miller and the MLBPA, pitchers Andy Messersmith and Dave McNally elected not to sign contracts for the 1975 season, and instead chose to 'play out their option' on their 1974 contracts. The standard baseball player's contract of that era (almost all of which were for one year) contained an option clause, which allowed teams to unilaterally renew a player's contract for the following year, his so-called option year. Of course, without free agency, the player would still ultimately have to re-sign with the team once the option year was completed.

The MLBPA took the Messersmith and McNally cases to arbitration and argued that, by playing out their option year, the players should be declared free agents and thus should no longer be bound to their current teams, the Los Angeles Dodgers and Montreal Expos, respectively. On December 23, 1975, arbitrator Peter Seitz rendered his decision, and agreed with the players; Messersmith and McNally were suddenly free agents, as was almost every player in baseball.

Miller and the MLBPA eventually negotiated a deal with the owners whereby only those players with at least six years of Major League service would be eligible for free agency; while this seems counterintuitive in the face of such a landmark victory, Miller knew that it was critical to limit the supply of free agents on the market at any one time if player salaries were to rise. Players' salaries did rise; in fact they skyrocketed. In the five years preceding free agency, salaries rose an average of 8.8 percent per year; in contrast, under the first five years of free agency, salaries rose an average of 26.3 percent per year. Work by Scully (1974) found that MLB players in the reserve clause era earned only about 20 percent of their marginal revenue products (MRPs).

In the 20 years subsequent to the Seitz decision, players in the other three major pro leagues also eventually gained free agency. The players' associations in these three leagues were not as strong as the MLBPA, and the battle to gain free agency was often long and difficult.

Rival Leagues

In the era prior to players winning free agency rights in their sports, the only instances where teams did not have full monopsony power over their players was when a rival league existed.

Rival leagues were particularly prominent in football – the NFL faced four different rival leagues in the 40 years following the Second World War. The most successful of these was the American Football League (AFL), which started play in 1960, and within six years negotiated a merger agreement with the NFL that saw all eight AFL teams join the NFL. The last rival league to challenge the NFL was the United States Football League (USFL), in the mid-1980s. The USFL had several high-profile owners and was established with much fanfare, but the league survived only three seasons, and failed to gain any type of merger with the NFL.

In basketball, the NBA began play in 1946 under the name Basketball Association of America (BAA), and was itself a rival league to the established National Basketball League (NBL). The BAA proved to be too much competition for the NBL, and the NBL was absorbed into the BAA in 1949, with the league becoming known as the NBA. The NBA faced serious competition for nine seasons beginning in 1967, with the formation of the American Basketball Association (ABA). The two leagues merged in 1976, with four ABA franchises absorbed into the NBA.

At about the same time, the NHL faced competition from a rival league in the form of the World Hockey Association (WHA). The WHA existed for seven years during the 1970s, and had four teams absorbed into the NHL when the two leagues merged in 1979.

Major League Baseball (MLB) is the only one of the Big 4 leagues not to face competition in the post-Second World War era. In fact, no rival leagues have existed in baseball in over a century – the last being the Federal League, which ceased operations in 1917. The lack of rival leagues in baseball is largely attributable to a 1922 Supreme Court decision that granted baseball an exemption from antitrust law. This allowed baseball to potentially engage in activities that would otherwise be illegal to prevent the formation of rival leagues. For example, in the late 1950s the Continental League was formed to challenge MLB, but the upstart league never did play a game, in part because MLB suddenly decided to expand (after 60 years of not expanding) to some of the cities targeted by the Continental League, and in part because MLB had hundreds of players in its minor leagues who were perpetually tied to their MLB clubs, thus ensuring that potential rivals would be unable to access a sufficient number of quality players.

Rival leagues were created on the basis of opportunities in both the output and input market. In the output market, rival leagues would attempt to capitalize on the monopolistic tendencies of the established leagues to severely limit expansion, thus leaving many viable markets unserved. On the input side, the monopsonistic power of the established leagues resulted in players being highly underpaid, relative to their MRPs, and made players amenable to switching leagues to increase their salaries. Not coincidentally, no rival league has ever emerged in a sport after players in the established league gained free agency rights.

1.3   THE CURRENT ENVIRONMENT: COLLECTIVE BARGAINING AGREEMENTS AND THEIR IMPACTS ON PERSONNEL DECISIONS IN SPORT

Despite differences in specifics, the history of employer-employee relationships has been remarkably similar across all of the Big 4 leagues: in the earlier years, the complete monopsony control of players through the reserve clause, alleviated occasionally and temporarily by the formation of rival leagues (except in baseball); followed by the more modern era, with the development of stronger unions, the eventual demise of the reserve clause, and the corresponding absence of any further rival leagues. With these similar histories, it is not surprising that the *current* state and structure of employer-employee relations is also very similar across the Big 4.

In all four leagues, collective bargaining agreements (CBAs) form the foundation for player-owner relations. CBAs have an impact across a wide range of personnel functions – from recruiting, to pay and performance, to training and development. The discussion below examines some of the specific areas in which CBAs set the institutional rules for the player-owner relationship.

Roster Size and Make-Up

In non-sport businesses, one of the core personnel decisions that individual firms must make is to decide *how many* employees to hire. This decision is removed for sport firms, as roster sizes are strictly set at the league level and are identical across all teams in the league. In addition, given the structured nature of the game being played on the field, how teams use these specific rosters spots, in terms of how many workers are hired at each playing position, tends to vary only minimally across teams.

In hockey, for example, NHL active rosters are limited to 23 players at any given time, only 20 of which can actually 'dress' for any particular game. Of these 20, teams will almost always carry 12 forwards – divided equally amongst centers, right-wingers, and left-wingers – six defensemen, and two goaltenders. In football, NFL rosters are limited to 53 players – of these, 22 are 'starters', with 11 on offense and 11 on defense. Rosters in basketball are small – only 13 players, relatively evenly divided between front-court players and guards. In baseball, MLB teams will generally use their 25-player roster to carry four or five starting pitchers and eight or nine relief pitchers, with the remainder being position players.

What this means is that all personnel decisions that ultimately follow – who to hire, how much to pay, etc. – must be undertaken within these constraints of a fixed roster size. NBA teams, for example, need never consider the relative costs and benefits of expanding their rosters to 20 players, for such decisions are beyond the individual teams' purview.

Entry Rules: Player Drafts

The typical entry point for players into the Big 4 is through the draft system

The draft system allocates incoming players to specific teams. Drafts are generally conducted in some type of reverse order, whereby the poorest performing teams of the prior season receive the first selections. As such, leagues justify the draft on the basis that it contributes to competitive balance. However, there is considerable evidence, both theoretical and empirical, to question such claims. First, the invariance principle states that resources – in this case, players – will flow to their highest-value use, regardless of who initially owns the resource. This suggests that, while the draft may initially allocate the best incoming players to the poorest performing teams (often small-market teams), these players will eventually find their way to the large-market teams, meaning that any competitive balance benefits of the draft are, at best, temporary and fleeting. Empirical evidence has generally supported these theoretical predictions, and has uncovered little to no evidence that drafts improve competitive balance.

To economists, the more plausible explanation as to why all four leagues have drafts is that drafts limit the bargaining power of incoming players. The draft system creates a monopsony situation, whereby players can only negotiate with the club that drafted them. This causes the salaries of incoming players to be lower than under an open bidding system. However, unlike the pre-free agency era, drafts can now only bind incoming players to particular teams for a specified length of time, and not in perpetuity.

The number of rounds in the draft varies by league – 40 in MLB, seven in both the NFL and NHL, and two in the NBA.

Player Mobility: Free Agency

In all of the Big 4 leagues, veteran players (i.e. those not on rookie/entry-level contracts) are able to gain free agency rights after reaching a pre-specified number of years of service in the league.

There is a critical distinction between what are typically referred to as 'restricted' versus 'unrestricted' free agents. Restricted free agents can sign with other clubs, but the signing club must compensate the player's former club, either through draft picks or other players (or, in more modern-day versions of being 'restricted', the player's current club has the right to match the offer and retain the player). Compensation requirements greatly reduce demand for the player – often to the point of zero – as other clubs are reluctant to lose players or draft picks. In contrast, with unrestricted free agency, the signing club does not compensate a player's former club, creating a much more active market for that player. Because the compensation requirements of restricted free agency are so harsh, most economists consider only unrestricted free agents to be 'true' free agents, in that they are the only players not facing a monopsonistic employer.

In the days before the owners and players formally negotiated the specifics of free agency through the CBA process, a few players would become restricted free agents by 'playing out their option', essentially challenging their team's perpetual claim on their services. The leagues were, of course, strongly opposed to such actions, and devised methods to limit voluntary player movement. In the NFL, for example, R. C. Owens of the San Francisco 49ers played out his option and signed with the Baltimore Colts. Pete Rozelle, the NFL commissioner at the time, intervened and unilaterally adopted a policy where the commissioner could arbitrarily award compensation (in the form of a player or players) to the team losing a free agent – the policy became known as the Rozelle Rule. The other three major pro leagues all followed suit and soon adopted some form of their own Rozelle Rule. Any instances in the 1960s and 1970s of players challenging the monopsony control of their teams were isolated and infrequent, and often resulted in long court battles. As players' associations became powerful, free agency provisions began to become codified into CBAs.

Baseball was the first sport of the Big 4 where players gained true free agency, which was the result of the aforementioned decision of arbitrator Peter Seitz in December 1975. Following the decision, baseball owners and the MLBPA quickly agreed on a set of rules that would govern free agency. Starting for the 1976 season, all players that had accrued six years of Major League service were eligible to become unrestricted (i.e. no compensation) free agents. Remarkably, this six-year time frame to free agency still holds today, over 40 years later. In addition, players with three years of service can now file for salary arbitration, providing them some degree of bargaining power, even without full free agency rights.

Currently in the NFL, players can become unrestricted free agents after four years of NFL service. However, unlike baseball, football players have earned free agency rights only relatively recently. The NFL's first foray into free agency occurred in 1989 with the so-called 'Plan B' free agency system. Plan B was implemented unilaterally by the NFL (i.e. rather than being negotiated with the NFL Players' Association (NFLPA)). The 1987 NFL players' strike had ended disastrously for the NFLPA, with the NFL bringing in replacement players, forcing the regular players back to work without a settlement. In an apparent effort to avoid antitrust issues, the NFL decided to provide players with limited free agency, whereby each team 'protected' 37 players who were not eligible for free agency, but all others were free agents when their contract expired. Of course, the protected players were those who were of the highest quality, so Plan B only benefited the more marginal NFL players. This changed with the Freeman McNeil court case, where Plan B free agency was ruled a violation of antitrust laws, ultimately paving the way for NFL players to acquire full free agency rights in 1994.

With the other two leagues, NBA players won unrestricted (i.e. no compensation) free agency in 1988. Current NBA players generally acquire unrestricted free agency rights after completing their second NBA contract. Hockey was the last of the Big 4 sports where players gained unrestricted free agency. Currently, NHL players achieve unrestricted free agency after they have reached 27 years of age, or have played in the league for at least seven years.

Team Payrolls and Individual Player Salaries

Three of the four major professional leagues have some form of a salary cap, with MLB being the only league without a cap. The term 'salary' cap is somewhat of a misnomer because generally what are capped are team payrolls, rather than the salaries of individual players (although the NBA CBA does restrict individual salaries for some types of players).

Both the NHL and NFL have hard caps, while the NBA has a soft cap. The difference is that hard caps provide a strict and unyielding upper limit on team payrolls; a limit that cannot be exceed under any circumstances. A soft cap also specifies a numerical upper-limit on team payrolls, but there are several allowable ways in which team can exceed this limit.

Luxury taxes are different from salary caps. With luxury taxes, an upper-limit payroll threshold is established and teams that exceed that threshold must pay a tax on the amount by which they exceed the threshold. Both the NBA and MLB have a luxury tax system.

The Case of European Soccer

The above discussion has focused on the Big 4 leagues in North America, simply because in these leagues much of the employer-employee relationship is regulated by CBAs. In contrast, European soccer is a more open and competitive market, and functions much closer to the way most non-sport firms would operate.

In Europe, the top domestic leagues compete with each other for players, drastically reducing the monopsony power of individual clubs or leagues. While Europe had its own version of the reserve clause at one time, the 1995 'Bosman' ruling essentially granted soccer players the same free agency rights that North American players first gained with baseball in 1975.

Players in European soccer leagues do not collectively bargain with their employers over monetary issues like salary or payroll caps. Furthermore, there are no roster limitations, so clubs can determine unilaterally the size of their squad.

In many ways, we would expect European soccer, rather than North American leagues, to be able to provide better insights into the non-sport world. However, a limitation for researchers is that individual performance in soccer is notoriously difficult to measure; in addition, salary data for individual players has generally not been publicly available. Thus, any potential gains to researchers from studying a more unregulated market have often been nullified by these measurement and data restrictions.

1.4 APPLICATIONS AND IMPLICATIONS FOR SPORT

As Oyer and Schaefer (2010) note, strategic management researchers ask whether persistent differences in performance across firms are (at least partially) attributable to differences in HR practices. Applied to sport, this question becomes whether certain clubs in a league can consistently outperform its peers (either on the field and/or in terms of profitability) because of superior HR practices. Given the highly structured nature of the closed North American leagues – with roster limitations, the draft system, and salary caps – individual clubs have fewer choice variables on which they can differentiate themselves, compared to, say, European soccer clubs, or to firms in non-sport industries.

In thinking about applying personnel economics to sport, many broad observations are possible, and several questions arise that are important to ponder. Below are a few summary thoughts in each of the functional areas of HR management.

Recruiting and Hiring

- In non-sport industries, firms often use higher pay than their competitors to attract better quality applicants. However, in the Big 4 leagues, entry-level (i.e. rookie) contracts are generally dictated by CBAs, and even salaries for veteran free agents will often be constrained by salary caps.
- How many resources should clubs devote to the screening of entry-level players? Most teams in a league have the same public information about prospective players, sometimes through league-wide screening processes like the NFL draft 'combine', or the NHL's Central Scouting rankings of draft-eligible players. Individual clubs are able to gain a competitive advantage over other clubs only if they have consistently better private information than others, which can only be gained by superior scouting techniques.
- Even if a club were to consistently draft better players, two questions arise. First, how costly was it to achieve the better draft results? Second, how long can the player be retained by the club at a below-market wage? With the latter, free agency provisions generally allow players to leave their drafting clubs after four to seven years, depending on the league, meaning that any economic rents achievable through superior drafting methods are relatively fleeting.
- Is drafting 'risky' players an effective HR strategy? It would seem that it could be, in that players can be easily released if they fail to perform to expectations – there is little to no protection for players in this regard. Risky players would seem to be more likely found when clubs go beyond their usual geographic recruiting territories (as in the early days of Europeans entering the NHL and NBA, where these players were higher risk because of the lack of reliable information on their

talent levels) or when they recruit college players who have played in the lower divisions (say, Division II or III football players). However, despite the potential benefits of recruiting riskier players, agency issues may lessen the likelihood of this occurring. In preserving their own jobs, general managers may be very sensitive to not drafting players – particularly with early picks – who have a higher probability of being 'busts'. Their own survival sense may incentivize them to 'play it safe'.

- With veteran free agents, as opposed to entry-level players, the issues are different. Issues of asymmetric information, adverse selection, and the winner's curse all increase the risk to teams when signing free agents.

Training and Development

Sport clubs must determine their investment level in training and development activities. In North America, these activities typically occur within the club's minor league teams, while in Europe they occur within the club's youth training academy. The NHL and MLB have long maintained very extensive minor league systems to house players who have been drafted and signed by the club. Player development in these sports, particularly baseball, can be lengthy, with most 18-year-olds, for example, not ready to play at the top level. In Europe, the top soccer clubs all maintain youth academies whereby they bring players into the club at a young age, so the clubs have control and influence over a player's development for much longer than teams in North America sports.

The critical question here is the extent to which a player's professional prospects with the club are influenced by their skills related to the sport itself, versus their club-specific knowledge and skills. The former are transferable to other competitor clubs, while the latter are not.

While teams always talk about seeking incoming players that are a good 'fit' with the club's culture, current players, and/or coaching style, all of these factors can change abruptly, particularly the latter, as coaches are hired and dismissed with great frequency. When that occurs, is the player that was drafted, or was taken into the youth academy, no longer as valuable to the club as they once were? Casual observation would suggest that while club-specific factors are not necessarily unimportant in some situations, the fact that most veteran players switch clubs without significant performance changes would suggest that it is the general sport-related skills, rather than any club-specific match, that are the most important factors in their personal performance.

To the extent, then, that this is the case – i.e. that the club-specific match is secondary to the sport-related skills – this would suggest that development systems, like the minor leagues in North America and the training academies in Europe, are more valuable to teams as long-term screening mechanisms (i.e. probationary periods) than as knowledge-impartment mechanisms. This is certainly a fruitful area for further research.

Performance, Pay, and Incentives

The output of a professional athlete is generally much easier to measure than it is for workers in non-sport firms. However, this ability to measure player output varies greatly by sport – where on-field teammate interaction is low (baseball), it is easier to measure individual contributions, compared to sports where interaction is high (football, hockey, soccer). Each of these sports has now been subject to the analytics revolution – the attempt to better measure the performance of players through the use of advanced technological tools that more effectively capture on-field activities, and through using this information to create new, 'advanced', performance metrics. This (presumed) increased ability to better measure player performance will continue to encourage clubs to find market inefficiencies – i.e. to find disconnects between player value and player pay. Exploiting these inefficiencies is profit-generating for the clubs, at least until other clubs gain knowledge of the inefficiency and bid it away in the market.

The better the understanding a club has about true player performance, the more likely it is to make effective decisions in the free agent market. For example, understanding age-performance profiles lessens the chances of clubs offering long-term contracts to players who are 'past their prime' and whose performance is likely to decline very soon.

Directly attaching pay to performance at the micro level is difficult in the sport industry, in that 'performance bonuses' are not a major component of players' compensation packages. In other words, to use broader HR terms, most pay is base pay, not piece-rate pay. There are at least two important reasons for this. First, players' associations are generally opposed to performance pay, as are most unions in the non-sport world. Second, the clubs themselves must be careful here, since performance bonuses, by their very nature, reward individual players, and may have negative impacts on teamwork and cohesive behavior.

The Roles of Teammate Effects and Management

In sports that require high interaction among teammates, like soccer, hockey, and basketball, team output is much more than the sum of the individual talents of the players. The most effective teams are those that, for a given level of individual talent, generate the most output. Clubs can gain a competitive advantage over other teams in the league by essentially being better at team-building – in other words, finding the right mix of players. Several questions arise here:

- How large is this team effect? To what degree can finding the right combination of players overcome individual talent deficiencies?
- All else equal, are teams more effective if they are homogenous or if they are heterogeneous? Teams can be heterogeneous along many dimensions – age, experience, geographic origin, race, language, national origin, etc. For example, holding average age of the team constant, is it better to construct a team of primarily mid-career players, or a team where there is a mix of younger and older players? As another example, are players better when they have teammates that are similar to them in terms of geographic origin, or language, or culture? Or, does the effect work the other way? Or, does it not matter either way?
- For a given level of talent, how important is coaching to the team's success? Coaches perform multiple roles – selecting the specific mix of players, training, motivation, game strategy, etc. Given that coaches are paid much less than average players in most professional sports leagues, does this then imply that the coach's role is much less significant to team success? It this is the case, then coaches should be relatively interchangeable with each other, without any discernible performance change in the team.
- As professional sports have become more sophisticated – with advances in training methods, in-game strategic decision-making, motivation techniques, etc. – has the requirements to be an effective coach changed? Are educated generalists more effective in today's game than more narrow specialists (for example, former players)?

Several of the questions raised in this section have been examined, to various degrees, in the literature, while others have received little attention to date. The chapters that follow in this book touch on several of these issues, and help to provide a larger context for the discussion of personnel economics in sport.

NOTE

1. Since much, if not most, of the intellectual foundations of personnel economics are attributable to Ed Lazear, this section relies heavily on his (and his co-authors') countless

contributions to the discipline over the past three decades. For more detail and discussion on each of the topics discussed in this section, see Lazear and Gibbs (2014).

REFERENCES

Lazear, E. (2012) 'Leadership: a personnel economics approach', *Labour Economics* **19** (1), 92–101.

Lazear, E. and M. Gibbs (2014) *Personnel Economics in Practice*, Hoboken, NJ: John Wiley & Sons.

Lazear, E. and P. Oyer (2012) 'Personnel economics', in Robert Gibbons and John Roberts (eds), *The Handbook of Organizational Economics*, Princeton, NJ: Princeton University Press, pp. 479–519.

Lazear, E. and S. Rosen (1981) 'Rank-order tournaments as optimum labor contracts', *Journal of Political Economy*, **89**, 841–864.

Lazear, E., K. Shaw and C. Stanton (2015) 'The value of bosses', *Journal of Labor Economics*, **33** (4), 823–861.

Oyer, Paul and S. Schaefer (2010) 'Personnel economics: hiring and incentives', in O. Ashenfelter and D. Card (eds), *Handbook of Labor Economics*, Amsterdam: Elsevier, pp. 1770–1823.

Scully, G. (1974) 'Pay and performance in Major League Baseball', *American Economic Review*, **64** (4), 915–930.

Spence, M. (1973) 'Job market signaling', *The Quarterly Journal of Economics*, **87** (3), 355–374.

PART I

Recruiting and human capital development

2.   The failed promise of the draft in the NFL and NBA

David Berri

In 1934 the Minnesota Golden Gophers were widely considered the best team in college football.[1] The 'Hook 'Em Cows' finished the year with a mark of 8-0; scoring 270 points while allowing their opponents to score just 38 points.[2] These numbers, however, do not do justice to the dominance of this team. A *Time* magazine article[3] from 1934 noted that the Golden Gophers tried to limit how badly they beat their opponents. The team's strategy was to punt on second down in the first half. Only in the second half would Minnesota make every effort to score.

The star of this team was Clarence ('Stockyard Stan') Kostka. Here is how the *Time* magazine article described Kostka:

> Although he has not been a full-time player, in the first six games of the season he accounted for 532 yd. or more than a quarter of Minnesota's total ground gained by rushing. Minnesota's greatest ground-gainer, he can run 100 yd. in 12 sec. in uniform.
>
> A smiling, quiet-spoken, curly-haired youth of 21, Stan Kostka has been dubbed 'King Kong' by his hometown sportswriters because he is wedge-shaped and his arms seem to hang, apelike, below his knees.

After the 1934 season ended, a bidding war ensued among two National Football League (NFL) teams for 'King Kong's' service. Although college football had been played since the 1860s, the NFL had only existed since 1920.[4] In 1934 the league consisted of only 11 teams. Two of these were the Philadelphia Eagles and Brooklyn Dodgers[5] and each wanted to hire Kostka. In the end, the Dodgers agreed to pay him $5,000. This is only about $90,000 in 2017; so relative to NFL players today this is not very much money.[6] But in 1935, the Dodgers were paying 'King Kong' essentially the wage paid to Bronco Nagurski – a player many considered the best player in the NFL.

Bert Bell – owner of the Philadelphia Eagles (i.e. the team that lost the bidding war) – decided that bidding for new talent was not a great idea. For Bell, a better idea was a reverse-order draft. Starting in 1936, Bell's draft would give the worst teams in the NFL the first choice in choosing the best college talent. Once a player was chosen, that player could not negotiate with any other team. Therefore the bidding war for Kostka – a bidding war Bell lost – would not happen anymore.

Clearly, Bell had a reason to prefer a draft over a bidding process. The self-interested nature of the proposal does not stop there. Bell's Eagles were also the worst team in 1935. That meant that Bell was proposing an institution that would let him pick first in 1936. Fate would have the last laugh, however. Bell chose Jay Berwanger with the very first pick in 1936. Berwanger turned down Bell's offer of $125 to $150 per game (or $1500 to $1800 for a 12-game season). Berwanger was then traded to the Chicago Bears but Berwanger's demand for $25,000 over two years led George Halas – owner of the Bears – to pass on Berwanger.[7] Ultimately, Berwanger never played in the NFL. Berwanger was not the only drafted player to make that decision in 1936. Of the 81 players drafted, only 28 players actually played in the NFL.[8]

Although the draft did not work out for Bell in 1936, the institution of the draft remained. The National Basketball Association (NBA) adopted a draft when it was founded in 1947. And in the 1960s, both Major League Baseball (MLB) and the National Hockey League (NHL) also adopted the draft.[9] The drafts in baseball and hockey, however, are different from the NFL and NBA. In the latter leagues, drafted players tend to play immediately for the NFL or NBA team that selected them.[10] In baseball and hockey, many players begin their career in the minor leagues and then work their way up to the top league.

Given these differences, we are going to focus our discussion on the NFL and NBA, where most drafted players move to the highest professional ranks in their first professional season. Our specific focus will be on how well teams make these choices. Specifically, how often do the worst teams in these leagues actually select the 'best' talent?

Before we get to that question, we must address the more fundamental question: Why does the draft exist as an institution in the first place?

2.1   WHY DO LEAGUES EMPLOY A DRAFT TO SELECT TALENT?

The story of Bert Bell and the draft makes it clear why the draft was proposed. Bell lost a bidding war for Stan Kostka's talent. When Bell selected Berwanger in the 1936 draft, Bell's initial offer was more than $3,000 less than what Kostka was offered by the Dodgers for the 1935 season. Clearly, Bell preferred the draft because it lowered his player costs.

Krautmann et al. (2009) offered evidence in support of that hypothesis. In MLB, the NFL, and the NBA, younger players have restricted bargaining power. These authors offered evidence that in all three leagues younger players with restricted bargaining power received lower wages than free agents in their sports. So restricting bargaining power – as the draft appears designed to do – will lower player salaries.

Leagues, however, tend to focus on a different reason for the draft. According to the leagues, the reverse-order draft is designed to promote competitive balance. The argument is very simple to follow. The league's worst teams are given the first choices in the draft. With those first choices they will select the best amateur talent. And with those new – and better – players, the worst teams will get better and be more competitive.

For all this to happen, teams have to be able to select the 'best' talent. Unfortunately – as this chapter will show – published research suggests that in the two leagues where the draft receives the most attention (i.e. the NFL and NBA), decision-makers often fail to identify the best talent.

2.2   CHICAGO CONTESTS RATIONALITY

The idea that decision-makers do not consistently make the best choices contradicts a fundamental idea in neoclassical economics. Economists have historically argued that decision-makers conduct relatively complex calculations to make decisions. Individuals seek to maximize utility by considering marginal benefits and marginal costs. Firms seek to maximize profits by considering marginal revenue and marginal costs. For some, such calculations seemed beyond the power of a normal human being. As Thorstein Veblen sarcastically noted in 1898:

> The hedonistic conception of man is that of a *lightning calculator of pleasures and pains* who oscillates like a *homogeneous globule of desire of happiness* under the impulse of stimuli that shift him about the area, but leave him intact. (Veblen (1898): p. 389, emphasis added)

Veblen's argument that people are essentially not capable of what economists were proposing was addressed by Milton Friedman and L. J. Savage (1948). Friedman and Savage suggested that economists think about billiard players in considering how human beings process information. The game of billiards (or pool) can be modeled with advanced physics. But Friedman and Savage argued that no one thinks that billiard players actually know advanced physics. The players who excel at this sport just behave as if they do. Furthermore, if they do not they cannot excel. Likewise, firms may not understand the advanced economics that describe their decision-making. But firms that excel have to behave like they understand these ideas. Therefore economists are correct in assuming that human beings are rational. Or using Veblen's words, Friedman and Savage's argument would suggest that maybe human beings can be 'lightning calculators'.

Milton Friedman spent a significant part of his career at the University of Chicago. Although Friedman did persuade many economists, he did not ultimately persuade everyone at Chicago. For example, Nobel Laureate Herbert Simon – a graduate of the University of Chicago – argued in the 1950s that the ability for human beings to process information could best be described by the concept of 'bounded rationality'. As *The Economist* noted in a brief biography of Simon:[11]

> Contrary to the tenets of classical economics, Simon maintained that individuals do not seek to maximise their benefit from a particular course of action (since they cannot assimilate and digest all the information that would be needed to do such a thing). Not only can they not get access to all the information required, but even if they could, their minds would be unable to process it properly. The human mind necessarily restricts itself. It is, as Simon put it, bounded by 'cognitive limits'.

Another Nobel Laureate and University of Chicago economist – Richard Thaler – continued the attack on the core rationality assumption in economics by helping to create the field of behavioral economics. Behavioral economists combine insights from economics and psychology to describe not only areas where human beings depart from the tenets of the rationality assumption but also how these departures are predictable.[12]

So we have two views on human behavior from researchers at the University of Chicago.[13] When we look at the reverse-order draft in the NFL and NBA, which view is most consistent with the choices made by decision-makers? We will start our discussion with the NFL draft, to which Thaler – and his co-author Cade Massey – have contributed some research.

2.3   FALLING IN LOVE ON DRAFT DAY OFTEN LEADS TO SO MUCH HEARTBREAK LATER

In 2012 the NFL's Washington franchise held the 6th pick in the annual draft. But the team decided it definitely wanted to draft Robert Griffin of Baylor University. Perhaps this is not surprising. The scouting report at NFL.com stated:[14]

> Many would argue that RG3 is not only the most physically gifted quarterback in the 2012 draft, but that he is the most talented player overall. His intangibles are making so many general managers swoon.

Yes, Griffin's talent definitely seemed to make Washington fall in love. To acquire 'the most talented player in the draft overall', Washington traded its sixth overall pick, its second round pick, and its first round pick in 2013 and 2014 for the rights to move up to the second pick in the 2012 draft held by the St Louis Rams.

Was this a 'fair' trade? The answer to this question begins with what Cade Massey and Richard Thaler (2013) describe as 'The Chart'.[15] This was a creation of Mike McCoy (a part-owner of the Dallas Cowboys) in 1991, and is based on trades from 1987 to 1990. The values in the chart reveal what teams are willing to pay when making trades. For example, the first overall pick in the draft is worth 3000 points, the second is worth 2600 points, etc.; by the 33rd overall pick (the first pick in the second round), the value drops to 580 points, and eventually falls to only three points for the last pick in the seventh (and final) round.

In the Griffin trade, Washington obtained the second pick in the draft, valued at 2600 points. For this pick, Washington in 2012 gave up the sixth overall pick, worth 1600 points, and also a second round pick (the 39th overall pick), worth 510 points.

Those two picks – according to 'The Chart' – were not enough. So Washington also sent a 2013 first round pick. This turned out to be the 22nd overall pick, valued at 780. But since it was next year, there was a discount associated with that price. One might think that would have been enough, but Washington also decided to send another first round pick in 2014 which ended up being the second overall pick in that draft. By the standards of 'The Chart', it seems clear that Washington overpaid for Griffin. But it gets even worse. It turns out that according to Massey and Thaler (2013), 'The Chart' does not price draft picks correctly.

Massey and Thaler looked at the difference between each player's salary and economic value that a player's production would be worth if the player was a free agent. Because drafted players lack bargaining power, economic value tends to exceed salary. In other words, there is a surplus. Massey and Thaler wondered where the surplus value was the highest. One might expect – given the values seen in 'The Chart' – that the highest value would be in the first round. But Massey and Thaler found that the highest value was at the top of the second round. In sum, 'The Chart' was incorrect. The top pick in the second round (valued at 580 points) was worth more than the top pick in the draft (worth 3000 points). That suggests that – unlike what Washington did in 2012 – teams would be better off trading down in the draft.

Here is how Massey and Thaler summarized their findings (p. 1493).

> Our findings are strikingly strong. Rather than a treasure, the right to pick first appears to be a curse. If picks are valued by the surplus they produce, then the first pick in the first round is the worst pick in the round, not the best. In paying a steep price to trade up, teams are paying a lot to acquire a pick that is worth less than the ones they are giving up. We have conducted a wide range of empirical tests and every analysis gives qualitatively similar results. The same is true under the 2011 labor agreement. The new rookie salary cap reduced the cost of the very top draft picks, but not enough of them to alter our results.

We should note that Washington did not have to read research in an academic journal to know their trade for Griffin was not the best move. Years before this draft, Dan Snyder – owner of Washington's NFL team – had a chance to hear directly from Richard Thaler about this research. Years later, here is how Thaler described this conversation:[16]

> So we had two lessons for [Dan Snyder]: Trade down and loan picks this year for better picks next year. So Cade and I get a six-pack, start watching the draft that year keen to see what the Redskins are gonna do. What do they do? They trade up and they give up a better pick next year to have a better pick this year. We moved onto another team after that.

The 2012 draft indicated that Washington and Snyder were still not listening to Thaler. But over-valuing the second pick in the draft was not the only mistake Washington made in 2012. Robert Griffin was not the only quarterback Washington selected that year. In the fourth round Washington selected Kirk Cousins. For the next three seasons Griffin was the team's primary starter. But after the 2014 season, Cousins became the team's starter. Griffin eventually moved on from Washington and after the 2016 season appeared to be out of the league.[17] In sum, what seemed like love on draft day in 2012 led to much heartbreak just a few years later.

Griffin started 40 games in his NFL career. Prior to the 2017 season, Cousins had started 41 games. In addition, Ryan Tannehill – taken with the eighth pick in 2012 (two picks after Washington's original pick) – had started 77 times before the 2017 season. Russell Wilson – taken with the 75th pick overall in 2012 – had started 80 games by the end of the 2016 season and won a Super Bowl in 2013.

In sum, there appears to be a few quarterbacks who performed better than Griffin in the NFL. One of these quarterbacks was actually selected by Washington without the need of a trade that contradicted the advice of a Nobel Laureate in economics.

Could Washington have known that Griffin was not really the best quarterback in the 2012 draft? Maybe not, but they could have suspected that Griffin was not likely to be an immensely better quarterback than the other signal callers selected that year.

The history of the draft has an abundance of examples where teams spent a high pick on a quarterback that did not work out. A partial list would include Tim Couch (first overall pick in 1999), David Carr (first overall pick in 2002), JaMarcus Russell (first overall pick in 2007), Rick Mirer (second overall pick in 1993), Ryan Leaf (second overall pick in 1998), Heath Shuler (third overall pick in 1994), Akili Smith (third overall pick in 1999), Joey Harrington (third overall pick in 2002), and Vince Young (third overall pick in 2006). All of these quarterbacks were supposed to be franchise quarterbacks in the NFL who would lead their respective teams to many appearances in the playoffs. But that never really happened for these players.

Of course, a series of anecdotes is not the same as systematic evidence. Berri and Simmons (2011) addressed two questions related to quarterbacks in the draft.

1. What factors impact where a quarterback is drafted in the NFL draft?
2. How does performance in the NFL relate to where a quarterback is selected in the draft?

For the first question, Berri and Simmons considered the following list of factors: height of the quarterback, body mass index, the Wonderlic score,[18] a quarterback's 40-yard dash time, a dummy variable for quarterbacks not playing NCAA Division I football, and a wide variety of college performance measures. They tested nine different models and found that height, the Wonderlic score, the 40-yard dash time, playing for a non-Division I team, and various summary measures of performance[19] were significant. Of these, the most important were the non-performance measures. As the authors note, 20 percent of the variation in draft position is explained by the non-performance metrics. Adding in a measure of performance only increases explanatory power another three percent.

Although these factors helped explain where a quarterback was selected, when Berri and Simmons turned to predicting NFL performance, a different story emerged. As the authors noted:

> In all of our formulations, we never found that the combine factors, or the college performance with respect to Wins Produced per 100 plays or QB rating, had a significant impact – of the expected sign – on NFL Wins Produced per play or NFL QB Rating at any level of experience in the NFL.

In sum, the factors that get you drafted do not seem to predict future performance. In fact, Berri and Simmons also noted that where

Table 2.1   NFL performance by position in the draft: career performance after four years (1980–2012)

	Pick 1–10	Pick 11–50	Pick 51–100	Pick 101–180	Pick After 180
Completion Percentage	56.8%	58.4%	56.6%	54.9%	55.7%
Yards per Attempt	6.616	6.920	6.682	6.631	6.419
Touchdowns per Attempt	0.038	0.042	0.036	0.037	0.036
Interceptions per Attempt	0.033	0.034	0.035	0.038	0.035
Total Plays	61,347	50,885	30,245	19,370	15,782
Total Wins	390.6	337.2	180.1	115.8	90.8
NFL's Quarterback Rating	75.7	79.4	74.4	71.8	72.5
Wins Produced per 100 plays	0.637	0.663	0.595	0.598	0.575
Observations	40	44	48	44	39

a quarterback is selected also fails to predict what we see in the NFL.[20] Since decision-makers may consider much more than the factors Berri and Simmons considered in selecting players, draft position should do a better job of predicting NFL performance.

Table 2.1 updates what Berri and Simmons found. The table reports total and average performance for quarterbacks taken at different spots in the draft from 1980 to 2012. Career performance after four years is considered.[21] The results indicate that if you look at total Wins Produced, the expected pattern emerges. Players drafted first – on average – perform better.

However, that seems to be because quarterbacks taken first get many more opportunities to play. If we consider measures of performance like the NFL's Quarterback Rating or Wins Produced per 100 plays we do not see quarterbacks selected first doing better than those taken later. In fact, quarterbacks selected with picks 11 to 50 seem to do more – on average – than those taken with one of the first 10 choices.

A similar story is told if we look at the correlation between NFL performance and draft positions. Draft position only explains 4 percent of the variation in career NFL Wins Produced per 100 minutes after four years in the league. Berri and Simmons (2011) offered a more sophisticated model looking at how experience and draft position both predicted performance. As they noted:

> Regardless of the selected NFL performance metric, experience determines performance independently of draft pick, with no significant role for draft choice. Put another way, comparing two quarterbacks with the same NFL experience, the player selected earlier in the draft is not predicted to have significantly different NFL performance levels than a player picked later in the draft. *Draft pick is not a significant predictor of NFL performance.* (Emphasis added)

This result should not be surprising. As noted in *The Wages of Wins* (Berri et al., 2006) and Berri and Burke (2012), performance of veteran NFL quarterbacks is very inconsistent. Quarterbacks do not do much by themselves. Their performance depends on their receivers, the offensive line, the running game, the play-calling of their coaches, and the talent and decisions made by their opponents on defense. All of these factors can change from game to game and certainly from season to season. In addition, injuries can impact the performance of all these players and the quarterback themselves. Consequently, the performance of quarterbacks tends to vary much more than that of athletes in baseball and basketball.

Given that the play of veteran quarterbacks cannot be predicted with much accuracy, it is not surprising that NFL decision-makers cannot predict the performance of quarterbacks as they move from college to the NFL. However, it is clear that decision-makers act as if they can predict performance. Consequently, decision-makers – like Dan Snyder – give up significant resources to acquire quarterbacks who may not (and ultimately were not) better than quarterbacks they could have taken later.

So the promise of the NFL draft did not just fail Bert Bell in 1936. The work of Massey and Thaler (2013) and Berri and Simmons (2011) suggests that decision-makers are hardly expert billiard players when it comes to the NFL draft. Is the story different when we turn to the NBA?

2.4   WHY ONE SHOULD NOT 'TRUST THE PROCESS' IN THE NBA

Sam Hinkie was hired by the Philadelphia 76ers in 2013 to be the team's general manager. In 2013–14, the Sixers finished with a mark of 19-63. The next season the team managed to get even worse, finishing with a record of 18-64. Although one might think it still could not get worse, it did. In 2015–16 the Sixers finished with only 10 wins. Hinkie, however, did not finish the season. In April 2016 Hinkie departed the Sixers front office.

Given this record, Hinkie's reign in Philadelphia was a disaster. But before we judge this record we have to consider what Hinkie was trying to accomplish. During Hinkie's years the phrase 'Trust the Process' became popular in Philadelphia. What is 'the Process'? Although Hinkie may not have explicitly stated this, it was generally believed that what Hinkie hoped to do was:

1.   lose as much as possible;
2.   accumulate high draft picks;
3.   acquire amazing talents and then win.

In sum, Hinkie hoped to take advantage of the NBA draft to acquire top talent.

As we saw in football, this is actually the promise of the reverse-order draft. But for this to work, teams have to be able to identify the top talent. Unfortunately, the evidence suggests this does not happen as often as people might suspect.

The result we see in basketball is similar to what we see in football. Specifically, we often see teams do not select the 'best' talent first. The reasons for this outcome, however, are different in basketball.

Let us begin with the disconnect between how players are evaluated in basketball and what actually determines wins. It is not very difficult to determine why basketball teams win. The link between the box score statistics and wins has been laid forth in a number of publications and online forums.[22] The basic story this empirical work tells is simple. Teams win when they:

1. Take the ball from the opponent without the opponent scoring. This primarily means they must grab defensive rebounds and force turnovers.
2. Keep the ball away from the opponent. This means the team should avoid turnovers and grab offensive rebounds when they miss.
3. Ultimately convert possessions into points. This means the team should shoot efficiently from the floor and get to the free throw line.[23]

Which box score statistics primarily matter most in terms of team wins? The answer is shooting efficiency from the floor, free throw attempts, offensive and defensive rebounds, turnovers, and steals. The other factors – like assists, blocked shots, and personal fouls – matter and are included in the measure of how many wins a player produces. But these factors seem to matter less.

Given this list, how are players evaluated? Numerous studies have noted that the one factor that drives player evaluation is total points scored.[24] A player can increase their scoring by shooting more efficiently and getting to the free throw line. But they can also increase scoring by taking more shots from the field.

Consider the classic case of Andrew Wiggins. The 2014 draft was considered so good that people wrote articles speculating about which team was losing the most to get a chance to select Wiggins.[25] Andrew Wiggins was widely considered the best player in the 2014 draft and no one was surprised when he was selected by the Cleveland Cavaliers with the first pick in that draft. However, a look at Wiggins' college stats might have given pause for thought. Not only was Andrew Wiggins not the most productive player in

Division-I men's NCAA basketball in 2013–14, he was not even the most productive player on his college team. In 2013–14 the Kansas Jayhawks were led in Wins Produced by Joel Embiid, Perry Ellis, and Naadir Tharpe. Wiggins 3.4 Wins Produced was only fourth on his own team. His Wins Produced per 40 minutes of 0.118 was only slightly above average for a college player.[26] Wiggins was not even an elite college player as a freshman in college.

Again, these stats are only from one season. So perhaps it could be argued that a young player like Wiggins would get better. Unfortunately, across his first three NBA seasons there is not much evidence that this happened. As BoxScoreGeeks.com reported,[27] across Wiggins' first four seasons he was consistently below average (relative to the position he played in the NBA) with respect to shooting efficiency from the field, defensive rebounds, steals, and turnovers. In sum, when it comes to much of what determined wins, Wiggins was below average.

However, in terms of field goal attempts and total points scored, Wiggins was well above average. Given how players are evaluated in basketball, perhaps it is not surprising that the Minnesota Timberwolves gave Wiggins the maximum salary an NBA player of his experience could receive.[28]

The anecdotal story with respect to Wiggins is consistent with the systematic study of the NBA draft. Berri, Brook, and Fenn (2011) looked at what factors determined where college players were selected in the NBA draft. This work is updated in Table 2.2.

The results indicate that teams prefer younger players who play for college teams that have success. Appearing in the Final Four the year a player is drafted has a significant impact on where a player is selected. However, if a player returns to college after a Final Four appearance the benefit of this success vanishes. In other words, if a player is in the Final Four they must declare for the draft for this to help.

The NCAA tournament is a single elimination tournament, so advancing requires some luck. But if a team fails to advance there is still hope for the player. Playing for a winning team – by itself – definitely helps. In fact, the average college player drafted from 2001 to 2016 played for a team that won 72 percent of its games.

The results with respect to team success are consistent with a working paper by Greer, Price, and Berri (2017). This study looked at what factors determined whether or not a college player was drafted. The results indicated that scoring totals were also the most important box score statistics. In addition, team success mattered. Specifically, this study indicated that college players who played on teams that won less than 40 percent of their games were very unlikely to be drafted at all. That means that the NBA typically ignores thousands of players in choosing the best incoming talent simply because those players have poor teammates.[29]

Table 2.2 *Factors determining where a college player is selected in the NBA draft. Dependent variable: place taken in draft sample 2001 to 2016 (observations: 664)*

Independent Variables[a]	Marginal Value	Standard Deviation	One-Standard Deviation Change	p-value
Box Score Statistics				
Points per 40 minutes***	−1.337	4.018	−5.373	0.000
Blocked shots per 40 minutes***	−2.819	0.899	−2.533	0.000
Steals per 40 minutes***	−3.174	0.564	−1.789	0.000
Rebounds per 40 minutes***	−0.692	1.932	−1.336	0.006
Adjusted Field Goal Percentage***	−25.574	0.050	−1.272	0.006
Personal fouls per 40 minutes**	1.610	0.789	1.270	0.013
Turnover Percentage*	−0.253	3.654	−0.926	0.091
Assists per 40 minutes	−0.603	1.299		0.140
Free Throw Percentage	−0.541	0.096		0.923
Non-Box Score Statistics				
Age when drafted***	4.864	1.393	6.773	0.000
Team winning percentage***	−21.533	0.131	−2.823	0.000
Dummy variable, Final Four Team***	−3.524			0.008
Dummy variable, Final Four Team Last Year	1.926			0.245

Notes:
*** significant at the 99% level
** significant at the 95% level
* significant at the 90% level
[a] The model also controlled for year of the draft, position played by the player, and whether the player played in a power conference or a small conference.

Beyond ignoring a large population of talent, NBA teams also do not do a good job of evaluating those players they do consider. The results indicate that of all the box score statistics[30] tabulated for college players, points scored has the largest impact on where a player is selected. But shooting efficiency and rebounding are less important. When it comes to predicting future success, Berri, Brook and Fenn (2011) noted that scoring more points in college is not linked to increased productivity in the NBA. Shooting efficiency and rebounds, however, do predict better performance. Again, shooting efficiency and rebounds explain wins in basketball.[31]

Therefore, the factors that drive draft position are not necessarily the factors that drive winning. Not surprisingly – just as we saw in the NBA – where a player is drafted does not tell us much about a player's NBA performance. Let us consider the performance of the players that teams 'won' in the NBA lottery. The NBA lottery decides the first three picks in the draft. The teams that win these picks often hope they have landed a franchise-changing player. As Table 2.3 indicates, however, often the players the teams draft are not even above average talents.

An average player will produce 0.100 wins per 48 minutes (WP48).[32] From 1991 to 2013 there were 66 players selected with one of the top three choices.[33] Of these, 34 – or more than half – had a below average career WP48 after four years in the league. Eight of these below average performers were taken with the first pick overall. So the aforementioned Andrew Wiggins was not the first number one choice to do less than expected.

When we turn to the second pick overall the picture is even worse. Across these 20 years, the majority of second round picks (61 percent) were below average performers after four years in the league. The third choices were better. But this group also included players like Adam Morrison, Ben Gordon, and Jerry Stackhouse, none of whom ever contributed much to any NBA team.

Table 2.4 extends our analysis to the average performance of all first round draft picks. Once again, an average player has a 0.100 WP48. Of all these picks, the very first pick is generally the most productive. But on average, the top pick is not very much better than average. There were a few outstanding players taken with the first pick from 1991 to 2010. Shaquille O'Neal, Chris Webber, Tim Duncan, Yao Ming, LeBron James, Dwight Howard, and Anthony Davis were all taken with the first pick and all were productive NBA players. But as noted, many number one picks never lived up to that promise. Hence the average is not far above average.

In looking over this list we see that the expected pattern – top picks are better than later picks – is not what many expect. There is a positive correlation between draft position and NBA productivity.[34] If we look at average Wins Produced after four years and where a player is selected, we see that 55 percent of the variation in a player's total production can be explained by where he was drafted. This result, however, is driven by the link between minutes played and draft position, where draft position explains 85 percent of the variation in minutes played. Players who are drafted first tend to get more minutes regardless of how decision-makers perceive their performance.[35]

Table 2.3   Below average lottery picks from 1991 to 2013: career average WP48 after four years in the NBA

Player	Year	Career WP48 After 4 Years
First Pick		
Anthony Bennett	2013	−0.041
Andrea Bargnani	2006	−0.024
Kwame Brown	2001	0.069
Kenyon Martin	2000	0.061
Michael Olowokandi	1998	−0.031
Allen Iverson	1996	0.054
Joe Smith	1995	0.038
Glenn Robinson	1994	0.028
Second Pick		
Victor Oladipo	2013	0.078
Derrick Williams	2011	0.051
Evan Turner	2010	0.045
Hasheem Thabeet	2009	0.094
Michael Beasley	2008	−0.009
LaMarcus Aldridge	2006	0.086
Marvin Williams	2005	0.084
Darko Milicic	2003	0.037
Jay Williams	2002	0.013
Mike Bibby	1998	0.098
Keith Van Horn	1997	0.018
Antonio McDyess	1995	0.060
Shawn Bradley	1993	0.054
Kenny Anderson	1991	0.073
Third Pick		
Bradley Beal	2012	0.057
Enes Kanter	2011	0.086
O. J. Mayo	2008	0.064
Adam Morrison	2006	−0.112
Ben Gordon	2004	0.040
Carmelo Anthony	2003	0.027
Mike Dunleavy	2002	0.094
Chauncey Billups	1997	0.058
Shareef Abdur-Rahim	1996	0.098
Jerry Stackhouse	1995	0.014
Christian Laettner	1992	0.081

Table 2.4 *Average performance[a] of each first round NBA draft pick: 1991–2013*

PICK	Average Wins Produced After 4 Years	Average WP48 After 4 Years	PICK	Average Wins Produced After 4 Years	Average WP48 After 4 Years
1	24.4	0.126	16	6.6	0.074
2	16.2	0.098	17	6.8	0.066
3	20.4	0.110	18	7.4	0.086
4	16.1	0.092	19	3.6	0.046
5	16.3	0.101	20	5.6	0.073
6	10.3	0.070	21	10.8	0.109
7	11.5	0.073	22	8.7	0.107
8	9.5	0.073	23	8.2	0.089
9	17.4	0.122	24	9.5	0.095
10	11.6	0.086	25	3.5	0.066
11	7.5	0.079	26	8.9	0.125
12	6.4	0.066	27	6.4	0.094
13	11.0	0.090	28	4.6	0.069
14	5.4	0.056	29	5.0	0.090
15	8.8	0.100	30	7.7	0.124

Notes: [a] This is a weighted average. It is found by looking at total Wins Produced and total minutes played by every player at that spot in the draft.

Once one controls for this bias the link between draft pick and performance essentially vanishes. In this sample there is no statistical relationship between where a player is drafted and WP48. The top pick is the best, but productivity from the ninth pick, 26th pick, and 30th pick are similar. Essentially, one can find productive players after the top three picks and even after the first half of the first round.

No team better illustrates this point than the San Antonio Spurs. Starting in 1997–98, the Spurs have won at least 61 percent of their regular season games – or at least 50 games in an 82-game regular season – every single year. In 1997 the Spurs took Tim Duncan with the number one pick in the draft. But after that, the highest they have ever drafted was the 24th pick in the draft.[36] Despite never having a high draft pick, the Spurs – unlike every other NBA team – keep winning year after year.

One might think this was entirely due to Tim Duncan. Certainly Duncan was an outstanding player in his career. Across his 19 NBA seasons he produced 218.2 wins. But in those years the Spurs won 1,072 regular season games, so about 854 wins were not about Duncan. Furthermore, if the

Spurs replaced Duncan with a player who produced no wins they would still have won 56.5 percent of their games. And if Duncan was replaced by an average NBA player the Spurs would have won 63 percent of their games across these 19 seasons.

This tells us that the Spurs were much more than Duncan. Other players also produced wins. The list of such players includes:

- Manu Ginobili (112.7 Wins Produced from 2002–03 to 2015–16);
- Tony Parker (86.6 Wins Produced from 2001–02 to 2015–16);
- Kawhi Leonard (61.8 Wins Produced from 2011–12 to 2015–16).

None of these three players was taken in the NBA lottery. Even when we add the productivity of these three players to Duncan's production we still do not get to half the wins the Spurs accumulated in Duncan's career.

What the Spurs have shown is that productive players can be found in all sorts of places. They have demonstrated for more than two decades that a team does not have to endure years of failure to be competitive.

However, the Sixers ignored this example. Instead, Sam Hinkie tried to build a title contender through the draft lottery. Hinkie did accumulate many more lottery picks than the Spurs. But these lottery picks failed to produce very many wins. Here were the specific draft picks:

- 2013 drafted Michael Carter-Williams with the 11th pick and traded Jrue Holiday and Pierre Jackson to the New Orleans Pelicans for Nerlens Noel (sixth pick overall).[37]
- 2014 drafted Joel Embiid with the third pick and Elfrid Payton with the 10th pick. Payton was sent to the Orlando Magic for Dario Saric (the 12th pick), and second round pick in 2015 and a first round pick in 2017.[38]
- 2015 drafted Jahlil Okafor with the third pick.

The following is what these lottery picks did for the 76ers:

- Michael Carter-Williams won the NBA Rookie of the Year in 2014. However, Hinkie traded him to the Milwaukee Bucks (as part of a three-team trade) for what ultimately became an unprotected draft pick in 2018. In the end, Carter-Williams produced 3.3 wins for the Sixers.[39]
- Nerlens Noel was with the Sixers for less than three seasons. In this time he produced 13.5 wins.[40] Although Noel was easily the most productive Hinkie selection, Hinkie traded Noel to the Dallas Mavericks for two second round picks, Justin Anderson (former

21st pick in the draft) and Andrew Bogut (who the Sixers promptly waived). In sum, it could be argued that Noel was just given away.

- Joel Embiid was injured and missed both his first and second seasons. Injuries also limited his third season to just 786 minutes and only 1.4 Wins Produced.[41] In 2017–18 Embiid was healthy enough to play in 63 of the team's 82 regular season games. Although Embiid was above average with respect to points scored and rebounds, his shooting efficiency wasn't far above average, and his turnovers were far below average for his position. So his WP48 was only 0.115. This is an above average mark but not exactly what the Spurs received from Tim Duncan from 19 seasons.

- Dario Saric played 2129 minutes in his rookie season in 2016–17 (he was in Europe until that season). In that time he produced −2.6 wins (i.e. a negative mark).[42]

- Jahlil Okafor played 2750 minutes with the Sixers in little more than two years. In that time he produced −2.0 wins (a negative).[43] Okafor was then traded to the Brooklyn Nets (along with Nik Stauskas) for journeyman Trevor Booker.[44]

What did these lottery picks do for the Sixers through the 2016–17 season? The five picks produced a combined 13.6 wins and most of those were produced by Nerlens Noel, a player the Sixers essentially gave to the Dallas Mavericks. To put that in perspective, in 2016–17 Kawhi Leonard – a former 15th choice in the NBA draft – produced 15.0 wins for the San Antonio Spurs.

Of course, the inability of all these lottery picks to produce wins did keep returning the Sixers to the lottery. In 2016 – after Hinkie left – the Sixers took Ben Simmons. Although Simmons missed his rookie season due to injury, in 2017–18 he produced 16.5 wins and posted a 0.289 WP48.[45] It is clearly early in Simmons' career, but it is possible that he will be an immensely good player. But even if Simmons becomes as consistently as productive as Tim Duncan, the Sixers will need much more to be title contender.

To illustrate, the New Orleans Pelicans selected Anthony Davis with the first pick in the 2012 draft. Across his five seasons Davis produced 50.7 wins and posted a WP48 of 0.211.[46] But the Pelicans only averaged 34 wins across those five years because the Pelicans – unlike the Spurs – have failed to find many players who can produce wins besides Davis.

So are the Sixers with Simmons going to be like the Pelicans or the Spurs? It is too early to say. But we can say that the Sixers accumulated many lottery picks and so far most of those picks have failed to produce many wins. Given what we have learned about the draft, this is not surprising. Because the process of choosing draft picks is imperfect, the results are not very reliable.

2.5 THE FAILED PROMISE OF THE DRAFT

We have seen in both the NFL and NBA that the draft does not live up to its promise. The reasons, however, are not entirely the same. In the NFL it is very difficult to forecast future performance for veterans. So it not surprising that NFL decision-makers cannot forecast the NFL productivity of college players. Of course, the inability to forecast suggests that significant resources should not be expended for players who it is not certain are any better than later choices.

In the NBA, the issue is not entirely an inability to forecast the future. Although one cannot forecast future NBA performance perfectly, college statistics do tell us something about the future. But NBA decision-makers fail to understand this data. By over-emphasizing scoring and team wins – two factors that do not predict higher productivity in the NBA – decision-makers often make mistakes in choosing players. As a result, many top picks are no more productive than picks chosen later.

In the end, it appears that the draft in the NBA and NFL is more consistent with the vision of those who critiqued the assumption of rationality in economics (i.e. Veblen, Simon, and Thaler) and less consistent with the idea that decision-makers are like expert billiard players (offered by Freidman and Savage). So one should be hesitant to put much faith in the 'the Process' in the NBA. And if a Nobel Laureate like Thaler gives you advice in football . . . well, maybe you should pay close attention to what he is saying.

NOTES

1. The story of Stan Kostka and the birth of the NFL draft was also told in *Stumbling on Wins* (Berri and Schmidt, 2010) and *Sports Economics* (Berri, 2018).
2. See https://www.sports-reference.com/cfb/schools/minnesota/1934.html.
3. 'Football', *Time* magazine, 2 November 1934 (http://www.time.com/time/magazine/article/0,9171,882323-1,00.html).
4. The American Professional Football Association came into existence in 1920. In 1922 the league was renamed the National Football League. See https://www.pro-football-reference.com/years/.
5. The Eagles still exist today. The Brooklyn franchise folded after the 1944 season.
6. See http://www.bls.gov/data/inflation_calculator.htm.
7. See http://www.nytimes.com/2002/06/28/sports/jay-berwanger-88-winner-of-the-first-heisman-trophy.html.
8. See http://www.pro-football-reference.com/years/1936/draft.htm. Kostka did play, but

not much. The Dodgers only had his services for the 1935 season, where he played in nine games and rushed for 249 yards. So the Dodgers paid Kostka $555.56 per game in 1935, or $20.08 per yard (http://www.pro-football-reference.com/players/K/KostSt20. htm).

9. The NHL adopted the draft in 1963, while baseball held its first draft in 1965.
10. Both the NFL and NBA have experimented with minor leagues. But in general, most drafted players in both leagues will play (if they play at all) for the team in the major league that chose them in the draft.
11. *The Economist* (March 20, 2009). 'Herbert Simon' (http://www.economist.com/node/13350892).
12. Dan Ariely (2008) – another critic of the rationality assumption in economics – wrote a book called *Predictably Irrational*. This book (consistent with the work of Thaler) not only argues that human being are irrational but that their irrationality is predictable (as the title suggests).
13. To complete the story, Veblen also spent part of his career at the University of Chicago. Of course one should also emphasize that people outside the University of Chicago have also discussed these ideas.
14. See http://www.nfl.com/combine/profiles/robert-griffin,%20iii?id=2533033.
15. See http://sports.espn.go.com/nfl/draft06/news/story?id=2410670.
16. See http://ftw.usatoday.com/2017/10/nfl-richard-thaler-nfl-draft-nobel-prize-dan-snyder-redskins.
17. On March 10, 2017 Griffin was released by the Cleveland Browns. The Browns' record in 2016 was 1-15. Although Griffin was only 27 years old when he was cut, being released by the worst team in the NFL does not suggest that your career has a promising future.
18. The Wonderlic test is a 50-question exam designed to measure a person's intelligence. The questions are not about football, and the test has been used by a large number of non-sports firms.
19. These included a measure of Wins Produced (see Berri (2007) and Berri and Burke (2012)) and the NFL's quarterback rating measure.
20. Berri and Simmons (2011) noted that completion percentage in college explained 20 percent of the variation in completion percentage in the NFL. But no relationship was found for performance metrics that sought to consider much of what a quarterback did on the field (like Wins Produced and the NFL's quarterback rating).
21. A quarterback still had to be in the league after four years. One could also just look at all quarterbacks after four years (regardless of whether they were still in the league after four years). The results, however, are similar.
22. Measuring performance in basketball is detailed in Berri, Schmidt, and Brook (2006), Berri (2008, 2018), and Berri and Schmidt (2010). The basic Wins Produced metric can also be seen at The Wages of Wins Journal (http://wagesofwins.com/how-to-calculate-wins-produced/) and Box Score Geeks (boxscoregeeks.com).
23. Players tend to shoot much more efficiently from the free throw line than they do from the field. Because of this, getting to the free throw line – by itself – is important.
24. The primacy of scoring in the evaluation of basketball talent was noted with respect to salaries by Berri, Schmidt, and Brook (2006), Berri, Brook, and Schmidt (2007), and Berri and Simmons (2011). Scoring was also seen as the driving force behind the allocation of minutes per game (see Berri, Deutscher, and Galletti (2015)) and the allocation of post-season awards (see Berri and Schmidt (2010) and Berri, Van Gilder, and Fenn (2014)).
25. See http://bleacherreport.com/articles/1714034-the-reverse-nba-power-rankings-whos-tanking-hardest-for-andrew-wiggins.
26. An average team will win 0.500 games. So in college, an average team will win 0.500 games per 40 minutes. This means that an average player will produce 0.100 wins per 40 minutes.
27. See https://www.boxscoregeeks.com/players/1463-andrew-wiggins.

28. In October 2017 it was reported that Wiggins signed a five-year contract that would pay him $146.5 million. Given the league's collective bargaining agreement, this was the maximum Minnesota could pay him (see http://bleacherreport.com/articles/2722896-andrew-wiggins-timberwolves-agree-to-5-year-148-million-contract-extension).

29. Berri (2018) notes that the most productive men's college basketball player since 2002–03 was Anthony Davis. In 2011–12, Davis produced 12.96 wins for the University of Kentucky. That year Kentucky played 40 games. So by himself, Davis would have only given Kentucky a 0.325 winning percentage.

30. Except for turnover percentage, adjusted field goal percentage, and free throw percentage, the box score statistics were adjusted for position played and measured per 40 minutes played.

31. It should be noted that turnover percentage is also significant in the model explaining draft position. But the sign suggests that the more a player turns the ball over the better will be their draft position. That is likely because players who handle the ball more commit more turnovers. Of course, committing more turnovers does not help a team win.

32. As noted, an average team will win 0.500 games. In other words, an average team will produce 0.500 wins per 48 minutes. So one player – or one-fifth of a team – will produce 0.100 wins per 48 minutes.

33. Numbers from 1991 to 2010 were compiled by the author. From 2011 to 2013, numbers provided by Andres Alvarez of BoxScoreGeeks.com. The underlying numbers to calculate Wins Produced can all be found at basketball-reference.com.

34. The analysis presented here is of the 30 observations in Table 2.4.

35. This result was noted in Camerer and Weber (1999) and Berri and Schmidt (2010).

36. See https://www.basketball-reference.com/teams/SAS/draft.html.

37. This trade also sent Orlando's first round pick (who became Elfrid Payton) in 2014 to the Philadelphia 76ers. See https://www.basketball-reference.com/players/n/noelne01.html.

38. See https://www.basketball-reference.com/players/p/paytoel01.html.

39. See https://www.boxscoregeeks.com/players/1411-michael-carter-williams.

40. See https://www.boxscoregeeks.com/players/1413-nerlens-noel.

41. See https://www.boxscoregeeks.com/players/1516-joel-embiid.

42. See https://www.boxscoregeeks.com/players/1520-dario-saric.

43. See https://www.boxscoregeeks.com/players/3089-jahlil-okafor.

44. See http://www.espn.com/nba/story/_/id/21703295/brooklyn-nets-acquire-jahlil-okafor-nik-stauskas-trading-trevor-booker-philadelphia-76ers.

45. See https://www.boxscoregeeks.com/players/3131-ben-simmons.

46. See https://www.boxscoregeeks.com/players/1287-anthony-davis.

REFERENCES

Ariely, Dan (2008) *Predictably Irrational: The Hidden Forces that Shape Our Decisions*, New York, NY: HarperCollins.

Berri, David J. (2018) *Sports Economics*, New York, NY: Worth Publishers/Macmillan Education.

Berri, David J. (2012) 'Measuring performance in the National Basketball Association', in Stephen Shmanske and Leo Kahane (eds), *The Handbook of Sports Economics*, Oxford, UK: Oxford University Press, pp. 94–117.

Berri, David J. (2008) 'A simple measure of worker productivity in the National Basketball Association', in Brad Humphreys and Dennis Howard (eds), *The Business of Sport*, Westport, CT: Praeger, pp. 1–40.

Berri, David J. (2007) 'Back to back evaluation on the gridiron', in James H. Albert and Ruud H. Koning (eds), *Statistical Thinking in Sport*, Boca Raton, Florida: Chapman & Hall/CRC, pp. 235–256.

Berri, David and Brian Burke (2012) 'Measuring performance in the NFL', in Kevin Quinn (ed.), *The Economics of the National Football League: The State of the Art*, New York, NY: Springer Publisher, pp. 137–158.

Berri, David J. and Martin B. Schmidt (2010) *Stumbling on Wins: Two Economists Explore the Pitfalls on the Road to Victory in Professional Sports*, Princeton, NJ: Financial Times Press.

Berri, David J. and Rob Simmons (2011) 'Catching a draft: on the process of selecting quarterbacks in the National Football League amateur draft', *Journal of Productivity Analysis*, **35** (1), 37–49.

Berri, David J., Stacey L. Brook, and Aju Fenn (2011) 'From college to the pros: predicting the NBA amateur player draft', *Journal of Productivity Analysis*, **35** (1), 25–35.

Berri, David J., Stacey L. Brook, and Martin B. Schmidt (2007) 'Does one simply need to score to score?', *International Journal of Sport Finance*, **2** (4), 190–205.

Berri, David J., Christian Deutscher, and Arturo Galletti (2015), 'Born in the USA: national origin effects on time allocation in US and Spanish professional basketball', for special issue of *National Institute Economic Review*, May, R41–R50.

Berri, David J., Martin B. Schmidt, and Stacey L. Brook (2006) *The Wages of Wins: Taking Measure of the Many Myths in Modern Sport*, Stanford, CA: Stanford University Press.

Berri, David J., Jennifer Van Gilder, and Aju Fenn (2014) 'Is the sports media color-blind?', *International Journal of Sport Finance*, **9**, 130–148.

Camerer, Colin and Roberto A. Weber (1999) 'The econometrics and behavioral economics of escalation of commitment in NBA draft choices', *Journal of Economic Behavior & Organization*, **39**, 59–82.

Friedman, Milton and L. J. Savage (1948) 'The utility analysis of choices involving risk', *The Journal of Political Economy*, **56** (4), 279–304.

Greer, Tiffany, Joshua Price, and David Berri (2017) 'Jumping in the pool: what determines which players the NBA considers in the NBA draft?', Originally presented at the Western Economic Association; Honolulu, Hawaii: July 2015.

Krautmann, Anthony, Peter Von Allmen, and David J. Berri (2009), 'The underpayment of restricted players in North American sports leagues', *International Journal of Sports and Finance*, **4** (3), 155–169.

Massey, Cade and Richard H. Thaler (2013) 'The loser's curse: decision making and market efficiency in the National Football League draft', *Management Science*, **59** (7), 1479–1495.

Veblen, Thorstein (1898) 'Why is economics not an evolutionary science', *The Quarterly Journal of Economics*, **12**, 373–397.

3. The golden generation: the personnel economics of youth recruitment in European professional soccer

Joachim Prinz and Daniel Weimar

3.1 INTRODUCTION

In 1998 and 2000 respectively, the German national soccer team closed the World and European Soccer Championships with disappointing results. As a consequence, and based on the fact that in Europe elite youth education is in charge of the soccer clubs themselves (and not schools and colleges), the German Soccer Association (DFB) and the German Soccer League[1] (DFL) profoundly restructured the youth education and youth recruitment system in German soccer (DFB, 2015). From 2001, the clubs of the top soccer division (and later, second division clubs as well) were required to operate a so-called 'elite youth academy' as a core requirement to receive a playing license for the top two divisions (DFB, 2015). Since 2002, the DFB operates 366 training bases for regional and federal youth selections (U12–U15). Today, this change is considered to be one of the key antecedents to Germany's 2014 World Cup victory.[2] Thus, human resource management of youth elite human capital (also called talent identification and development (TID)) is one crucial determinant of the success of soccer clubs and national teams, and thus seems worthy to be discussed in more detail (Williams and Reilly, 2000; Unnithan et al., 2012).

From a personnel economics point of view, the time spent on youth teams endows young athletes with general soccer-related human capital (Becker, 1962) and with team- and club-specific human capital (Jovanovic, 1979b) – with both types of human capital determining the probability of entering professional soccer (Göke et al., 2014).

For a club, the youth recruitment process serves as both an education function to disseminate soccer-related skills and personal skills, and as a long-term screening vehicle with a filter-function so as to better assess the quality of the match between the club and the player (Jovanovic, 1979a; Spence, 1973).[3] Therefore, considering the traditional life cycle model (Vernon, 1966), the period of TID can be seen as the first and second career stage of soccer athletes (see Prinz and Weimar, 2016). The economic utility of clubs and young athletes from TID are congruent: TID increases a young player's marginal productivity, and in the process helps clubs to develop a professional soccer player (Ashworth and Heyndels, 2007). With the latter, a player can become a professional in one of two ways: either within his youth team or by being transferred to another club. For the club, youth players whose marginal productivity is too low to justify the (youth) education can either be sold, or they can be leased out to other clubs and returned later. Unlike North American major sports leagues, where the draft system regulates the transition from youth (high school or college teams) to professional teams, youth players in Europe are allowed to be traded between clubs – before and after leaving the youth leagues (U19). Thus, and in line with classical product markets, youth players are viewed economically as future 'innovations' necessary for potential advantages in the market (Rogers, 1983). Since the 'true' talent of a young player is more uncertain in their early years, clubs have the incentive to screen as many young players as possible to select the most promising ones (Schmidt et al., 2017; Unnithan et al., 2012). This means that every year some players who might be valuable to other (lower) teams have to leave the club. This process helps the best players to find the best clubs (and vice versa) and is called assortative matching, which is particularly evident in the sports sector due to the high transparency and observability of talent (Drut and Duhautois, 2017; Gandelman, 2008). Therefore, the selection process in European youth soccer can be defined as an open innovation process (Chesbrough, 2003), whereby youth players either continue with the current club, change clubs, temporarily change clubs (on lease), or even exit soccer due to higher opportunity costs[4] such as school, alternative hobbies or relationships (Barnsley et al., 1985; Schmidt et al., 2017). In the case of a club change, the player adds utility to the 'innovation process' of another club. In higher age groups (U19+, these teams only play in senior leagues), the remaining roster slots are very restricted, and thus many youth players have to be capitalized by selling or lending them to other clubs. Leasing is an especially attractive option for the youth club, since a player can increase his human capital without losing the comeback option, which might be valuable if the player achieves a performance improvement beyond the U19.[5] Since youth players are young and have no information about their future market value and talent outcomes, they make decisions under uncertainty, leading to high drop-out rates during the TID processes (Schmidt et al., 2017). This assumption of TID as an economic open innovation process is examined further by Prinz and Weimar (2016).

Despite similarities between recruitment in soccer and recruitment in broader labor markets, there are crucial differences when discussing organizational and personnel implications for TID policies and investments. To illustrate the European peculiarities of human resource management in youth soccer, we first discuss the structure of the German youth recruitment system and the TID regulations of the international soccer association (FIFA). Then, we examine differences between the soccer players' labor market and the general labor market, and the resulting implications for youth recruitment. Following that, the specific economic peculiarities of youth recruitment are examined in more detail: first, the matching process and the determinants of a professional career are considered; second, we discuss an important phenomenon and market inefficiency of youth education in soccer by presenting original data and analysis on the 'relative age effect'. The German soccer market is used as a reference market for the European youth soccer structures.[6]

3.2   THE GERMAN YOUTH RECRUITMENT SYSTEM

Unlike North American youth recruitment systems, German schools and colleges primarily offer sporting activities in the form of voluntary sport groups. These sports groups only aim to provide soccer participation without any (or at a low level of) competition.

Instead, soccer education is basically under the control of the soccer clubs.[7] From 'Under 5' (U5) to 'Under 19' (U19) there are municipal, communal, regional and (from U17 on) nationwide leagues controlled by the DFB and 21 regional soccer associations (Landesfussballverbände). Each age group consists of players of the two lower age cohorts (e.g. U19 are players aged 18 and 17; U18 are players aged 17 and 16, etc.). Youth players can always play in older age groups, but not in lower ones. The last separately organized age group is U19. After that, youth players must enter senior teams. Professional and semi-professional teams often possess U21 and U23 teams, which play in lower senior divisions (they can only be promoted to the third division, at best). Youth players who are aged 16 or older can be provided with an official player contract. Within an age group, leagues are open to relegations and promotions as in senior soccer (Hoehn and Szymanski, 1999). For elite soccer education, there are structures provided by the DFB (training camps, youth national teams) and by professional soccer clubs in the form of elite youth academies. Unlike in North America, where players who do not enter the major leagues often quit playing the sport (as an organized competition), every youth soccer player can find a club in a senior team in one of current 25,075 registered soccer clubs (DFB.de).[8] Thus, there are no sunk costs for youth players after passing through the youth system.

Until 2000, there were few regulations for soccer clubs regarding TID. However, from an organizational perspective there is one crucial problem when clubs are deciding on investment into youth academies: free riding. This means that while one team invests in the development of a youth player, another club could capitalize on the benefit if no contract exists, or when the contract with the youth player ends. Since agreements are restricted to five years (and only for players older than 16) and player performance is observable for outside bidders, clubs tend to under-invest in youth soccer development (Bougheas and Downward, 2003; Kesenne, 2007). Generally, even in the case of a transfer fee, the emitting club faces incomplete information on the future market value of the player, which leads to incomplete transfer agreements and contracts (Schmidt et al., 2017; Tirole, 1999). Teams therefore avoid investments in their own youth academies, with the result that the overall quality of soccer education decreases (Bougheas and Downward, 2003). Consequently, there was a fundamental market inefficiency in the German TID process (which became publicly apparent after the 1998 and 2000 disasters), and was the reason the DFB decided to clarify the property rights over youth athletes. To strengthen the property rights over a youth player, and thus to increase the incentives to invest in youth academies, the DFB, the DFL and FIFA set up two core regulations (Kesenne, 2007): (1) an obligation for clubs of 1. Bundesliga and 2. Bundesliga to run an elite youth academy (since 2001) and (2) the FIFA youth compensation regulations.

Since 2001, professional teams have been required to operate elite youth academies under DFL law (§ 3 No. 2 Lizenzierungsordnung). There are very specific and detailed descriptions of how the elite youth academies have to be organized and equipped (see Table 3.1 for an overview). To induce quality maximization of elite youth soccer education, elite youth academies are frequently rated by a specialized agency (DFL, 2015). This rating includes eight main categories and 300 subcategories, whereby the main categories are weighted by their importance (Table 3.2).

These weights can be interpreted as a DFL market evaluation of different education priorities and of the overall quality of soccer education. Based on the overall score, elite youth academies are ranked from zero stars (low quality) to three stars (high quality).[9] Currently, all 36 first and second division clubs and 10 clubs from the third division run their own elite youth academies. In 2013–2014, 5601 youth players were registered in youth teams (U12–U23) connected to elite youth academies (DFL, 2015).

Table 3.1   *Minimum requirements for elite youth academies according to DFL law (Anhang, No. 2, LO)*

Category	1. Bundesliga Clubs	2. Bundesliga Clubs
Facilities	• 3 pitches, 2 with floodlights • Technikparcours • Training hall • Boarding home • Canteen	• 2 pitches, 1 with floodlights • Technikparcours • Training hall • Boarding home • Canteen
Staff	• 7 head coaches with at a least a B-License, 3 full time, 2 with an A-License • 1 goalkeeper coach, part time • Obligatory participation at training courses held at the academy	• 7 head coaches with at least a B-License, 2 full time, 1 with an A-License • 1 goalkeeper coach, part time • Obligatory participation at training courses held at the academy
Medical Care	• Medic room • 2 massage rooms • Sauna • Revitalizing pool • Medic, part time • Physiotherapist, full time • Rehabilitation/coordination coach, full time • Annual medical examination of all youth athletes	• Medic room • Massage room • Medic, part time • Physiotherapist, part time • Rehabilitation/coordination coach, part time • Annual medical examination of all youth athletes
Concept	Elaboration of a youth development concept	
Education	Appropriate cooperation with a public school	

Table 3.2   *Weighted evaluation criteria for elite youth academies (Bonarius, 2015)*

Criterion	Weights
Strategy and Finances	5.8 %
Organization	4.8%
Soccer Education	26.3 %
Support and General Education	9.2 %
Qualification of Staff	22.2 %
Communication/Cooperation	8.6 %
Infrastructure	7.3 %
Effectiveness (Promotion of Youth Players)	15.8 %

2002/2003–2015/2016

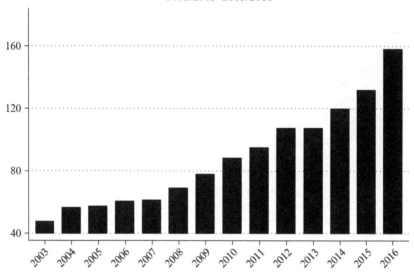

Note: Data is drawn from the Bundesliga reports published yearly by the German Soccer League (DFL).

Figure 3.1   Expenses for youth recruitment in the first and second Bundesliga

Furthermore, to further increase the incentive to invest in their own elite youth academy, the DFL requires all professional teams to list at least eight players in the professional roster who were educated in a German elite youth academy, while four of these players must have passed through (for at least three years) their own youth academy (§ 5b, Lizenzordnung Spieler). As depicted in Figure 3.1, the expenses for clubs' investments in TID have significantly increased since 2003. Therefore, the restructuring of the German TID concept is widely considered to be both successful (rising investments) and effective (World Cup Champions 2014).

Apart from regulations pertaining to the quality of youth TID processes, FIFA law prescribes the financial compensation of youth players. The basic economic dilemma of youth soccer education is in the temporal shift between human capital development (youth academies) and human capital evaluation (senior team). More precisely, the true value of a youth player is only revealed after some seasons in senior soccer, while contracts made by the training club (e.g. transfer fees, salaries) are 'deeply' incomplete as a result of imprecise property rights (Schmidt et al., 2017; Tirole, 1999). To overcome this dilemma, FIFA prescribes different schemes to compensate

Table 3.3   Compensation fees according to FIFA law (Circular 1537)

	Category I	Category II	Category II	Category IV
AFC	–	$40,000	$10,000	$2,000
CAF	–	$30,000	$10,000	$2,000
CONCACAF	–	$40,000	$10,000	$2,000
CONMEBOL	$50,000	$30,000	$10,000	$2,000
OFC	–	$30,000	$10,000	$2,000
UEFA	€90,000	€60,000	€30,000	€10,000

Notes: Examples: Category I: England, Germany, Argentina, Brazil; Category II: Austria, Costa Rica, Morocco, Egypt; Category III: Gambia, Sudan, Bolivia, Croatia; Category IV: Liechtenstein, Fiji, Panama, Zambia.

youth clubs (for providing training), even after a player has left the club. The regulations are codified by the 'FIFA Regulations on the Status and Transfer of Players (RSTP)'. First, if a player is less than 23 years of age, the new club has to pay a training compensation fee 'when a player signs his first contract as a professional, and each time a professional is transferred until the end of the season of his 23rd birthday' (Article 20, RSTP). Compensation fees are announced annually by FIFA circulars. Table 3.3 shows the 2016 compensation fees.

Furthermore, and most importantly, according to the FIFA Article 21 RSTP, 5 percent of every transaction fee has to be shared proportionally among the former youth clubs where the player was trained between his 12th and 23rd birthdays ('solidarism mechanism'). More precisely, the percentage share of the transaction fee is divided[10] by the players' team tenure.[11] By offering emitting youth clubs future compensation where the player becomes a star, even smaller clubs have incentives to invest in their own youth education. It would be pointless for a small club to hold back a youth player from moving to a bigger club, since the probabilities of incoming cash flows from a youth player are higher in a professional team, which makes smaller clubs more open to recommending a move to better teams. To sum up, the RSTP expanded the property rights over players and reduced market inefficiency.

Besides the RSTP, the DFB youth regulations (§ 3 Jugendordnung) determine basic transaction fees for youth players moving to other clubs, depending on the division of the club to which the player is moving (Table 3.4).[12] These transaction fees do not have to be paid if the player is signing his first professional contract, or he has no contract and regularly changes clubs (within the transfer window). In such cases, FIFA training compensation fees (Table 3.3) have to be paid. The regulations are of great

Table 3.4   Basic transaction fees for youth players (§ 3, No. 2, JO)

Division	Basic Fee U16–U18	Basic Fee U13–U15	Fee per Season	Total Fee U12 or Younger
1	€2,500	€1,500	€200	–
2	€1,500	€1,000	€150	–
3	€1,250	€750	€125	–
4	€1,000	€500	€100	–
5	€750	€400	€50	–
6	€500	€300	€50	–
7	€400	€200	€50	–
8	€300	€150	€50	–
9	€200	€100	€25	–
10	€100	€50	€25	–
11	€50	€25	€25	–

importance, especially for youth transactions at the amateur level and for the players themselves.

3.3   GENERAL IDIOSYNCRASIES OF THE LABOR MARKET FOR YOUNG ATHLETES

Compared to non-sport labor markets and industries, the soccer business is characterized by a variety of peculiarities regarding the human capital development of players. However, one aspect is the same: as with other (non-sport) workers, the general aim of the soccer player is to maximize marginal productivity and lifetime earnings (Ashworth and Heyndels, 2007). This is especially true for elite youth soccer education (rather than youth teams of amateur clubs), which will be considered in the following discussion.

The most differentiating factor in youth elite soccer education lies in its organization and its financing of basic human capital development (Becker, 1962). While in traditional industries, human capital is developed in the firm, in schools, and in higher education institutions, teams in the soccer business are in charge of developing basic and soccer-related human capital by themselves. Since only a few youth academies exist, youth players have to decide early in their lives where to improve their basic soccer education. Such decisions are often influenced by uncertainties (Schmidt et al., 2017), as they may require that youth players and their families move from home, abandoning their social networks. The decision to enter an elite youth academy as a very young athlete (compared to traditional school education) leads to two critical economic issues. First, since joining a youth academy is often associated with the relocation of a player and his family, the young player enters a locked-in situation, as a move to another club would be associated with sunk costs at the current club and additional costs to the family. Thus, once they have entered a youth academy, most youth players only leave the club after finishing the U19 level, or upon receiving a professional contract. This locked-in situation increases the costs for the player (in terms of effort, pressure, costs incurred by the parents for equipment and further personal training, etc.). A departure would lead to the loss of almost all sunk costs. In traditional education, young pupils enter and re-enter different schools, losing only social capital, and experience little loss of sunk costs. After basic schooling, the acquired general human capital can be capitalized into a wide range of opportunities, such as higher education, vocational training or entrepreneurship. In contrast, in elite youth soccer education, only a small fraction, about 2 to 5 percent (Göke et al., 2014; Kassis et al., 2017), enter professional soccer, meaning that 95 to 98 percent face a partial or total depreciation of their soccer-related human capital. Even though there is more than one way to become a professional, the youth soccer market displays strong 'winner-take-all' market characteristics (Frank et al., 1996). Although young players are aware of the overall low probability of becoming a professional player, they still often believe that the odds are with them and may become overconfident (Jung et al., 2012). The more a youth player has already invested in his soccer-specific human capital the more likely he will continue with elite soccer until he is selected by the coach, instead of losing his sunk costs and accepting an alternative career path. Schmidt et al. conclude (2017, p. 18), 'the longer individuals [youth players] survive this selection process, the more willing they are to sacrifice, for example higher educational degrees for an uncertain career trajectory'. Additionally, continuing high-risk soccer education could be explained by a success bias associated with success at early stages during the youth selection process. In addition, young players with lower socio-economic or migrant backgrounds accept higher risks when it comes to investments in soccer training (Schmidt et al., 2017).

Another important difference between the non-sport labor market and the labor market for young soccer players is based on the fact that, in the latter, performance is publicly available for rival soccer clubs. This leads to a greater frequency of outside offers to youth soccer players by external clubs. Borland and Lye (1996, p. 144) state: 'Whereas studies of matching generally assume that workers control separation decisions, the market for soccer . . . is a "thin" market in which firms initiate separations'. Thus, outside of sports, it is the employees who mainly initiate the process of leaving their employer; however, in soccer and youth soccer, external clubs (who offer youth players higher salaries or a better chance of becoming a professional player) mainly initiate such departures (Borland and Lye, 1996; Göke et al., 2014). This drives salaries and transfer biddings, especially if two different clubs enter into a bidding war for a particular player.

The possibility of major injuries and their significant impact on a successful youth development process also distinguishes youth soccer players from young workers outside the sports business. Even if students or young workers become sick, they rarely suffer from a deep decline in productivity. In the case of young soccer players, however, injuries are critical to their career and occur more frequently. According to Price et al. (2004), players of youth soccer academies face 0.40 injuries per player per year.

Moreover, difficulties are present for any potential switch to other sports. One reason for this is the limited transference of the general sports-related human capital generated by soccer training (endurance, athleticism, flexibility, reaction) to other sports, like handball, basketball or running. In schooling, there might be some competition between private and public schools; however, both strands end in the same labor market. In the case of soccer, moving to another sport is associated with sunk costs for the soccer industry (even in older age ranges, clubs in other sports do not have to pay compensation or transfer fees).

When comparing youth investments to investments in goods innovations, the investment of clubs in TID is equally costly, but is not listed on the club's balance sheets, as such investments are intangible human resources. Only transaction fees can be linearly depreciated over the contract length. This peculiarity makes a corporate valuation of soccer clubs complicated, since the most valuable assets (future incoming paybacks from youth players) cannot be considered, and/or are very uncertain.

The role of parents is another aspect when developing young soccer players. Sometimes, attending a youth academy puts stress on the family environment, which might then influence the player's performance (Harwood et al., 2010). As a consequence, parents' socialization and identification with the youth academy is as important as it is for the player himself (Clarke and Harwood, 2014), which makes the market for youth athletes more complex compared to the general workforce (where decisions are generally made without parental interventions). In all negotiations, parents have to be present. From a club's perspective, negotiations and decisions must not only benefit the youth player, but also the player's parents. This, in turn, increases transaction costs and uncertainty, since the utility of parents is sometimes not fully compatible with the utility of the youth player.

In summary, the general peculiarities in the personnel economics of youth soccer – such as incomplete contracts, high turnover rates caused by outside offers, high exit rates through injuries, or considerable parental involvement – are associated with an increased risk of sunk costs for the clubs. The resulting uncertainty about the future development and capitalization of the investments make strategic financial planning very challenging in the soccer industry.

3.4 MATCHING AND THE DETERMINANTS OF A PROFESSIONAL CAREER

Operating a youth soccer academy has two (personnel) economics objectives: increasing a youth player's marginal productivity, and collecting information about a player's hidden characteristics. The latter are especially important benefits for clubs in operating their own youth systems, since performance on the pitch can be considered public information and can be observed by all. Thus, internal 'private' information, or exclusive information, becomes an important part of the matching theory provided by Jovanovic (1979a). Following this matching theory, soccer clubs operate youth teams primarily to accumulate private information about the players (e.g. personality, motivation, team building, team identity) so as to better approximate the player's future productivity, and to better assess the matching compatibility with the youth club, thus reducing outcome uncertainty (Gandelman, 2008; Mortensen, 1988; Prinz and Weimar, 2016; Prisinzano, 2000; Unnithan et al., 2012). In a similar vein, youth players will also be uncertain about their true talent and their compatibility with the present club (Schmidt et al., 2017). Göke et al. (2014, p. 452) appropriately state on matching processes in youth soccer education: 'At this early stage, neither the worker nor the firm can correctly assess the true quality of the match, hence match quality is regarded as an experience-good since information deficits are stepwise diminished by the duration of the partnership'.

The more private information a youth club gathers about a player, the better the chance of a good future match, and hence the better the chance of the player being promoted to the senior team. Therefore, from a club's perspective, the time a player spends at the club's youth academy team acts like a probation period (or a long-run screening process), helping the club to make decisions about a potential future contract (Göke et al., 2014; Mortensen, 1988; Stiglitz, 1975). However, youth players rarely go through a linear development; instead, their development is a process of selection and de-selection (turnover in youth academies: 24.5 percent; turnover in

U-national teams: 41 percent), mainly influenced by injuries and/or the player's physical growth (Güllich, 2014).

Besides gathering private information to assess matching quality, passing through a club's youth academy helps the player to acquire valuable club-specific human capital (Jovanovic, 1979b). This club-specific human capital reduces the transaction costs compared to buying an external youth player, and thus generates additional benefits to the club (e.g. commitment to the team philosophy, knowing places and staff, having a place to live or being part of a social network). Team-specific human capital also helps a player to be content with his situation, since he has fewer uncertainties about the club (Gandelman, 2008; Prinz and Weimar, 2016). Hence, Prisinzano (2000, p. 278) argues, 'good matches are more productive and result in relatively longer tenure and higher wages'.

A stable match between a youth player and his educating team can be disrupted by four events: first, if the player's performance diminishes (including the effects of injuries), or is not improving as well as other players; second, if misbehavior and/or opportunistic behavior is observed (e.g. shirking, being disrespectful, not obeying the rules); third, if parents move to another city or no longer allow the player to attend the youth academy; fourth, if there is an outside offer which cannot be matched by the current club (Göke et al., 2014). In the case of underperformance, youth players often enter into a 'job shopping' cascade (Johnson, 1978) until they find a better match with another club. While the basic soccer-related human capital generates utility at any other club, the team-specific human capital is completely depreciated (Prinz and Weimar, 2016).

Job separation because of (better) outside offers usually decreases the probability of a professional debut and reduces future earnings (Prinz and Weimar, 2016). This downward spiral relates to an assortative matching process, which has often been evident in sports (Gandelman, 2008; Drut and Duhautois, 2017). More precisely, the theory of assortative matching describes a multiple period selection process where outstanding players are selected to star teams, while less-talented players are selected to lower division clubs. In the end, players are allocated to the club where their value of marginal product is highest. However, it can also be argued that, especially in youth teams, a 'perfect' assortative matching and selection is not achieved. Young players often do not move to the club with the highest utility, since the peculiarities of youth education and the decision-making processes of young players are influenced by uncertainty, coaching decisions, regional roots, and the subjective favoritism of teams[13] (Schmidt et al., 2017).

The longer a player has been at a youth academy, the more likely he will enter professional soccer (Göke et al., 2014). Hence, tenure at his last club is an important determinant when a player begins his professional soccer career. Apart from tenure, other determinants have been found to positively affect the career prospects of a young player. The most obvious of these is the evidence that high performance leads to a higher probability of staying with the club and thus prolonging a professional career (Dilger and Prinz, 2004; Geyer, 2010; Ohkusa, 2001). In addition, entering an elite youth academy as early in life as possible helps a player to gather more soccer-specific human capital (Unnithan et al., 2012). Göke et al. (2014) and Leeds and Leeds (2009) indicate that the number of games played in youth national teams is associated with a higher chance of becoming a professional soccer player. They argue that nomination to a youth national team is a precious job market signal (Spence, 1973) to clubs of a player's superior quality. In addition, being a native player also helps to prolong contracts (Frick, 2007). Physical advantages, such as body size, have also been found to positively affect the probability of becoming a professional player (Fry et al., 2014; Göke et al., 2014). Kassis et al. (2017) show that personality and cognitive factors are in general not very important to promotions in youth soccer teams. Furthermore, the quality and reputation of the youth academy significantly increases the chance of it promoting a youth player's professional career (Radoman and Voia, 2015). Also, acquiring scarce skills during youth education (e.g. two-footedness) might increase the chance of the player receiving a professional contract (Bryson et al., 2013). The absence of major injuries has also been found, not surprisingly, to be another key factor for a player's successful promotion to a professional team (Göke et al., 2014; Price et al., 2004).

3.5 RELATIVE AGE EFFECTS

The performance of youth players is a multiplicative production function in terms of effort and talent (Lazear et al., 2015). In this context, talent, as well as the human capital formation of youth players, is a multiplicative composition of physicals skills, technical/motorial skills, and intellectual/psychological skills such as anticipation and logic (Williams and Reilly, 2000). The younger the athletes, the more pronounced are age differences, since the marginal utility from each additional month of physical maturity is crucial (Ashworth and Heyndels, 2007; Unnithan et al., 2012). Hence, to assess and evaluate talent, only a comparison of players of the same age is useful. If youth soccer competitions could be organized into monthly age groups, all players participating in a specific age cohort would be equally old and physical advantages would be smaller. As a consequence, TID processes would be efficient to separate the less talented from the more talented players.

However, youth soccer competitions in Europe are organized into yearly age group intervals. Since 1997, the cutoff date for every age group is 1 January (before that, the cutoff date was 1 August: Ashworth and Heyndels, 2007). In this regard, a youth player born on 31 December participates in the same cohort as a player born almost a year earlier. Clearly, this leads to strong physical and, in turn, competitive advantages for players born early (maximum variance at the age 13–15) in the year; in addition, younger players might feel frustrated about their physical disadvantage and choose to quit (Barnsley et al., 1985; Barnsley and Thompson, 1988; Sagar et al., 2007; Musch and Grondin, 2001). There are also particular benefits in certain positions related to body size and weight, such as goalkeeper or attacker (Musch and Grondin, 2001). As a result, younger players 'underperform' compared to older ones, which reduces the probability of being selected into the starting formation. Assuming a random talent distribution of young players over a period of different months, older players within an age group are preferred simply due to growth-related physical advantages, rather than other skills, thus leading to inefficiencies in TID processes (Barnsley et al., 1985; Glamser and Vincent, 2004). Even if two players are equally talented, each is viewed by the coach at different stages in their age development; coaches will often select the best current player, and not the best at a specific age. Since the cutoff date of age group selection is constant from U8 to U19, relative age effects exist within one cohort and between different cohorts. The latter is disadvantageous for young players who in general are late developers and only perform significantly better when entering senior soccer (irrespective of the month they are born).[14] Both cases might induce potentially good players to quit, resulting in a loss for the whole youth system (Baker et al., 2010; Barnsley et al., 1985, 1992; Musch and Grondin, 2001).

These age (selection) effects were first referred to as relative age effects by Barnsley et al. (1985), who looked at minor league hockey players. This phenomena also relates to the 'Matthew effect',[15] which states that people who are better endowed initially always retain that advantage. Players selected early into elite academies due to relative age effects receive a significantly better soccer education and develop higher human capital (Ashworth and Heyndels, 2007; Baker and Logan, 2007; Merton, 1968; Unnithan et al., 2012). Today, there is empirical evidence supporting relative age patterns for German soccer, world and youth soccer championships, US soccer, Belgian soccer, Dutch soccer, French soccer, English soccer, Brazilian soccer, Australian soccer, Basque soccer, North American hockey, North American baseball, cricket, handball, rugby, swimming, gymnastics, tennis, volleyball, and skiing (Ashworth and Heyndels, 2007; Baker and Logan, 2007; Bjerke et al., 2016; Glamser and

Vincent, 2004; Hurley et al., 2001; Mujika et al., 2009; Nolan and Howell, 2010; Sims and Addona, 2016). See also Musch and Grondin (2001) for a good literature review up to 2000, and Baker et al. (2010) up to 2009.

Although the negative effects of age intervals within the TID process in sports has been known for many years, we still see strong relative age patterns in current German soccer. As shown by Figure 3.2, the distribution of current (2011–2015) native players in the Bundesliga over the birth months is skewed to the left. Players born in January compose the highest fraction among native Bundesliga players, while players born in September also had minor advantages (probably due to the former cutoff date). Non-native players in the Bundesliga show similar patterns.

To see whether current youth teams try to overcome the potential biases of relative age effects, we look at German, English, Italian and French U16–U21 national squads. Indeed, the German youth teams show strong distribution patterns of relative age selection effects – players who are born early in a year play in a higher proportion of youth teams than players born in later months. In addition, English, French and Italian youth soccer also displays relative age patterns.[16] If Gini coefficients are used (0 = equal distribution; 1 = unequal distribution) for comparison purposes, all youth squads show very similar values of unequal distributions over months of birth. The strongest relative age cohort effect was identified in France (Gini = 0.365) where the proportion of birth months is strongly left skewed, followed by Germany (Gini=0.359), Italy (Gini = 0.356) and England (Gini = 0.330). Hence, in terms of age groups, the English youth TID system seems to be the most efficient among the four leagues in question.

While it seems practical to look at the 'pure' birth month distributions, the literature also suggests taking into account the general birth rates (Ashworth and Heyndels, 2007; Thompson et al., 1991; Glamser and Vincent, 2004). Some months might, on average, be characterized by higher birth rates, leading to a higher fraction of youth players entering youth academies. Indeed, Figure 3.3 illustrates an unequal distribution of male birth rates across different months. Part one shows the corresponding birth rates (1979–1996) for current Bundesliga players, and part two the corresponding birth rates (1994–2002) for the current youth national teams in Germany. Basically, a higher fraction of births is observed in the summer months. November and December are generally months with lower birth rates on average. In order to detect the net value of relative age effects among German Bundesliga and youth national team players, we analyze the fractional differences between general male birth months and birth months of soccer players, using differences in percentage points (Ashworth and Heyndels, 2007). The distribution of the net effect depicted in Figure 3.4 confirms the results from Figure 3.2, indicating selection benefits for

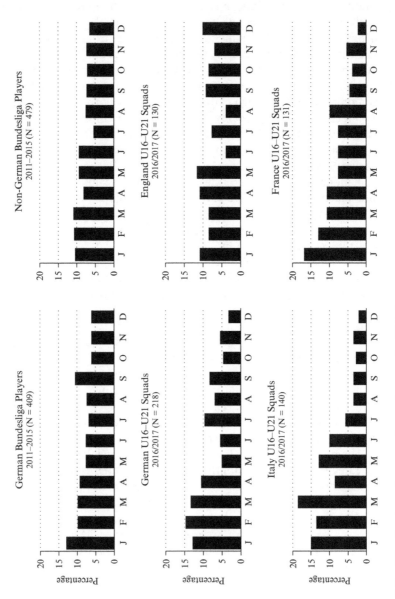

Figure 3.2   Distribution of soccer players by month of birth

62

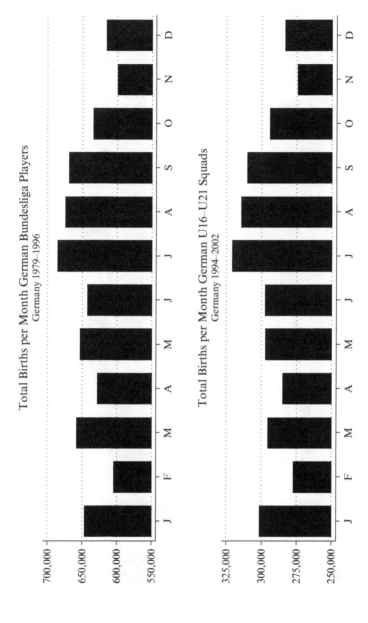

Figure 3.3   Distribution of births per month in Germany

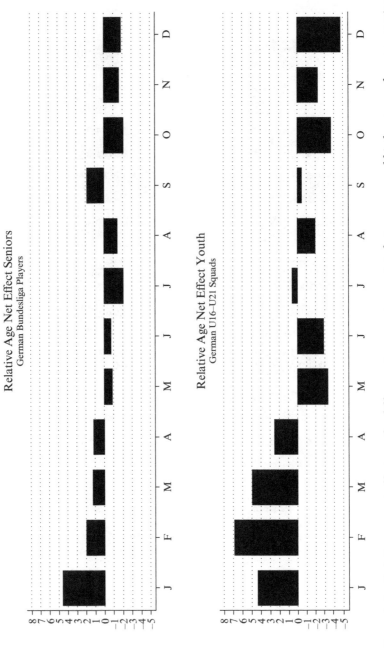

Figure 3.4   Relative age net effects as the difference in percentage points between general birth rates and representation among soccer players

players born early. For example, among current players on German youth national teams, there is an overrepresentation of players born in February by seven percentage points, while players born in December are underrepresented by four percentage points. Comparing the figures to current Bundesliga players (Gini = 0.281) and current youth national players (Gini = 0.310), we see an increase in the net age effect among players. This seems surprising, as we would have expected to see a lower net effect since the relative age effect has been discussed for almost 30 years, and hence is well known and well understood by decision-makers.

One economic reason for this rising adverse selection might be the increasing incongruence between a club's utility from youth education and a coach's utility based on information asymmetries. While the club is primarily interested in maximizing talent outcomes (market values) at the end of the youth academy (U19), coaches are interested in outcome maximization at the end of every youth season. With the latter, hidden motivations arise because the success of a coach's youth team decides his future employment at the club (or outside offers) and (almost more importantly) his reputation among youth coaches at the club and among other elite youth academies' coaches. Since competition among youth academies and investments are rising, competition among coaches should have increased, leading to higher incentives to maximize their own utility by selecting the current best teams and ignoring the relative age discussion.

Given the overwhelming evidence of age group effects for youth players, the issue has been raised as to whether these effects are detrimental to developing star players (Baker et al., 2010). One general argument used in this discussion is the observation that physically less-talented players focus more strongly on specific human capital – e.g. positioning and timing – which are important when entering senior soccer (Baker et al., 2010; Prinz and Weimar, 2016). Ashworth and Heyndels (2007) and Sims and Addona (2016) argue that players born later, who are thus required to undergo a more difficult process, are on average more productive due to the increased challenges they face. While physical deficiencies can be reduced later in life, intelligent playing styles and technical skills are difficult to learn later. To put it simply, young players who always benefited from their strong physical advantages have fewer incentives to develop further technical or match intellectual skills when young, and therefore have performance deficiencies in senior teams.

From a soccer club's point of view, relative age (selection) effects increase the uncertainty of elite youth education and lead to an inefficient TID (Ashworth and Heyndels, 2007; Prinz and Weimar, 2016). To maximize (talent) outcomes of elite youth academies, clubs are interested in solutions to reduce the relative age effects. Since the competition structure is a given, clubs can only change recruiting evaluation mechanisms within their own teams. As an alternative to only looking at performance in league games, young players could frequently participate in 'laboratory' tests to compare skills to those at the same age. When deciding on promotions of youth players or roster decisions, coaches should base their nominations on evaluation tests, instead of performance in past games or subjective evaluations (Unnithan et al., 2012). Clubs could also introduce a monthly or quarterly quota in starting rosters to counter the coach's tendency to select the current best players (Barnsley and Thompson, 1988; Hurley et al., 2001). Groups of clubs could also frequently organize closed tournaments, where only players of the same year and month of birth play against each other. The DFB could also introduce narrower age intervals or shift cutoff dates, meaning that deadlines will change every year by one month to increase efficiency (Barnsley et al., 1985; Barnsley and Thompson, 1988; Glamser and Vincent, 2004; Hurley et al., 2001). In addition, instead of using chronological age, the umbrella association could also use biological age for youth group selection (Musch and Grondin, 2001).

3.6   CONCLUDING REMARKS

In terms of personnel economics peculiarities, the market for youth athletes seems to be as complex as the market for senior athletes. What makes the personnel economics of youth education even more challenging for both clubs and athletes is the lack of scientific and practical learnings from outside the sports world, since in the non-sport world, employers are separated from the education function. In addition, investment in youth players is riskier and characterized by more uncertainties than for the senior sports market. From a club's perspective, investing in a youth player means that 2 to 5 percent of players have to generate a return on investment for the remaining 95 to 98 percent, which makes investment in youth education generally less attractive. Besides this, age grouping effects lead to further peculiar inefficiencies. Thus, a completely unregulated market of youth sport education is extremely inefficient and has to be guided by regulations of umbrella sports organizations.

Operating a youth sports academy helps a club to reduce information asymmetries about the players and to assess matching quality with the player. Investing in sport-specific human capital only pays off for a small fraction of young players. They should only continue their investments when they are nominated early for youth national teams, as this will allow them to generate a valuable signal in the senior sports market. Besides this, youth players should enter early into the elite youth academy of their preferred club so as to avoid later moves, thus allowing them to generate as much club-specific human capital as possible and correspondingly increasing their chances of becoming a professional player. In addition, youth players born later in the year should concentrate their training on additional non-physical related skills to counteract age grouping discrimination. In contrast to the club's perspective, where the drop-out of every youth player is associated with absorbing the full sunk costs of the investment, youth players can always use their accumulated sports-specific human capital for other sports or for entering amateur sport leagues of the same sport.

NOTES

1. While the DFB regulates the Senior and Youth national teams as well as the third division, the DFL governs the top two soccer divisions in Germany (1. Bundesliga and 2. Bundesliga).
2. In soccer, extraordinarily successful age cohorts are often called the 'golden generation', a term which is associated with the Dutch team in the 1980s, the French team in the late 1990s, the Portuguese team in the early 2000s, the Spanish team in the late 2000s and the German team in the early 2010s (Mourão and Cima, 2015).
3. According to science, six core skills related to soccer-specific human capital exist and are associated with higher chances of being promoted to professional soccer: awareness, resilience, goal-directed attributes, intelligence, sport-specific attributes and environmental factors (Jokuschies and Conzelmann, 2016; Mills et al., 2012).
4. This is even more important for youth players, as youth athletes are found to have a 'black and white view of reality and approach problems more dualistically than older adults' (Creed et al., 2002, p. 42).
5. Indeed, the fraction of professional players who entered professional soccer with the same club in which they passed their TID is very small (e.g. Kevin Großkreuz, Thomas Müller, Sami Khedira, Phillip Lahm).
6. Even though every European soccer association has its peculiarities, the German example should be comparable to other top leagues since the soccer market is highly standardized by the law of FIFA, regulations of the European Soccer Association (UEFA), and the European labor law by the European Union (EU).
7. In Germany, there is currently one professional first division (1. Bundesliga), one professional second division (2. Bundesliga), one professional third division (3. Liga), four semi-professional fourth divisions (Regionalliga), 14 fifth divisions (Oberliga). After that, there are organized leagues down to an eleventh division.
8. The European and German football systems offer competitions up to municipal divisions. In Germany, there are 11 divisions from professional, to semi-professional and to amateur football.
9. In 2012, three stars were given to 11 clubs, two stars to four clubs, one star to one club and zero stars to two clubs (Eberhardt, 2012).
10. From a player's 12th to 15th birthday, 25 percent of the total compensation; and from a player's 16th to 23rd birthday, 50 percent of the total compensation.
11. For example, after his 12th birthday, Mesut Özil was trained by Rot-Weiss Essen (for five years) and Schalke 04 (for three years). When Özil moved from Werder Bremen to Real Madrid (for €18 million in 2010 at the age of 21), Rot-Weiss Essen received €270,000 in compensation, Schalke 04 received €180,000 and Werder Bremen €162,000. When moving from Real Madrid to Arsenal at the age of 23, Rot-Weiss Essen was

compensated by €750,000, Schalke 04 by €650,000, Werder Bremen €500,000 and Real Madrid €600,000.

12. Up to the age of 10 (U11), youth players can change clubs without the permission of the current club and without a freeze period. Thus, no compensation has to be paid in the case of a transfer. From U12 to U19, youth players can only change clubs without penalties if the emitting club gives permission or the corresponding compensation fee (see Table 3.3) is paid. If the new club does not pay, and the emitting club denies permission, the youth player faces a three-to-six-month freeze period in the case of an in-season transfer, or until 1 November in the case of a transfer within the transfer window (June and July). A transfer with permission but outside the transfer window is penalized with a three-month freeze period (§ 3 No. 3 Jugendordnung).

13. For instance, a youth player at Borussia Dortmund might struggle to move to Schalke 04 even if the prospects are better.

14. One anecdotal example is Lionel Messi, who was a physically late developer and would have been selected-out in early stages by most coaches due to his underdeveloped physical skills.

15. In reference to the gospel of Matthew (25:29): 'For unto every one that hath shall be given and he shall have abundance; but from him that hath not shall be taken away even that which he hath'.

16. For England, the summer months (June, July, August) are the lowest representation, which is associated with a different deadline for entering the next age group. While in France, Italy and Germany the deadline is 1 January, in England the deadline is 1 September (Baker et al., 2010).

REFERENCES

Ashworth, J. and Heyndels, B. (2007) 'Selection bias and peer effects in team sports: the effect of age grouping on earnings of German soccer players', *Journal of Sports Economics*, **8**(4), 355–377.

Baker, J. and Logan, A. J. (2007) 'Developmental contexts and sporting success: birth date and birthplace effects in National Hockey League draftees 2000–2005', *British Journal of Sports Medicine*, **41**(8), 515–517.

Baker, J., Schorer, J., and Cobley, S. (2010) 'Relative age effects', *Sportwissenschaft*, **40**(1), 26–30.

Barnsley, R. H. and Thompson, A. H. (1988) 'Birthdate and success in minor hockey: the key to the NHL', *Canadian Journal of Behavioural Science/Revue canadienne des sciences du comportement*, **20**(2), 167–176.

Barnsley, R. H., Thompson, A. H., and Barnsley, P. E. (1985) 'Hockey success and birthdate: the relative age effect', *Canadian Association for Health, Physical Education, and Recreation*, **51**, 23–28.

Barnsley, R. H., Thompson, A. H., and Legault, P. (1992) 'Family planning, football style: the relative age effect in football', *International Review for the Sociology of Sport*, **27**(1), 77–87.

Becker, G. S. (1962) 'Investment in human capital: a theoretical analysis', *The Journal of Political Economy*, **70**, 9–49.

Bjerke, Ø., Lorås, H., and Pedersen, A. V. (2016) 'Variations of the relative age effect within and across groups in elite alpine skiing', *Comprehensive Psychology*, **5**, 1–6.

Bonarius, A. (2015) 'Leistungszentren, *Zeitschrift für Fußball Training*, **8**, 1–5.

Borland, J. and Lye, J. (1996), 'Matching and mobility in the market for Australian rules soccer coaches', *Industrial and Labor Relations Review*, **50**(1), 143–158.

Bougheas, S. and Downward, P. (2003) 'The economics of professional sports leagues: some insights on the reform of transfer markets', *Journal of Sports Economics*, **4**(2), 87–107.

Bryson, A., Frick, B., and Simmons, R. (2013) 'The returns to scarce talent: footedness and player remuneration in European soccer', *Journal of Sports Economics*, **14**(6), 606–628.

Chesbrough, H. W. (2003) *Open Innovation: The New Imperative for Creating and Profiting from Technology*, Cambridge, MA: Harvard Business Review Press.

Clarke, N. J. and Harwood, C. G. (2014) 'Parenting experiences in elite youth soccer: a phenomenological study', *Psychology of Sport and Exercise*, **15**(5), 528–537.

Creed, P. A., Patton, W., and Bartrum, D. (2002) 'Multidimensional properties of the LOT-R: effects of optimism and pessimism on career and well-being related variables in adolescents', *Journal of Career Assessment*, **10**(1), 42–61.

DFB (2015) '25 Jahre Fußball-Einheit: Erfolgsgeschichte Leistungszentrum', available at: http://www.dfb.de/news/detail/25-jahre-fussball-einheit-erfolgsgeschichte-leistung- szentrum-135321/?no_cache=1&cHash=9789adb207687e1820592a44ce d81c3a.

DFL (2015) 'Bundesliga Report', available at: https://s.bundesliga.de/as-sets/doc/510000/501988_original.pdf.

Dilger, A. and Prinz, J. (2004) 'Hazard-raten in der NBA', *The German Journal of Sports Science*, **34**(3), 327–340.

Drut, B. and Duhautois, R. (2017) 'Assortative matching using soccer data: evidence of mobility bias', *Journal of Sports Economics*, **18**(5), 431–447.

Eberhardt, H. (2012) 'Griff nach den Sternen', *Sponsors*, **16**(2), 32–34.

Frank, R. H., Cook, P. J., and Rosen, S. (1996) 'The winner-take-all society', *Journal of Economic Literature*, **34**(1), 133–134.

Frick, B. (2007) 'The football player's labor market: empirical evidence from the major European leagues', *Scottish Journal of Political Economy*, **54**(3), 422–446.

Fry, T. R., Galanos, G., and Posso, A. (2014) 'Let's get Messi? Top-scorer productivity in the European Champions League', *Scottish Journal of Political Economy*, **61**(3), 261–279.

Gandelman, N. (2008) 'Mobility among employers and assortative matching: field evidence from soccer data', *Journal of Sports Economics*, **9**(4), 351–370.

Geyer, H. (2010) 'Quit behaviour of professional tennis players', *Journal of Sport Economics*, **11**(1), 89–99.

Glamser, F. D. and Vincent, J. (2004) 'The relative age effect among elite American youth soccer players', *Journal of Sport Behavior*, **27**(1), 31–38.

Göke, S., Prinz, J., and Weimar, D. (2014) 'Diamonds are forever: job-matching and career success of young workers', *Journal of Economics and Statistics*, **234**(4), 450–473.

Güllich, A. (2014) 'Selection, de-selection and progression in German soccer talent promotion', *European Journal of Sport Science*, **14**(6), 530–537.

Harwood, C., Drew, A., and Knight, C. J. (2010) 'Parental stressors in professional youth soccer academies: a qualitative investigation of specialising stage parents', *Qualitative Research in Sport and Exercise*, **2**(1), 39–55.

Hoehn, T. and Szymanski, S. (1999) 'The Americanization of European soccer', *Economic Policy*, **14**(28), 204–240.

Hurley, W., Lior, D., and Tracze, S. (2001) 'A proposal to reduce the age discrimination in Canadian minor hockey', *Canadian Public Policy/Analyse de Politiques*, **27**(1), 65–75.

Johnson, W. R. (1978) 'A theory of job shopping', *The Quarterly Journal of Economics*, **92**(2), 261–278.

Jokuschies, N. and Conzelmann, A. (2016) 'Das sieht man doch, dass das ein Talent ist!', *Zeitschrift für Sportpsychologie*, **23**(2), 44–55.

Jovanovic, B. (1979a) 'Job matching and the theory of turnover', *Journal of Political Economy*, **87**(5), 972–990.

Jovanovic, B. (1979b) 'Firm-specific capital and turnover', *Journal of Political Economy*, **87**(6), 1246–1260.

Jung, V., Schmidt, S. L., and Torgler, B. (2012) 'Antecedents of attitudes towards risky career choices', https://papers.ssrn.com/sol3/papers.cfm?abstract_id=2185429.

Kassis, M., Schmidt, S. L., Schreyer, D., and Torgler, B. (2017) 'Who gets promoted? Personality factors leading to promotion in highly structured work environments: evidence from a German professional football club', *Applied Economics Letters*, **24**(17), 1222–1227.

Kesenne, S. (2007) 'Belgian soccer – a comment', *Journal of Sports Economics*, **8**(6), 670–674.

Lazear, E., Shaw, K., and Stanton, C., (2015) 'The value of bosses', *Journal of Labor Economics*, **33**(4), 823–861.

Leeds, M. A. and Leeds, M. E. (2009) 'International soccer success and national institutions', *Journal of Sports Economics*, **10**(4), 369–390.

Merton, R. K. (1968) 'The Matthew effect in science', *Science*, **159**(3810), 56–63.

Mills, A., Butt, J., Maynard, I., and Harwood, C. (2012) 'Identifying factors perceived to influence the development of elite youth soccer academy players', *Journal of Sports Sciences*, **30**(15), 1593–1604.

Mortensen, D. T. (1988) 'Matching: finding a partner for life or otherwise', *American Journal of Sociology*, **94**, S215–S240.

Mourão, P. R. and Cima, C. (2015) 'Studying the golden generations' effects and the changes in the competitive balance of the Portuguese Soccer League', *International Journal of Sport Finance*, **10**(1), 42–61.

Mujika, I., Vaeyens, R., Matthys, S. P., Santisteban, J., Goiriena, J., and Philippaerts, R. (2009) 'The relative age effect in a professional soccer club setting', *Journal of Sports Sciences*, **27**(11), 1153–1158.

Musch, J. and Grondin, S. (2001) 'Unequal competition as an impediment to personal development: a review of the relative age effect in sport', *Developmental Review*, **21**(2), 147–167.

Nolan, J. E. and Howell, G. (2010) 'Hockey success and birth date: the relative age effect re-visited', *International Review for the Sociology of Sport*, **45**(4), 507–512.

Ohkusa, Y. (2001) 'An empirical examination of the quit behavior of professional baseball players in Japan', *Journal of Sports Economics*, **2**(1), 80–88.

Price, R. J., Hawkins, R. D., Hulse, M. A., and Hodson, A. (2004) 'The soccer association medical research programme: an audit of injuries in academy youth soccer', *British Journal of Sports Medicine*, **38**(4), 466–471.

Prinz, J. and Weimar, D. (2016) 'Spielermärkte', in Deutscher, C., Hovemann, G., Pawlowski, T., and Thieme, L. (eds), *Handbuch Sportökonomie*, Schorndorf, Germany: Hofmann-Verlag, pp. 179–196.

Prisinzano, R. (2000) 'Investigation of the matching hypothesis: the case of Major League Baseball', *Journal of Sports Economics*, **1**(3), 277–298.

Radoman, M. and Voia, M. C. (2015) 'Youth training programs and their impact on career and spell duration of professional soccer players', *Labour*, **29**(2), 163–193.

Rogers, E. M. (1983) *Diffusion of Innovation* (5th edn, 2003), New York: Free Press.

Sagar, S. S., Lavallee, D., and Spray, C. M. (2007) 'Why young elite athletes fear failure: consequences of failure', *Journal of Sports Sciences*, **25**(11), 1171–1184.

Schmidt, S. L., Torgler, B., and Jung, V. (2017) 'Perceived trade-off between education and sports career: evidence from professional football', *Applied Economics*, **49**(29), 2829–2850.

Sims, J. and Addona, V. (2016) 'Hurdle models and age effects in the Major League Baseball draft', *Journal of Sports Economics*, **17**(7), 672–687.

Spence, M. (1973) 'Job market signaling', *The Quarterly Journal of Economics*, **87**(3), 355–374.

Stiglitz, J. E. (1975) 'The theory of "screening," education, and the distribution of income', *The American Economic Review*, **65**(3), 283–300.

Thompson, A. H., Barnsley, R. H., and Stebelsky, G. (1991) '"Born to play ball" the relative age effect and Major League Baseball', *Sociology of Sport Journal*, **8**(2), 146–151.

Tirole, J. (1999) 'Incomplete contracts: where do we stand?', *Econometrica*, **67**(4), 741–781.

Unnithan, V., White, J., Georgiou, A., Iga, J., and Drust, B. (2012) 'Talent identification in youth soccer', *Journal of Sports Sciences*, **30**(15), 1719–1726.

Vernon, R. (1966) 'International investment and international trade in the product cycle', *The Quarterly Journal of Economics*, **80**(2), 190–207.

Williams, A. M., and Reilly, T. (2000) 'Talent identification and development in soccer', *Journal of Sports Sciences*, **18**, 657–667.

PART II

Pay, performance, and incentives

4. Determining the drivers of player valuation and compensation in professional sport: traditional economic approaches and emerging advances

Christian Deutscher

4.1 INTRODUCTION

One goal of personnel economics is to improve our understanding of worker pay and performance issues. However, the major challenge in the literature to empirically analyzing performance determinants and salaries stems from the general lack of availability of pertinent data. While tremendously valuable to scholars, individual worker performance, personal characteristics, and optimal salary are often hard to measure and assess even for employers themselves; furthermore, to the extent that employers are able to do some of this, it is vital that they keep this information confidential. While personnel economics researchers occasionally manage to obtain data for individual firms, extensive empirical research is not available for any single industry sector besides professional sports. In sports, firm inputs, outputs, and compensation are observable – detailed worker and company performance information, enriched by individual income and team spending data, are publicly and continuously available over several decades. Furthermore, knowing the identity of players allows one to track career development, relate performance to compensation schemes, and determine market shortcomings such as discrimination (Kahn, 2000; Rosen and Sanderson, 2001).

The literature assumes that all parties are maximizing agents (Zimbalist, 2003). Players maximize utility, with clubs in North American leagues predominantly aiming at profits and clubs in European sports focusing on wins (e.g. Sloane, 1971, 1976; Ferguson et al., 1991). In their attempt to realize their goals, clubs acquire suitable personnel with a focus on expected future performance and marketability. In professional sports, as well as in any other industry, it is of major importance to understand the determinants of player success, and, relatedly, the determinants of salary, with the latter typically being estimated with a Mincer-like earnings function (Mincer, 1974).

Early studies linked well-known concepts from the personnel economics literature to data from professional sports for an empirical approach inherently hard to perform in any other industry sector. As professionalization and revenues have increased in sports throughout the last two decades, so have information processing systems and performance tracking equipment. Hence, recent literature on performance evaluation and remuneration enriches established concepts from personnel economics with newly available information detailing players' behavior and performance on the field.

This chapter provides a literature overview of both traditional as well as novel drivers of player valuation and salaries in professional sport. The focus is on research of the most prominent sports in North America – namely baseball, basketball, (American) football and (ice) hockey – and Europe, namely soccer. After a short discussion of salary development, empirical evidence on the sports mentioned above is presented. Subsequently, shortcomings of current research as well as future paths are outlined.

4.2 DISTRIBUTION OF INCOME IN PROFESSIONAL SPORTS

Salaries in professional sports are characterized as right skewed over all athletes, with many of them earning relatively 'low' salaries and a few earning considerably more.[1] For individual sports such as golf or tennis, this can be explained by the skewed distribution of prize money in tournaments, for example the PGA Tour or the ATP World Tour. The rationale behind small prize differences at the bottom and large differences at the top can be linked to the arguments of Lazear and Rosen (1981). They claim that, under certain circumstances, rank order tournaments are superior to other types of compensation, especially piece rates. In order to maintain incentives throughout the competition, prizes are concentrated towards the top positions in tournaments. They can be considered as an option value for everybody in the competition. Still, individual sports are typically dominated by a small group of athletes. Since they claim the majority of prize money, top athletes earn salaries substantially more than CEOs of large companies, while the 100th-ranked golf or tennis player earns salaries comparable to division managers (with considerably shorter careers).

Although related to a different rationale, large differences in salaries can also be explained by the 'superstar' approaches of Rosen (1981) and Adler (1985). Rosen (1981, 1983) assumes that the distribution of talent is fixed among market suppliers and freely observable to the demand side. Greater and lesser talent is an imperfect substitute and hence the demand for superior talent is over-proportionally higher. This results in small differences of talent at the top of the talent distribution leading to large differences in earnings. Adler (1985) puts the focus on network externalities of popularity as the main reason for emergence of superstars and consequently skewed distribution of income amongst the top earners. He rejects the idea of free observation of talent and claims that detecting the highest talent is costly. Search costs are minimized when focusing on popular suppliers of talent, again claimed to be superstars. Adler (1985) claims that popularity is determined by luck and not talent, and later argues (2006) that stars consciously use public appearances to enhance their popularity. Rosen and Sanderson (2001) claim that the marginal value-added per spectator by a star player is relatively low, but as the number of spectators is very high, the impact on individual salary is substantial.

To summarize, earnings are distributed unequally amongst athletes within sports. This can be traced to (a) organizers of competitions incentivizing athletes to provide effort throughout all rounds of competition, or (b) spectators' demand for highly talented or popular athletes. While the former can easily be observed by the distribution of prize money amongst ranks in a competition, the latter is less obvious. Although the ideas of talent and popularity are clear, the statistical proxies for both are not so straightforward (Connolly and Krueger, 2006). As part of the 'traditional' drivers of salary, the next section describes the approaches taken in the literature so far.

4.3   TRADITIONAL APPROACHES

I characterize 'traditional' drivers of player values and salaries as those originating in the concepts of human capital theory (Schultz, 1961; Becker, 1962). Income functions in labor research connect individual earnings to formal training, with this training presumably increasing productivity (Mincer, 1958). Building on this concept, Mincer (1974) developed and estimated what is now known as the 'earnings function', where an individual's earnings are modeled as a function of formal qualifications, i.e. the years of schooling and experience. Subsequent empirical studies apply data from different countries and/or time periods, seeking to identify the impact on wages of age and the highest school degree obtained (for an overview, see e.g. Card, 1999).

I categorize these traditional drivers into four broad areas – experience, performance, talent, and popularity – and look at each in turn, within the context of the sport industry.

Experience

Workers' experience has been found to positively impact productivity and, correspondingly, salary, albeit with decreasing marginal returns to experience. This is especially true for sports, where athletes gain experience but lose athleticism during their career, with the latter being the dominant factor at the end of careers (Fair, 1994). What results is an inverted u-shaped relationship between experience[2] and wages. As physical requirements vary between sports, so do career paths, with wages peaking at different ages. Thinking about careers of gymnasts and race car drivers illustrates how career earnings profiles are different between sports (e.g. young age in gymnastics and older age in car racing).

Empirical studies generally support inverted u-shape experience-income profiles. In soccer, maximum salaries are achieved between age 26 and 28 (Frick, 2007b; Lucifora and Simmons, 2003; Bryson et al., 2013), in the National Basketball Association (NBA) and the National Hockey League (NHL) salaries peak later, at around age 29 to 31 (Deutscher, 2009; Yang and Lin, 2012; Deutscher et al., 2017). For Major League Baseball (MLB), distinguishing between pitchers and non-pitchers is important for determining age-income profiles (Alm et al., 2012), while the distinction between positions is even more important in football, where task assignments vary drastically. Accordingly, salary estimations for the latter two only make sense for each position separately. It is important to note that career length is crucially dependent on player performance – many players get released or are not signed to new contracts because of insufficient output. Determining an experience-income profile must be done with the knowledge that much performance-related selection has already occurred – this very high level of performance-related sorting is evidenced by, for example, average career length in the NFL being only 3.3 years (Statista. com).

Performance

A player's (recent) performance also impacts their salary – higher past performance is perceived as an indicator of future performance, thus increasing the player's negotiating position. Depending on the sport, performance statistics differ. A number of studies account for the number of appearances in the previous season (e.g. Lucifora and Simmons, 2003; Franck and Nüesch, 2012). In soccer as well as hockey, goals scored is the most obvious performance indicator, again heavily dependent on the position on the field or ice, as scoring goals is the main objective for only certain positions, while other players have more defensive-oriented tasks (Lehmann and Schulze, 2008; Jones and Walsh, 1988). In basketball, defensive performance is determined more easily – the number of blocks, steals, and rebounds have all been found to positively impact salary (Simmons and Berri, 2011; Deutscher et al., 2017). Still, offensive performance is remunerated better than defensive performance (Berri et al., 2007; see also section 4.5 below). In baseball, slugging percentage and runs batted in are amongst the variables with the highest impact on players' salaries (Holmes, 2011). In football, job assignments differ the most; hence, performance comparisons between players playing different positions is very difficult.

Across many sports, sport analytics has taken hold, with the concept of wins-above-replacement (WAR) now being commonplace. The concept attempts to determine the number of wins a given player is producing above a fictional replacement, with the latter often determined by the average player at that position (see Koedel et al., 2014 for the NFL). The concept of WAR tries to provide a concise, summary, metric of performance, amalgamating several different measures of performance into a single statistic.

Talent

Talent is another driver of wage differentials. Talent is an intrinsic trait, not directly observable. Talent and performance are not necessarily synonymous – while players with more talent are more likely to be higher performers, players with lesser talent may be equally good performers if, say, they expend more effort than the more-talented players.

Since there is no clear-cut metric for measuring talent, different paths have been taken in the literature. For North American major leagues, papers frequently use the spot in the amateur draft where the player was selected as a proxy for talent. With the aim of creating competitive balance within the league, the league rewards the earlier choices in the draft to the worst teams of the previous season (Zimbalist, 2002). Depending on the roster size in the particular sport the draft contains different number of rounds (MLB (40), NBA (2), NFL (7), NHL (7)). The pick at which a player was drafted serves as the indicator of their initial talent at the time they entered the league and is regularly included in wage estimations.[3] As with experience, studies typically account for decreasing marginal effects

of the draft position, as talent is not equally distributed across a cohort
of players. Differences in talent are expected to be the largest at the very
first selections, with these differences declining throughout the later draft
selections. The significant positive impact of talent – as measured by an
earlier selection in the draft – on salary is supported for the NBA (Gius
and Johnson, 1998; Wallace, 1988; Hill, 2004; Prinz et al., 2012) and the
NFL (Kahn, 1992), and somewhat supported for the NHL (Jones and
Walsh, 1988; Idson and Kahane, 2000).[4]

Note that teams often stick to (bad) decision-making during previous
drafts. Staw and Hoang (1995) reveal significant sunk-cost effects in the
NBA, where teams retain and play highly drafted players more than their
performances would suggest (for a re-examination, see Camerer and Weber,
1999; for the NFL, see Keefer, 2015). Since draft systems are exclusive to
North American major leagues, research for European leagues, most
prominently soccer, has to rely on alternative variables to proxy talent.[5]
Bryson et al. (2013) describe two-footedness as a rare talent to be rewarded
by the German market. Lucifora and Simmons (2003) operationalize the
number of appearances in 21-and-under teams as an indicator for innate
talent in Italian soccer. While these talent indicators serve a useful purpose,
problems still remain. The wide array of proxies that have been used make
them difficult to compare to each other. Also, for any given proxy, the
chances for a high positive correlation with performance seem probable.

Popularity

Similar arguments also hold for the popularity of athletes. A variety of
proxies attempt to capture popularity, but again due to systematic differences a distinction between North American and European leagues
is important. North American leagues showcase so-called all-star games
as part of their yearly schedule. Here, fans' votes determine (some of)
the players who participate. Hence, all-star appearances, or, relatedly, the
number of votes that players receive prior to these events, appear natural
candidates as indicators of popularity. While the former compares the
popularity of a borderline all-star to that of the least popular player in the
league, the latter faces a similar problem, particularly due to controversies
in the voting system.[6] Both measures have been found to impact salary
positively in MLB (Molina, 2004), the NBA (Hausman and Leonard,
1997) and the NHL (Deutscher, 2009). In the NFL, the Pro Bowl is the
closest equivalent, but it is less important as players on the best teams often
miss it due to scheduling problems (it is played one week prior to the Super
Bowl). What results is a small to no impact on player remuneration in the
NFL (Leeds and Kowalewski, 2001). For Major League Soccer, Kuethe

and Motamed (2010) find a positive effect of all-star game appearances on pay.

Since all-star games are not played in European sports, researchers apply different measures to determine popularity. Franck and Nüesch (2012) count the number of articles in which German soccer players are mentioned at least once, and find a positive impact of the measure on salary. In a similar vein, Prinz et al. (2012) find no impact of popularity (as measured by the number of 'Facebook likes') on salary for the NBA. Lehmann and Schulze (2008) measure popularity by the number of hits on players in the online version of a German soccer magazine, and find a positive, but diminishing, return to popularity/media exposure. In a similar fashion, Garcia-del-Barrio and Pujol (2007) use Google hits to explain soccer players' economic values in Spanish soccer.

4.4   NOVEL APPROACHES

Bowles, Gintis, and Osborne (2001a, 2001b) have challenged the traditional view described in the previous section to argue that these 'standard' human capital variables leave a lot of variation in earnings unexplained. They find that variables that have been previously omitted in the empirical literature very often prove to be important determinants of individuals' labour market success. Among these omitted variables are 'non-cognitive skills', which describe work habits (e.g. effort, determination, and discipline) and personality traits (e.g. self-confidence, sociability, and emotional stability) (Borghans et al., 2008; ter Weel, 2008). While personality traits and work habits are hard to capture and research, and often rely on self-reported information, the sports economic literature has started to consider their potential impact on salary.

Leadership skills are one personality component often claimed to be important to team success. While leadership skills cannot be encapsulated in a singular metric, they are often assumed to be displayed by team captains in sports. The task of the captain is, almost by definition, to be the leader of the squad. Team captains are either voted by their team-mates or determined by their head coaches and are often supported by co-captains who act in their place if suspensions or injuries occur to the captain. If leadership skills are an attribute of value to team success, and if team captains possess leadership skills, then the data should show wage premiums to team captains in sports. The approach was first taken by Deutscher (2009) for the NHL – the paper determines the wage premium for team captains in ice hockey, controlling for various determinants such as player performance, and team and season characteristics. Since goalkeepers cannot serve as team captains, the estimation includes players for all remaining positions. The results estimate the additional salary for team captains to be 20 to 30 percent, depending on the specification of the model. A study by Battré et al. (2009) follows up on this approach, identifying the wage premium for captains of German Bundesliga teams to be between 25 and 35 percent, again including a variety of control variables.

Another concept focusing on the mental aspect of sports relates to the idea of performance under psychological pressure. Psychological pressure in sports exists in late-game situations of close contests. Hence, actions have to have an impact on the outcome of the contest, and possible mistakes cannot be reversed at a later point in time. Free throws in basketball serve as a very reasonable object of investigation, as this task is repeatedly conducted and success is independent of the venue or any actions taken by opposing players. The negative impact of psychological pressure on performance has been shown for the NBA by Cao et al. (2011), who show that success rates decline on average by 5 to 10 percentage points in crucial late game situations. To determine whether mental strength and the maintenance of performance under pressure are rewarded monetarily, Deutscher et al. (2013) also study free throws in the NBA. Here, the measure of mental strength compares individual player success rates under psychological pressure to success rates in other situations. The resulting variable 'mental strength' is implemented as an independent variable determining player salary and shows a significantly positive impact. Closely related, Hickman and Metz (2015) analyze the impact of monetary payoffs on performance in professional golf. Using data from the PGA Tour, they show that athletes underperform when the financial stakes increase. Perhaps not surprisingly, the negative impact of pressure on performance is greater for less-experienced golfers.

Confidence and leadership skills may be enhanced by physical attractiveness. Inspired by the work of Hamermesh and Biddle (1994) on beauty and the labor market, Berri et al. (2011) analyze the impact of physical attractiveness on salaries for quarterbacks in the NFL. They find a wage premium for beauty, measured as face symmetry, which could again be related to the communication and leadership skills required in the specific job description of quarterbacks. Since height is a driver of confidence and leadership, and important for players in such sports as basketball (Berri et al., 2005), the wage impact of certain positions in team sports mentioned in the previous section alternatively could be explained by differences in player height and the accompanying differences in player personality.

As stated above, team members' work ethic is most likely to boost team performance and hence should be rewarded monetarily. Just as with personality traits, work ethic is hard to capture and needs to be proxied in the context of sports. Recently, 'running' information became publicly available for soccer in Europe and basketball in North America. Running is hypothesized to measure effort, and not skill or performance. Again, the questions to be answered revolve around the impact of effort on sporting success, as well as the monetary rewards to the athletes in return for their effort. Weimar and Wicker (2017) show that the total distance ran by a team, as well as the number of 'intense' runs increased the chances of winning for soccer teams in the German Bundesliga. Applying the identical proxies for effort, Wicker et al. (2013) cannot find a positive impact of effort on players' market values. Since salaries are not publically disclosed in European team sports, measuring the impact of effort on remuneration has yet to be done.

In line with the hypothesis that salary is determined, in part, by differences in personality is the approach not just of estimating average performance and its impact on salary, but also of tracking volatility in performance and its impact on remuneration. Originating in the work of Bodvarsson and Brastow (1998), papers on hockey, soccer, and basketball show divergent results. Longley (2005) disentangles individual performance volatility into person-specific and systematic volatility. Analyzing salaries in the NHL, he finds that an increase in volatility of the systematic component decreases player salaries. Increased volatility in the person-specific component does not result in lower salaries. Deutscher and Büschemann (2016) analyze the impact of the variance in player performance (as evaluated by a German newspaper) on a proxy for player salary in the German Bundesliga. The paper finds a positive and significant impact of performance volatility on salary. Subsequent work by Deutscher et al. (2017) analyzes the impact of performance consistency in both scoring and non-scoring on actual player salaries in the NBA, and finds wage premiums for consistency in both performance categories. The differences in findings across studies could be explained by differences in measures of performance and salary, as well as differences concerning the rules, for example the number of substitutions allowed per match.

4.5   FUTURE PATHS

As this chapter has shown, while 'standard'/'traditional' concepts of human capital continue to be employed to explain workers' productivity and salaries, several new paths have recently emerged. With new measurement techniques and the availability of additional data, new opportunities arise. This is of major importance, since estimations typically fail to explain at least 30 to 40 percent of variance in salaries. This 'black box' is driven in part by (a) managerial inability to evaluate performance correctly, (b) rules and regulation enshrined in collective bargaining agreements in the US major leagues and (c) the unavailability of performance statistics.[7] Concerning (a) above – information processing inefficiencies – academics have used the 'moneyball' idea (Lewis, 2004) to show gaps between performance statistics that lead to team wins and performance statistics that lead to higher salaries. Subsequent work supported the finding of inefficiencies in player evaluation for various sports (e.g. baseball (Hakes and Sauer, 2006), basketball (Berri et al., 2007), and soccer (Weimar and Wicker, 2017)). Once evaluation inefficiencies become known publicly, pricing anomalies are corrected by the market, exemplified in the case of baseball (Hakes and Sauer, 2007). On a related note, revenue sharing systems in North America as well as Europe could alter managerial decision-making (e.g. Brown et al., 2004).

Regarding point (b), league regulations restrict minimum and maximum wages in North America,[8] and act as counters to the forces of unregulated markets. On a team level, salary caps specify the maximum amount to be spent, with regulations and penalties in case of violations (Késenne, 2000). In Europe, markets are less regulated, but individual player salaries are undisclosed for team sports (Dobson and Goddard, 2001). Further to (c) above, while salary information is unavailable in Europe,[9] reliable and effective performance statistics have largely also been unavailable. In North America, although baseball is traditionally well-covered by statistics enthusiasts, individual performance data is limited for hockey and basketball, and is incomparable with playing positions in football.

In addition, in most sports nearly all data pertains to information 'on the ball' or defending the ball, while other factors such as player positioning on the court, or 'sports IQ', is indisputably important in generating team wins but not measured or measurable. Hence, one promising way to proxy missing but important data is to use evaluation by experts and teams of experts. Academics assume a high correlation between proxies (as in expert evaluations on transfermarkt.de) and real salaries. For German soccer during selective seasons, Gerhards et al. (2014) show the correlation between the two to be at a very high level of 0.93. Given this similarity between official information and expert valuation, subsequent research should consider expert evaluation in more versatile ways.

In this regard, Peeters (2016) measures the value of collective judgment in forecasting soccer results by player evaluations on transfermarkt.de. Also applying the concept of the 'wisdom of crowds', sport simulation video games, like the NBA 2k series or FIFA Soccer, aim to present customers with gaming experience close to reality. In the process of programming the software, comprehensive data is created in order to realistically simulate player behavior on the field. Teams of experts evaluate abilities of players in more detail than conventional statistics could ever do and evaluate personality traits in detail. Yet to date, sport economic research has neglected this source of data.

It should be noted that expert evaluation is not without its downside: experts could themselves be wrong, following heuristics that misidentify performance (Frick and Wicker, 2016). Second, the above-mentioned sources are often vague as to how exactly the gathered information is utilized to estimate players' values or abilities. Still, following the concept of swarm intelligence appears to be a promising approach in an attempt to better understand human capital and the resulting player values and salaries.

NOTES

1. Since salaries are usually not normally distributed, academic work typically applies natural logs to salaries instead of absolute salary numbers. Quantile regression estimations are often added since log salary measures in sports tend to have even greater kurtosis values compared to standard occupations (Hamilton, 1997; Berri and Simmons, 2009; Vincent and Eastman, 2009).
2. Age, experience in years, and career games played are strongly correlated, leading to either one or a combination utilized in studies (Vincent and Eastman, 2009; Yang and Lin, 2012).
3. Note that newly drafted players are typically not allowed to negotiate their contracts without restrictions. The collective bargaining agreements prescribe the range of money that the two parties can negotiate over. Academia accounts for this by including free agents in papers conducting salary estimations.
4. For papers covering MLB, the position at which a player was picked is generally not accounted for. A possible reason is the high number of players in the draft and the comparatively low predictability of player development.
5. Since talent is assumed to be a constant factor, many studies implicitly control for it by employing fixed effects models.
6. Viral campaigns on the Internet led to distortions in the final voting, as sub-par NHL player John Scott was voted as team captain for the NHL all-star game (and ironically won the most valuable player award) in 2016. Zaza Pachulia was heavily voted in 2016 and 2017, only to miss the all-star team in the latter year due to precautionary measures by the NBA. The cases of Grant Hill and Yao Ming making the roster in previous years despite not playing in one game are other examples of the vulnerability of the concept of letting fans vote.
7. Especially in North American team sports, players at the later stages of their careers maximize their utility by joining championship caliber teams and forgoing personal income.
8. Note that state income taxes vary between states in the United States of America. Hence net salary is dependent on team location, giving advantage to teams located in favorable states (Engler, 2011). Empirical studies rarely include income taxes in their considerations (see Alm et al., 2012; Kopkin, 2012). Similar implications can be drawn in individual sports where athletes from different countries and tax systems participate (Akers, 2015).
9. For an exception using team wage bills in English soccer see Szymanski and Kuypers (1999); for German soccer see Frick (2007a).

REFERENCES

Adler, M. (2006) 'Stardom and talent', *Handbook of the Economics of Art and Culture*, **1**, 895–906.

Adler, M. (1985) 'Stardom and talent', *The American Economic Review*, **75**, 208–212.

Akers, M. (2015) 'A race to the bottom: international income tax regimes' impact on the movement of athletic talent', *University of Denver Sports & Entertainment Law Journal*, **17**, 11.

Alm, J., Kaempfer, W., and Sennoga, E. (2012) 'Baseball salaries and income taxes: the "home field advantage" of income taxes on free agent salaries', *Journal of Sports Economics*, **13**(6), 619–634.

Battré, M., Deutscher, C., and Frick, B. (2009) 'Salary determination in the German Bundesliga: a panel study', in No 0811, IASE Conference Papers, International Association of Sports Economists.

Becker, G. (1962) 'Investing in human capital: a theoretical analysis', *Journal of Political Economy*, **70**, 9–49.

Berri, D. and Simmons, R. (2009) 'Race and the evaluation of signal callers in the National Football League', *Journal of Sports Economics*, **10**, 23–43.

Berri, D., Brook, S., Frick, B., Fenn, A., and Vicente-Mayoral, R. (2005) 'The short supply of tall people: competitive imbalance and the National Basketball Association', *Journal of Economic Issues*, **39**, 1029–1041.

Berri, D., Brook, S., and Schmidt, M. (2007) 'Does one simply need to score to score?', *International Journal of Sport Finance*, **2**, 190–205.

Berri, D., Simmons, R., Van Gilder, J., and O'Neill, L. (2011) 'What does it mean to find the face of the franchise? Physical attractiveness and the evaluation of athletic performance', *Economics Letters*, **111**, 200–202.

Bodvarsson, Ö and Brastow, T. (1998) 'Do employers pay for consistent performance? Evidence from the NBA', *Economic Inquiry*, **36**, 145–160.

Borghans, L., Duckworth, A., Heckman, J., and ter Weel, B. (2008) 'The economics and psychology of personality traits', *Journal of Human Resources*, **43**, 972–1059.

Bowles, S., Gintis, H., and Osborne, M. (2001a) 'The determinants of earnings: a behavioral approach', *Journal of Economic Literature*, **39**, 1137–1176.

Bowles, S., Gintis, H., and Osborne, M. (2001b) 'Incentive-enhancing preferences: personality, behavior, and preferences', *American Economic Review*, **91**, 155–158.

Brown, M., Nagel, M., McEvoy, C., and Rascher, D. (2004) 'Revenue and wealth maximization in the National Football League: the impact of stadia', *Sport Marketing Quarterly*, **13**, 227–235.

Bryson, A., Frick, B., and Simmons, R. (2013) 'The returns to scarce talent: footedness and player remuneration in European soccer', *Journal of Sports Economics*, **14**, 606–628.

Camerer, C. and Weber, R. (1999) 'The econometrics and behavioral economics of escalation of commitment: a re-examination of Staw and Hoang's NBA data', *Journal of Economic Behavior & Organization*, **39**, 59–82.

Cao, Z., Prinz, J. and Stone, D. (2011) 'Performance under pressure in the NBA', *Journal of Sports Economics*, **12**(3), 231–252.

Card, D. (1999) 'The causal effect of education on earnings', in O. Ashenfelter and D. Card (eds), *Handbook of Labor Economics, Vol. 3*, Amsterdam: Elsevier, pp. 1801–1863.

Connolly, M. and Krueger, A. B. (2006) 'Rockonomics: the economics of popular music', in V. Ginsburgh and D. Throsby (eds), *Handbook of Economics of Art and Culture*, Amsterdam: Elsevier, pp. 667–719.

Deutscher, C. (2009) 'The payoff to leadership in teams', *Journal of Sports Economics*, **10**, 429–438.

Deutscher, C. and Büschemann, A. (2016) 'Does performance consistency pay off financially for players? Evidence from the Bundesliga', *Journal of Sports Economics*, **17**, 27–43.

Deutscher, C., Frick, B., and Prinz, J. (2013) 'Performance under pressure: estimating the returns to mental strength in professional basketball', *European Sport Management Quarterly*, **13**, 216–231.

Deutscher, C., Gürtler, O., Prinz, J., and Weimar, D. (2017) 'The payoff to consistency in performance', *Economic Inquiry*, **55**(2), 1091–1103.

Dobson, S. and Goddard, J. (2001) *The Economics of Football*, Cambridge, UK: Cambridge University Press.

Engler, M. (2011) 'The untaxed king of South Beach: LeBron James and the NBA salary cap', *San Diego Law Review*, **48**, 601–621.

Fair, R. (1994), 'How fast do old men slow down?', *Review of Economics and Statistics*, **76**, 103–118.

Franck, E. and Nüesch, S. (2012) 'Talent and/or popularity: what does it take to be a superstar?', *Economic Inquiry*, **50**, 202–216.

Ferguson, D., Stewart, K., Jones, J., and LeDressay, A. (1991) 'The pricing of sports events: do teams maximize profit?', *Journal of Industrial Economics*, **39**, 297–310.

Frick, B. (2007a) 'Salary determination and the pay-performance relationship in professional soccer: evidence from Germany', in P. Rodriguez, S. Kesenne and J. Garcia (eds), *Sports Economics After Fifty Years: Essays in Honour of Simon Rottenberg*, Oviedo, Spain: Ediciones de la Universidad de Oviedo, pp. 125–146.

Frick, B. (2007b) 'The football players' labour market: empirical evidence from the major European leagues', *Scottish Journal of Political Economy*, **54**, 422–446.

Frick, B. and Wicker, P. (2016) 'Football experts versus sports economists: whose forecasts are better?', *European Journal of Sport Science*, **16**(5), 603–608.

Garcia-del-Barrio, P. and Pujol, F. (2007) 'Hidden monopsony rents in winner-take-all markets: sport and economic contribution of Spanish soccer players', *Managerial and Decision Economics*, **28**, 57–70.

Gerhards, J., Mutz, M., and Wagner, G. (2014) 'Die berechnung des siegers: marktwert, ungleichheit, diversität und routine als einflussfaktoren auf die leistung professioneller fußballteams/Predictable winners: market value, inequality, diversity, and routine as predictors of success in European soccer leagues', *Zeitschrift für Soziologie*, **43**(3), 231–250.

Gius, M. and Johnson, D. (1998) 'An empirical investigation of wage discrimination in professional basketball', *Applied Economics Letters*, **5**, 703–705.

Hakes, J. K. and Sauer, R. D. (2007) 'The Moneyball anomaly and payroll efficiency: a further investigation', *International Journal of Sport Finance*, **2**, 177–189.

Hakes, J. and Sauer, R. (2006) 'An economic evaluation of the Moneyball hypothesis', *The Journal of Economic Perspectives*, **20**, 173–185.

Hamermesh, D. and Biddle, J. (1994) 'Beauty and the labor market', *American Economic Review*, **84**, 1174–1194.

Hamilton, B. (1997) 'Racial discrimination and basketball salaries in the 1990s', *Applied Economics*, **29**, 287–296.

Hausman, J. and Leonard, G. (1997) 'Superstars in the National Basketball

Association: economic value and policy', *Journal of Labor Economics*, **15**, 586–624.

Hickman, D. and Metz, N. (2015) 'The impact of pressure on performance: evidence from the PGA Tour', *Journal of Economic Behavior & Organization*, **116**, 319–330.

Hill, J. (2004) 'Pay discrimination in the NBA revisited', *Quarterly Journal of Business and Economics*, **43**, 81–92.

Holmes, P. (2011) 'New evidence of salary discrimination in major league baseball', *Labour Economics*, **18**, 320–331.

Idson, T. and Kahane, L. (2000) 'Team effects on compensation: an application to salary determination in the National Hockey League', *Economic Inquiry*, **38**, 345–357.

Jones, J. and Walsh, W. (1988) 'Salary determination in the National Hockey League: the effects of skills, franchise characteristics, and discrimination', *ILR Review*, **41**, 592–604.

Jones, J., Nadeau, S., and Walsh, W. (1997) 'The wages of sin: employment and salary effects of violence in the National Hockey League', *Atlantic Economic Journal*, **25**, 191–206.

Kahn, L. (2000) 'The sports business as a labor market laboratory', *The Journal of Economic Perspectives*, **14**, 75–94.

Kahn, L. (1992) 'The effects of race on professional football players' compensation', *ILR Review*, **45**, 295–310.

Keefer, Q. (2015) 'Performance feedback does not eliminate the sunk-cost fallacy: evidence from professional football', *Journal of Labor Research*, **36**, 409–426.

Késenne, S. (2000) 'The impact of salary caps in professional team sports', *Scottish Journal of Political Economy*, **47**, 422–430.

Koedel, C., Hughes, A., and Price, J. (2014) *Positional WAR in the National Football League* (No. 1410). Department of Economics, University of Missouri.

Kopkin, N. (2012) 'Tax avoidance: how income tax rates affect the labor migration decisions of NBA free agents', *Journal of Sports Economics*, **13**, 571–602.

Kuethe, T. and Motamed, M. (2010) 'Returns to stardom: evidence from US Major League Soccer', *Journal of Sports Economics*, **11**(5), 567–579.

Lazear, E. P. (2000) 'The future of personnel economics', *The Economic Journal*, **110**, 611–639.

Lazear, E. and Rosen, S. (1981) 'Rank-order tournaments as optimum labor contracts', *Journal of Political Economy*, **89**(5), 841–864.

Leeds, M. and Kowalewski, S. (2001) 'Winner take all in the NFL: the effect of the salary cap and free agency on the compensation of skill position players', *Journal of Sports Economics*, **2**, 244–256.

Lehmann, E. and Schulze, G. (2008) 'What does it take to be a star? The role of performance and the media for German soccer players', *Applied Economics Quarterly*, **54**, 59–70.

Lewis, M. (2004) *Moneyball: The Art of Winning an Unfair Game*, New York: W.W. Norton & Company.

Longley, N. (2005) 'The role of performance volatility in pricing human assets: adapting the capital asset pricing model to salary determination in the National Hockey League', *The Journal of Business and Economic Studies*, **11**(1), 1–18.

Lucifora, C. and Simmons, R. (2003) 'Superstar effects in sport: evidence from Italy', *Journal of Sports Economics*, **4**, 35–55.

Mincer, J. (1974) *Schooling, Experience, and Earnings*, New York: Columbia University Press.

Mincer, J. (1958) 'Investment in human capital and personal income distribution', *Journal of Political Economy*, **66**, 281–302.

Molina, D. (2004) 'Productive efficiency and salary distribution: the case of US Major League Baseball', *Scottish Journal of Political Economy*, **51**, 127–142.

Peeters, T. (2016) 'Testing the wisdom of crowds in the field: transfer market valuations and international soccer results', Erasmus Research Institute in Management Working Paper.

Prinz, J., Weimar, D. and Deutscher, C. (2012) 'Popularity kills the talent-star? Einflussfaktoren auf Superstargehälter in der NBA', *Zeitschrift für Betriebswirtschaft*, **82**, 789–806.

Rosen, S. (1983) 'The economics of superstars: reply', *The American Economic Review*, **73**, 460–461.

Rosen, S. (1981) 'The economics of superstars', *The American Economic Review*, **71**, 845–858.

Rosen, S. and Sanderson, A. (2001) 'Labour markets in professional sports', *The Economic Journal*, **111**, 47–68.

Schultz, T. (1961) 'Investment in human capital', *The American Economic Review*, **51**, 1–17.

Simmons, R. and Berri, D. (2011) 'Mixing the princes and the paupers: pay and performance in the National Basketball Association', *Labour Economics*, **18**, 381–388.

Sloane, P. (1976) 'Restrictions on competition in professional team sports', *Bulletin of Economic Research*, **28**, 3–22.

Sloane, P. (1971) 'The economics of professional football: the football club as a utility maximiser', *Scottish Journal of Political Economy*, **17**, 121–146.

Statista.com. Average playing career length in the National Football League (in years) at: https://www.statista.com/statistics/240102/average-player-career-length-in-the-national-football-league/.

Staw, B. M. and Hoang, H. (1995) 'Sunk costs in the NBA: why draft order affects playing time and survival in professional basketball', *Administrative Science Quarterly*, **40**, 474–494.

Szymanski, S. and Kuypers, T. (1999) *Winners and Losers*, New York: Viking Adult.

Ter Weel, B. (2008) 'The noncognitive determinants of labor market and behavioral outcomes', *Journal of Human Resources*, **43**, 729–737.

Vincent, C. and Eastman, B. (2009) 'Determinants of pay in the NHL: a quantile regression approach', *Journal of Sports Economics*, **10**, 256–277.

Wallace, M. (1988) 'Labor market structure and salary determination among professional basketball players', *Work and Occupations*, **15**, 294–312.

Weimar, D. and Wicker, P. (2017) 'Moneyball revisited: effort and team performance in professional soccer', *Journal of Sports Economics*, **18**, 140–161.

Wicker, P., Prinz, J., Weimar, D., Deutscher, C., and Upmann, T. (2013) 'No pain, no gain? Effort and productivity in professional soccer', *International Journal of Sport Finance*, **8**, 124–139.

Yang, C. and Lin, H. (2012) 'Is there salary discrimination by nationality in the NBA? Foreign talent or foreign market', *Journal of Sports Economics*, **13**, 53–75.

Zimbalist, A. (2003) 'Sport as business', *Oxford Review of Economic Policy*, **19**, 503–511.

Zimbalist, A. (2002) 'Competitive balance in sports leagues: an introduction', *Journal of Sports Economics*, **3**, 111–121.

5. Multi-period contracts as risk management in professional sports

Joel Maxcy

5.1 INTRODUCTION

Through much of the twentieth century, professional athletes in North American team sport leagues were required, by the standard player's contract they signed, to negotiate *only* with their current clubs. Courts and arbitration panels finally proscribed these league-mandated contractual restrictions in the 1970s; the restrictions had essentially *reserved* for clubs the rights to their players' services in perpetuity. The dissolution of the so-called reservation systems introduced *free agency* to players' labor markets, meaning that (some) players were free to negotiate with multiple clubs, and accept their most-preferred contract offer.

Free agency impacted player compensation in two different ways. First, the less restricted market for players' services coincided with an expected and well-documented upsurge in salaries (see Scully, 1989; Sommers and Quinton, 1982; Hadley and Gustafson, 1991; and Fort, 1992, for example). The second phenomenon of free agency was that long-term, or multi-period, contracts – which guaranteed earnings for future periods or seasons – were observed concurrent with free agent rights. With the latter, the compensation of professional team sport athletes is determined *ex ante* based on expected performance, and that pay is typically guaranteed, at least for the current season or period.[1] Thus, the contracts for team sport athletes have typically guaranteed set payments, which are determined before any contests are played, and are independent of the athlete's performance in those contests. Before the existence of player free agency, contracts that guaranteed salary beyond the current season of play were, if they existed at all, extremely rare. There was very little, if any, incentive for clubs to offer players such employment arrangements, because the reservation systems effectively represented a one-sided long-term contract in favor of the club. Multi-period contracts that guarantee compensation are now commonplace, yet hardly represent the majority of employment agreements in professional sports.

The institutional change that brought about free agency and multi-period contracts has captured the interest of economists. The analysis of athletes' employment contracts has followed two distinct, though related, paths. One is the exploration of the arguments that motivate multi-period contracts for professional athletes in the first place. The other is the issue of the effect of the long-term contracts on work incentives and performance. Both matters are identified in the initial work on the topic by Kenneth Lehn (1982) – who introduced the idea of the multi-period contract as a risk reallocation mechanism, and one that may also present work incentive problems – shortly after free agency was introduced to Major League Baseball (MLB) in the mid-1970s.

The standard labor market explanation for the existence of long-term employment arrangements is that the contracts are motivated by risk-averse workers, who accept lower pay in return for an assured level of income over time. However, this notion of lower pay for athletes holding multi-period contracts is not supported by most empirical economic studies on compensation from professional team sports. Those players who would be expected to prefer such an arrangement are rarely found to have this type of contract. Moreover, the existence of a premium being paid to, rather than paid by, players has been a persistent empirical finding. So, the degree of relative risk preferences between clubs and professional athletes appears to be more complex than the compensation wage differential explanation. Maxcy (1996, 2004a) offered a forward-market, risk-sharing explanation for the conundrum with an alternative risk-sharing model that provided the foundation for this subdivision of the literature, and a limited number of works have recently developed from that conception.

With the motivation for multi-period contracts established, Lehn (1982) analyzed the inherent principal-agent issues – specifically, the effect of such contracts on players' work incentives. He did not employ an actual measure of performance, but instead examined aggregate player availability, as represented by the time and frequency of spells that players spent on the disabled list (DL). He found empirical evidence that time spent on the DL – where injured players are formally identified and not permitted to play for a set period, but still collect their full salaries – increased with the presence of multi-term contracts. Lehn interpreted this as evidence of shirking on the part of players. He did not look directly at changes for individual players with or without multi-period contracts, but counted the cumulative time all ballplayers spent on the DL in the years directly preceding and following the dismantling of the reserve clause in MLB. A criticism of his work was that placement on the DL is the club's, not the player's, decision. Thus, DL time may not reflect shirking on the part of the player, but perhaps is simply a club protecting its investment.

The subsequent empirical work, much of it reviewed here, evaluated more explicit measures of performance.

The literature on shirking, though not widespread, has developed with examinations across several time periods, assorted sports, and multiple concepts of measurement of effort and performance.[2] Alternative measurements and methods are the likely cause of the disparate empirical findings to date. Principal-agent theory suggests contracts, which guarantee income so that it is disconnected from work output, alter the incentives to put forth work effort. Worker-players are encouraged – both during the multi-period contract and while in the pursuit of such contracts – to behave *strategically* in order to maximize utility in the effort-leisure-income balance, and the likelihood of shirking is hence increased. However, whether multi-period contracts actually do adversely affect players' performances is ultimately an empirical question, and the question the literature has sought to answer.

The purpose of this chapter is to consider and critically review both lines of literature. They are inherently linked by way of the changes in risk, performance incentives, and the risk reallocation brought about by more competitive markets for players' services. This review will consider the literature primarily in the context of that linkage, but will not attempt to thoroughly examine the full body of work devoted to shirking, as Solow and von Allmen (2016) have carried out a recent and comprehensive review of the economics of labor contracts in sports, to which we refer readers. The examination of multi-period contracts as instruments of risk reallocation will revisit the issues that prompt multi-period contracts in light of subsequent structural changes in sports labor markets. This inquiry brings about suggestions for further research and includes an abridged empirical examination, which provides a foundation for future studies.

5.2   MULTI-PERIOD CONTRACTS AND INCENTIVE ISSUES

Multi-period employment contracts that guarantee income are believed to create an incentive towards opportunistic behavior, typically called *shirking* in principal-agent models (Alchian and Demsetz, 1972; Hart and Holmstrom, 1987). Shirking, which may be excessive in the absence of corrective inducements, theoretically results in inefficient performance outcomes on the part of contracted agents. Cantor (1988) models shirking specific to the general industrial case of long-term labor contracts. He explains that when job performance directly determines compensation and when information sets on a worker's performance are subject to update, effort becomes increasingly incentive-compatible as workers approach the end of their current contract. Shirking, if it occurs, is therefore most likely to prevail early in the contract and diminish as re-contracting approaches. A pattern of regulating one's work effort in the periods encompassing contract negotiations represents *strategic behavior* on the part of a worker.

Professional sports have provided an archetype laboratory to test the shirking proposition. Prior to the year 2005, nearly all known economic research on the topic covered MLB, and several subsequent studies also utilized baseball data. More recently, some empirical tests have employed data from the National Basketball Association (NBA), and there is at least one (unpublished) study of professional ice hockey. The National Football League (NFL) does not offer guaranteed long-term contracts and is thus largely not suitable for examination. The consideration of the issue beyond North American sports is limited to a few football (soccer) studies, primarily from the German leagues where detailed players' contract information is available.

Baseball is by far the overrepresented sport in these studies for a number of reasons. First, it is historically the sport of choice for examinations by American sport economists. Moreover, from a functional standpoint, MLB provides an excellent opportunity for testing the shirking hypothesis. The sum of individual performances establishes the team results (see Scully, 1974). Thus, the effect of teammates' cooperation (or interference) on a given player's performance is minimal, and the assumption that a ballplayer's performance is directly derived from his effort is justifiable and realistic. Measures of MLB players' individual performances are highly quantified and compiled in exceptional detail. Likewise, contract terms, including length and salary, for all MLB players are now fully disclosed and available to the public.

The literature analyzing the principal-agent problem in baseball has produced uneven empirical conclusions. The research in response to Lehn's (1982) initial supposition undertook a search for declining post-contact individual performance, using measurements of skill, as the evidence of shirking. Choice of a particular performance metric was arbitrary, but proved critical to the conclusions drawn. For example, Krautmann (1990, 1993) used a pure performance measure, the annual calculation of *Slugging Average* for baseball hitters, following Scully's (1974) metric of choice for the determination of a baseball player's value (specifically, estimates of marginal revenue product). Krautmann rejected the existence of shirking in MLB based on his analysis of free agent ballplayers in the periods (seasons) directly before, and directly after, entering into multi-period contracts. He reasoned that the sub-par performances observed after the signing of a long-term contract were simply due to stochastic variation. Scroggins (1993) countered Krautmann's argument, claiming that if the performance measure accounted for playing time, in this case *Total Bases*, then evidence of shirking is found. Both papers considered the same small sample of only free agent position players (non-pitchers).[3] Maxcy (1997) reiterated that any measured skill performance is just a proxy for effort. He provided a more theoretical explanation of how Cantor's (1988) principal-agent explanation of shirking applies to professional sports, with the recognition that incentives are most effected – but in opposite directions – in the periods directly before, and just following, the contract negotiation. He followed Krautmann's (1990) example and modeled output as a random variable, a function of skill (talent) and effort, the latter of which is in the player's control, such that:

$$q_{it} = \rho S_{it} + \lambda E_{it} + \xi_{it}. \tag{5.1}$$

A player's observed level of production (output) in period t, q_{it} is a function of the player's skill level (S) and effort (E) put forth in that period, as well as the stochastic nature of performance represented by random term ξ_{it}.

Maxcy's (1997) empirical analysis incorporated both pure performance and playing time measures for the two broad categories of baseball players, hitters and pitchers (slugging average and total bases; earned run average and innings pitched, respectively). He examined a larger and more representative data set, which included players at all stages of negotiation – those under reserve, those arbitration-eligible, and free agents. The findings, controlling for age and re-contracting status, generally confirmed a lack of evidence for contract-induced shirking.

Maxcy, Fort, and Krautmann (2002) (MFK, 2002, hereafter) offered the most comprehensive analysis of the initial investigations of shirking in baseball. Theirs is also the one most consistent with the formulation of the principal-agent problem inherent in long-term sport contracts, and includes the impact of firm inputs T_{it} (e.g. coaching, teammates, technology) in the performance equation:

$$q_{it} = f\ (S_i, E_{it}, T_{it}, \xi_{it}) \tag{5.2}$$

where, again, output q_{it} is a function of the player's skill level (S), effort put forth in that period (E), team inputs (T), and stochastic variation as the random term ξ_{it}.

Importantly, this paper clarified the conception of opportunistic behavior on either side of the contract negotiation period, including the idea that effort above and beyond expectations is also strategic behavior. Thus, besides shirking in the period(s) right after entering a guaranteed contract, an above-normal performance in the period immediately preceding negotiation (the contract year) may likewise be evidence of strategic behavior on the part of a player. While this behavior may be considered a detriment – the player never before or again puts forth the same effort to reap this performance, but receives a contract and compensation based on that expectation – it may also be consistent with incentive-compatible efficiency gains.

The most important contribution of MFK (2002) is the point that some degree of strategic behavior should be expected, but, to minimize the inefficiency of shirking, contracts should include incentive-compatible mechanisms. The mechanisms, which explicitly target shirking behavior, may develop and adjust over time. It can be observed that shirking in baseball, and other professional team sports, is discouraged by methods ranging from direct monitoring, to significant financial rewards for revealed effort, i.e. specified superior or consistent performance. In the face of shirking problems, contractual mechanisms evolve to overcome a worker's propensity to shirk. For example, more monitoring, particularly of offseason training – i.e. contractually mandated extra training (mini-camps) and the like – and incentive clauses and bonuses for meeting specific performance targets, have become more frequent in the free agent era. However, the extensive use of bonuses may be limited by collective bargaining agreements.[4]

MFK (2002) put forth an empirical framework that is now standard for examination of strategic behavior in sports. The proper test of the shirking hypothesis must include a comparison between those players at a point where strategic behavior is most likely to occur, and other players who are not at such a point in time. The test is to compare players with incentives to behave strategically, with those without such contractual incentives, and then to determine whether the incentives affect effort and output. They calculated and examined expected performance (derived from a three-period moving average) relative to actual performance for both categories of baseball players (hitters and pitchers) to account for pure skill (slugging average, strike-outs to walk ratio, respectively), skill-governed playing time (*At Bats* and *Innings Pitched* for hitters and pitchers, respectively) and availability (total annual DL days for each player in the sample). No statistical evidence of strategic behavior was found for skill or playing time measures. However, the frequency of DL days was found consistent with strategic behavior – in particular they found a decrease in DL days in the period directly preceding a negotiation (the contract year). Perhaps the implication is that players about to re-contract are less likely to disclose injury because it could be interpreted as a signal that they are injury prone.

Baseball has continued as a fertile ground for tests of shirking, but conclusions remain mixed, though variation is largely dependent on the metric measuring performance and on the analytical methodology employed. An important paper, and one often misinterpreted, is Daniel Marburger's (2003) work that compares the pre- and post-reserve system eras. Contrary to Lehn, Marburger finds evidence of shirking *before*, but not *after*, the advent of free agency and multi-period contracts. He measured productivity of hitters using a comprehensive estimate of offensive production that controlled for fielding position.[5] He argued that the monetary incentives offered by free agency encouraged more, not less, effort and it was the comparatively poorly paid players of the reserve era who were found to shirk.

Krautmann and Donley (2009) revealed what has become a typical finding. Their approach was a comparison of two different comprehensive metrics of a ballplayer's offensive production, one based on pure performance and one reflecting economic value (an estimate of marginal revenue product (MRP)). A contradiction was found, as they uncovered that the MRP metric indicated strategic behavior, while the pure performance measure did not. The conclusion drawn was that tests for shirking are sensitive to the approach used in the analysis. O'Neill (2014) echoes this view that the choice of performance measure and econometric method are critical to shirking tests in baseball, and that conflicting results can be derived from the same data set. In a recently published paper on the MLB, Krautmann and Solow (2015) revert back to the consideration of DL time. They evaluate players at different points in their careers and find evidence of shirking when a player expects to retire at contract's end, but improved performance in the final years when a new contract negotiation follows the current contract's expiration.

Tests of shirking and strategic behavior have been conducted on other team sports following the general model of comparing performance in periods surrounding the contract negotiations. A difficulty in most other sports is the separation of team and individual performance. Nonetheless, the development of better analytical techniques for the analysis of many team sports has facilitated tests of shirking. Two studies of the NBA are noteworthy. Berri and Krautmann (2006) also find that the choice of metric can alter the conclusion. When they employ a basic measure of performance, shirking is detected around the contract year. However, when using a more complex metric, and one that is consistent with an economic conception of MRP, they do not detect shirking – actually, the opposite of Krautmann and Donley's (2009) similar comparison of MLB players. Stiroh (2007) finds shirking when using a metric similar to Berri and Krautmann's method; however, his sample is not as comprehensive and covers only those NBA players with multi-period contracts.

Tests of shirking outside the North American leagues are few. Complete contract data has generally not been available for most European football leagues. Data on contracts from the top German and Italian leagues are, however, now available. The tests of shirking in soccer are more supportive of strategic behavior. Frick's (2011) study of the German Bundesliga finds evidence of strategic behavior through significantly improved performance in the final year of a contract. Feess et al (2010) reach the same conclusion in their studies of German soccer. Buraimo et al (2015) likewise find significant contract-year performance improvements by players in the Bundesliga. Conversely, Rossi (2012), using a panel from the top Italian league, finds that performance falls significantly in the player's contract year.

The MFK (2002) interpretation of the strategic behavior found in soccer may contend that because free labor markets did not come to soccer until the mid-1990s – 20 years after baseball in North America – contractual mechanisms to deter opportunistic behavior have lagged in comparison. A good extension of this literature would be a comparison of contractual incentives across open and closed leagues for the purpose of evaluating whether the contractual instruments designed to limit shirking are effective. Yet, although MFK (2002) suggest that incentive-compatible contracts are promising as an antidote to shirking, the subsequent research has continued to focus on detection, and largely does not address the question of efficiency. Buraimo et al (2015) find that Bundesliga long-term contracts inherently motivate shirking, but are continually observed for top players, so the costs of shirking are outweighed by the incentives to gain a long-term contractual relationship.

The tools used to deter shirking have evolved over time. Much research on the subject is of the mind that the incidence of shirking represents a problem, or inefficiency. An inference that could be taken from the contest literature on individual sports is that perhaps leveraging the natural inclination of athletes to adjust their efforts is actually consistent with greater efficiency. Further research is advised on the efficiency of these tools, and on the variation in practices across sports leagues.

Multi-period contracts that guarantee income, though not uncommon, remain the exception, as most team sport athletes still work on single-period contracts. Strategic behavior may or may not be a problem in sports, but it is exposed in the case of multi-period contracts. The promise of earning a long-term guaranteed income is arguably motivation for high effort levels from players. A fundamental finding of Marburger's (2003) paper was that the significant rise of salaries and contract values, post-free agency, in fact actually motivated more effort on the part of players. The contract issue discussed in the next section likewise is explicit that a multi-year contract is a reward for high performance and the overall effect would motivate, not deter, effort. As noted above, only high performers typically

Table 5.1   Contract term for 2017 MLB signings

TERM	Frequency	Percent
ONE PERIOD	230	84.9
MULTI PERIOD	41	15.1
2	15	5.5
3	8	2.9
4	4	1.5
5	7	2.6
6	6	2.2
8	1	0.4
Total	271	100

hold multi-period contracts. For example, Table 5.1, which breaks down MLB player contracts for the most recent signing period, shows that multi-period contracts comprised only about 15 percent of those signed for the 2017 season. Accordingly, there exists an intrinsic linkage between effort, performance, and the contract term decision.

5.3   MULTI-PERIOD CONTRACTS AS RISK ALLOCATION MECHANISMS

Theoretically, the economic function of the long-term or multi-period labor contract is that of a facilitator of risk reallocation between worker and firm. A formal model deriving the basic assumptions, and summarized by Hart and Holstrom (1987), suggests that workers pay a risk premium in the form of a lower wage for the benefit of a guaranteed contracted wage. This arrangement is a type of compensating wage differential. The basic tenets of the theory are summarized as follows: the risk-averse worker, who wishes to smooth income (consumption) over his career, motivates the long-term contract; risk neutral (or less risk averse) firms are willing to provide this insurance with a contracted wage that is lower than the expected average spot market or one-period wage; the difference between the contracted wage and the expected spot market wage defines a risk premium collected by the firm.

Lehn (1982) and Kahn (1993) were the first to consider the long-term contract as risk allocation in professional sports labor markets with their analyses of MLB. In each case, the authors pointed out that free agency has imposed an additional source of risk on the clubs, and the newly observed multi-period contracts were motivated by clubs' desire to mitigate that risk. However, both authors maintained that – consistent with principal-agent theory – it is foremost the player's desire and willingness to pay to insure his income stream that results in long-term contracts in professional sports. Both authors expected that players with long-term contracts paid a risk premium for the arrangements. Kahn's empirical results, however, contradicted the assumption, as he found statistical evidence that the multi-period contracts in MLB contracts are associated with higher salaries, *ceteris paribus*. In other words, his results implied that, on average, a risk premium was paid by the clubs, not the players. This relationship of higher per-period pay via long-term contracts became a persistent finding (see e.g. Maxcy, 1996, 2004b; Frick, 2011; Buraimo et al, 2015; and Walters et al, 2017).

Krautmann and Oppenheimer (2002) also considered the relationship between MLB player salaries and contract length. Following standard worker-to-firm compensating wage differential theory, they suggested that players are more risk averse than owners, and thus trade off salary for longer contracts. They model hitters' performance (Slugging Average) as the determinant of salary and contract length for baseball hitters. They note that salary and contract length are determined simultaneously, and correct for the endogeneity with a two-stage least squares model. Their findings show that returns to performance decline with contract length – a result that runs counter to other research on the subject.

Maxcy's (2004a) theoretical model of the contracting process for skilled workers put forth that the compensating wage differential explanation was not well suited to a non-homogeneous labor force. When an individual laborer has unique skills, as do professional athletes, the uncertain cost of maintaining or replacing a given individual's productivity creates a source of risk for the firm.[6] Furthermore, not only will productivity vary across individuals, but a unique worker's production may vary across periods – for all of the reasons, including, but not limited to, strategic behavior, as discussed in the previous section. Shirking is a productivity risk to the firm; but so are injuries, age-associated declines, and stochastic variation. The productive uncertainty associated with the labor input becomes a consequential factor in motivating both worker and firm to reallocate risk by contractual agreement. In this state, the model predicts that firms prefer multi-period labor contracts when price uncertainty around the labor input is high. Likewise, greater uncertainty about the worker's future level of production lowers the chance that a firm will offer a long-term contract. Price and production risk were modeled respectively as follows:

$$V_{t+1} = \lambda V_t + \varepsilon_{t+1} \qquad (5.3)$$

where V_t is the actual dollar-value of a unit of player production to the club in year t. There is a trend variable λ, which is assumed to be non-linear over a player's career. The random shock term, ε_{t+1}, satisfies $E(\varepsilon_{t+1}) = 0$ for all t, $E(\varepsilon_{t+1}{}^2) = \sigma_{\varepsilon+1}{}^2$ for all t, and $E(\varepsilon_t\varepsilon_{t-s}) = 0$ for all $s \neq 0$.

$$K_{it} = \delta_t K_{t-1} + \gamma_t \tag{5.4}$$

The coefficient δ_t measures the mean marginal change in output K_i due to experience and aging, and is assumed known, but not constant. The value of δ_t is greater than one when the positive effects of experience outweigh the negative influence of skill deterioration associated with aging, and less than one when the converse is true. The random term γ_t captures individual shocks, and has the properties $E(\gamma_t) = 0$ for all t, $E(\gamma_t{}^2) = sg^2$ for all t, and $E(\gamma_t\gamma_{t-s}) = 0$ for all $s \neq 0$.

Professional athletes' skill levels and performance vary across players and time periods. Top level players hold especially unique skills, implying that the production levels of exceptionally skilled players are not easily replaced, because players of similar ability do not exist in the club's replacement talent pool (bench warmers or players in the minor leagues). If the club plans to maintain or replace a uniquely talented player who has free agent status, they must bid for those services against their rivals. Market uncertainty, caused by the bidding process, and not present before free agency, presents a significant risk to the club. The greater the relative skill of the player, the greater the level of risk in regard to the impending price of his service.

Given that even minimum salaries in major league sports are comparatively lucrative, and thus the opportunity costs of losing a job are high, the players who are most willing to insure their income by accepting a salary at less than the market wage would be those who are the most easily replaced. Following logic from Akerlof's (1981) theory of lemons, it can be surmised that paying an easily replaced player, one whose performance has fallen below his potential replacement, may impose a greater cost on the club than the benefit gained from the collection of a risk premium. Even though the absolute production of a worker is positive, the worker's guaranteed employment prevents the hiring of a more productive worker. Accordingly, given that roster size is fixed, clubs are unlikely to offer, even at a discount, guaranteed long-term contracts to players who are most likely to be replaced.

Performance fluctuations create another element of risk. A player is paid for his expected production based primarily on his (recent) past on-field performance. Salaries that are contractually guaranteed are determined in advance, and clubs are not able to forecast with certainty the future productivity of a player. Past levels of productivity are used to estimate future performance, but doubt as to the actual level of performance always exists. Production uncertainty enters the risk equation most emphatically when the prospect that the player's performance falls below the 'easily replaced' threshold is high. This also means that highly productive players pose less risk because even with a drop below expected output those players are still better options than their best potential replacement.

Maxcy (2004b) described the negotiating and contracting process in MLB. The employment contracts are explicit and stipulate a per-season base salary. The market price for player services is determined during the between-seasons period when most contracts are negotiated. The bargaining period characterizes a spot market for player labor services, and determines a wage reflecting the current market value for player services. The choice of contract term is determined simultaneously with salary and divides the labor market into two distinct sectors, those players with multi-year (long-term) contracts and those with single-season (spot) contracts.

A bivariate probit specification can be used to classify all multi-period contracts regardless of length, and determine the magnitude of the factors that increase the probability that multi-period contracts are observed. Maxcy's (2004b) sample was drawn from newspaper reports of contract signings and, though large, was not a comprehensive sample. His model included a Heckman (1976) correction for selection bias, with the instrument a variable identifying players who switched teams.[7] Market price uncertainty based on negotiation status showed the most convincing results for increasing the probability of long-term contracts. Increased market power for the players, at each of the three stages of arbitration on to free agent status, significantly increased the likelihood that a long-term contract is observed. Diminished price uncertainty given owner collusion in the 1980s was also found to have significantly reduced the likelihood of multi-period contracts. The effects of production uncertainty were less clear. Aging significantly decreased the probability of a long-term contract, and the coefficient estimates show that aging is a more damaging factor for pitchers than hitters. However, inconsistency of performance, as measured by dispersion, was found to have minimal effects and, if at all, reduced the likelihood of a multi-period contract only for hitters.

The papers by Kahn (1993) and Maxcy (2004b) suggest that several unanswered questions about contracting in MLB remain; many of these were set out by Hakes and Turner (2008). Yet, the subsequent work on multi-period contracts has been limited until very recently. Long-term contracts have been researched in European soccer (notably Frick, 2011, and Buraimo et al, 2015) with similar findings of wage premiums to the players correlated with contract length. Nonetheless, there are several reasons why revisiting these issues with more applications to baseball and soccer, but also beyond to other sports, could be illuminating. The available data on North American sports, and MLB in particular, is now richer and more complete, as there is much more information available on contracts. Econometric techniques for this type of analysis have also advanced. For example, ordered binary choice models can differentiate short multi-period contracts (two years) from longer ones (five or more years) and those in between. Additionally, analytical techniques that measure player performance and the value of performance have advanced considerably and are more complete and robust.[8]

A staple assumption is that risk management motivates multi-period contracting and determines the risk premium. However, attempts to measure risk aversion on the part of either party, or to measure the level of relative risk aversion, which determines the amount of the risk premium, had not been addressed prior to work by Krautmann (2017) and Walters et al (2017). Krautmann measured the degree of risk aversion on the part of MLB owners and showed that it is both a significant factor and that it varies across clubs, thus affecting contract outcomes. Walters et al provided an update of the Kahn-Maxcy approach, but use a sample of multi-term contracts limited to contract extensions signed with the player's current club. They employ more sophisticated econometrics and a modern and comprehensive performance measure (wins above replacement player, or WARP). Previous findings, with the exception of Krautmann and Oppenheimer's (2002), are reaffirmed. Multi-period contracts are found to be associated with higher wages. Market price uncertainty as reflected by the increasing levels of players' market power motivates long-term contacts.

The most important contribution of Krautmann (2017) and Walters et al (2017) are estimates of the relative risk aversion of owners and players. They show owners to be more risk averse than players on average, and hence on average pay the risk premium associated with the multi-period contracts, first suggested as possible, but not proven, by Maxcy (2004b). Maxcy suggested that payment of the premium could be on either side depending on the relative risk preferences and motivation for reallocation. Heretofore, all prior studies showed that, in aggregate and on average, the risk premium was paid by clubs. However, Walters et al (2017) found that while this holds true, their disaggregation and player-by-player estimates show that some (roughly 20 percent of their cases) players pay a premium, and more often than not they are the older players. Walters et al's (2017) sample did not enable them to account for a risk evaluation of players transferring teams. The empirical model here tests a small sample, and is presented to suggest extensions to the work of Kahn (1993), Maxcy

(2004b), Krautmann (2017), and Walters et al (2017). The primary purpose of this limited data study is to suggest further research that might extend this body of literature.

5.4 EMPIRICAL MODEL

This section conducts a limited empirical test that updates Maxcy's (2004b) model using *Baseball Prospectus*'s WARP metric and an ordered choice model. The data is derived from a small sample of all 271 hitters, with performance histories of at least 100 previous MLB plate-appearances, who signed new contracts with MLB clubs for the 2017 season.

The data includes several dimensions of players' performance and availability, including the traditional metric of choice, Slugging Average, along with the more modern on-base plus slugging (OPS) and WARP measures of performance. Playing-time, a key gauge of a manager's perception of value, but unrecognized in many sports economics studies, is represented here by *plate appearances* (PA). Playing-time is critical because it likely accounts for intangible attributes that indicate value to a manager, but that may not be accounted for in specific performance statistics. Plate appearances are especially indicative of these values for baseball players.[9] Players with higher PA indicate those who, in addition to playing in more games, are also less likely to be substituted for, and are placed in the batting order so as to maximize their hitting chances per game – e.g. a player in slots 1 through 3 will average nearly one more PA per game than a player hitting in the 7 through 9 slots. As with previous studies, variables indicating players' market power as one progresses through stages of negotiation, from first-year arbitration eligibility through to free agent status, are included, as are indicators for defensive position based on *a priori* expectations. The number of days the player was assigned to the DL is included to check the value of availability.

The full set of MLB position players (non-pitchers) contracts for 2017 is included, so there is no selection issue per Maxcy (2004b). However, in that sample, the players who changed clubs in the negotiation process were found to be negatively affected in terms of both salary and contract length. This sample, though lacking the depth of several periods, is broader than Walters et al (2017) by including both all re-signed players (extensions) and all transferring players.

The example of Krautmann and Oppenheimer (2002), which assumes that salary and contract length are endogenous, is followed, with a two-stage estimation model and employing a multinomial choice model to account for multiple contract length options. The specification of the multi-variate probit models is as follows:

$$\text{TERM}_i = \alpha_1 \text{NL}_c + \alpha_2 \text{SWITCH} + \alpha_3\, \text{AGE}_i + \alpha_4\, \text{AGE}_i^2 +$$
$$\alpha_5 \text{PA} + \alpha_6\, \text{WARP}_i\, (\text{SA}_i,\, \text{OPS}_i) + \alpha_7 \text{DL} + \alpha_8 \text{CATCHER}_i +$$
$$\alpha_9 \text{DH}_i + \alpha_{10} \text{FA}_i + \alpha_{11} \text{LNSAL} + e_{ic} \qquad (5.5)$$

$$\text{LNSALARY}_i = \alpha_0 + \alpha_1 \text{NL}_c + \alpha_2 \text{SWITCH} + \alpha_3 \text{PA} + \alpha_4 \text{WARP}_i$$
$$(\text{SA}_i,\, \text{OPS}_i) + \alpha_5 \text{DL} + \alpha_6 \text{CATCHER}_i + \alpha_7 \text{DH}_i + \alpha_8 \text{AE1}_i +$$
$$\alpha_9 \text{AE2}_i + \alpha_{10} \text{AE3}_i\, \alpha_{10} \text{FA}_i + \alpha_{11} \text{FA}_i + e_{ic} \qquad (5.6)$$

The variables are defined as follows:

TERM_i = length in years of the contract signed by player i in 2017.

LNSALARY_i = the natural log of player i's annual salary in 2017. For multi-period contracts this is calculated as the annual average of the total contract value (Total Value ÷ Term) regardless of the listed 2017 payment.

SWITCH_i = a dummy variable coded 1 if the player transferred clubs from the previous period, 0 otherwise.

NL = a dummy variable coded 1 if the player transferred to an NL club, 0 otherwise.

WARP_i = comprehensive sabermetric statistic calculating player i's 2016 Wins Above Replacement Player as calculated by *Baseball Prospectus*.

SA_i = player i's calculated Slugging Average in 2016.

PA_i = player i's number of plate appearances.

DL = player i's number of days on the disabled list.

OPS_i = the sum of player i's slugging average plus on-base-percentage in 2016.

AGE_i = the player's chronological age as of June 1 of the contract year (2017).

AGE^2_i = the player's chronological age squared as of June 1 of the contract year.

AE1_i = a dummy variable coded 1 for the first year of arbitration eligibility, 0 otherwise.

AE2_i = a dummy variable coded 1 for the second year of arbitration eligibility, 0 otherwise.

AE3_i = a dummy variable coded 1 for the third year of arbitration eligibility, 0 otherwise.

FA_i = a dummy variable coded 1 for free agent eligibility, 0 otherwise.

CATCHER_i = a dummy variable coded 1 if catcher is the player's position, 0 otherwise.

DH_i = a dummy variable coded 1 if Designated Hitter is the player's position, 0 otherwise.

e_i: disturbance term $E(e) = 0$ and $\text{Var}(e) = e^2$.

5.5 RESULTS AND DISCUSSION

The summary statistics are reported in Table 5.2. Nothing unusual is revealed. The average age is 27 years, the usual mean for MLB. About 30 percent of those players signing new contracts were eligible for arbitration, and 23.5 percent had reached free agent status. About one-fourth of the players transferred to a different club. The average salary is just short of $3.5 million per year. The average contract length is about 1.3 years, as expected given the information in Table 5.1 that only about 15 percent of players have contracts of more than one period.

Table 5.3 shows the simple OLS results for determinants of salary. These are considered with three alternatives for pure performance – SA, OPS, and WARP. It is revealed that WARP is a slightly better predictor of salary than OPS, which is in turn slightly better than SA. This shows that the modern measurement techniques are improvements, and WARP is thus employed in the two-stage model. Yet, the explanatory power of Slugging Average remains impressive. Playing time as reflected through PA is shown to be very important when included with all three skill measures. However, the magnitude is diminished when WARP measures performance, because WARP does reflect playing time. Curiously, defensive position is only

Table 5.2   Summary statistics

Variable	Observations	Mean	Standard Deviation
NL	271	0.456	0.499
SWITCH	271	0.246	0.432
AGE	271	27.62	3.55
AGE^2	271	772.56	210.51
PA	271	360.0	199.7
SLUGGING	271	0.407	0.079
OPS	271	0.725	0.112
WARP	271	1.373	1.718
CATCHER	271	0.210	0.408
DH	271	0.029	0.169
DL	271	19.88	37.43
AE1	271	0.125	0.331
AE2	271	0.096	0.295
AE3	271	0.081	0.273
FREE AGENT	271	0.235	0.425
TERM	271	1.397	1.138
ANNUAL SALARY	271	$3,458,424	$4,543,490
LNSALARY	271	14.354	1.164

Table 5.3 *OLS determinants of annual salary*

LNSALARY	Coefficient	T Value	Coefficient	T Value	Coefficient	T Value
Constant	11.465[a]	6.81	11.241[a]	6.69[a]	11.299[a]	6.79
NL	−0.122[c]	−1.78	−0.131[c]	−1.92	−0.167[c]	−2.42
SWITCH	−0.190[b]	−2.01	−0.190[b]	−2.02	−0.185[b]	−1.98
AGE	0.048	0.42	0.050	0.44	0.090	0.79
AGE^2	−0.001	−0.37	−0.001	−0.4	−0.001	−0.71
PA	0.002[a]	7.02	0.002[a]	6.94	0.001[a]	4.35
SLUGGING	1.068[b]	2.21				
OPS			0.918[a]	2.7		
WARP					0.097[a]	3.38
DL	0.001	1.06	0.001	1.03	0.001	0.86
CATCHER	−0.050	−0.56	−0.050	−0.57	−0.068	−0.78
DH	0.392	1.88[c]	0.412[b]	2.00	0.481[b]	2.35
AE1	1.024[a]	9.15	1.027[a]	9.22	1.056[a]	9.53
AE2	1.436[a]	11.19	1.431[a]	11.2	1.426[a]	11.25
AE3	1.724[a]	11.91	1.727[a]	11.99	1.724[a]	12.07
FREE AGENT	1.742[a]	12.97	1.735[a]	12.98	1.767[a]	13.40
TERM	0.277[a]	8.82	0.274[a]	8.75	0.261[a]	8.27
ADJ R^2	0.781		0.783		0.786	
F (14, 256)	69.75[a]		70.56[a]		71.96[a]	

Table 5.4   Determinants of contract length, ordered probit regression

TERM	Coefficient	Z Value	Coefficient	Z Value
NL	−0.382[c]	−1.69	−0.137	−0.55
SWITCH	−0.505[c]	−1.69	−0.227	−0.72
AGE	0.764[c]	1.71	0.703	1.51
AGE^2	−0.014[c]	−1.78	−0.013	−1.65[c]
PA	0.001	0.58	−0.001	−1.42
WARP	0.275[a]	3.4	0.165	1.80[c]
CATCHER	0.055	0.19	0.193	0.62
DH	0.073	0.14	0.029	0.06
DL	0.000	0.07	−0.004	−0.75
AE1	0.181	0.53	−1.159	−2.63[c]
AE2	−0.649	−1.21	−2.230	−3.73[c]
AE3	0.395	0.88	−1.708	−2.90[c]
FREE AGENT	1.258[a]	3.2	−0.844	−1.61
LNSALARY			1.140[a]	6.28
PSEUDO R^2	0.297		0.1655	
Chi^2 (14, 256)	104.84[a]			58.53[a]

relevant for designated hitters (DH), who are paid more. There is no premium for catchers, the position most-valued for its defense. (This was also true for shortstop, second base, and centerfield, none of which were included in the final model reported here, but were found relevant in Krautmann's (2017) analysis.) Progression though each of the three stages of increased market power (AE1 through to FA) yield significant increases in pay, as expected. Players signing with new clubs earned less. Productive uncertainty, as measured by days of injury (DL), does not appear to factor into salary determination.

The determinants of contract length are first checked by ordered probit regression, without consideration of salary as endogenous. The results are shown in Table 5.4. There are two observations of note. First, the age (AGE, AGE^2) variables are significant, whereas they were not for salary. The age variables behave as predicted, showing a concave pattern where contract length initially increases with age but at a declining rate that results in a peak, and then falls. Second, only the full market power of free agency matters, with no level of arbitration eligibility being significant. The latter contradicts Maxcy (2004b), where, with each increment of a player's market power, the probability of a long-term contract increased.

The two-stage model results are shown in Table 5.5. Free agent status and performance as measured by WARP are the two clearly important

Personnel economics in sports

Table 5.5 Determinants of contract length, two-stage ordered probit with salary endogenous

TERM	Coefficient	Z Value	LNSALARY	Coefficient	Z Value
NL	−0.279	−1.30	CONSTANT	12.935[a]	111.81
SWITCH	−0.423	−1.53	NL	−0.205[a]	−2.72
AGE	0.595	1.59	SWITCH	−0.256[b]	−2.52
AGE^2	−0.011[c]	−1.73	PA	0.001	4.54
PA	0.000	0.36	WARP	0.134	4.35
WARP	0.240[a]	3.11	DL	0.001	1.01
DL	−0.002	−0.36	CATCHER	−0.042	−0.45
CATCHER	0.142	0.52	DH	0.420[c]	1.88
DH	0.367	0.77	AE1	1.072[a]	9.52
FREE AGENT	1.160[a]	3.54	AE2	1.430[a]	11.42
LNSALARY	−0.007	−0.04	AE3	1.817[a]	12.94
			FREE AGENT	1.970[a]	18.29
Correlation (TERM-LNSALARY)	0.5656[a]	5.55			
WALD Chi² (11)	41.800[a]				

factors in the determination of contract length. The signs on the age variables likewise imply the expected concavity. The persistent finding, which holds up, is that top level players with full market power negotiate for both greater salary and job security. Also, the results, counter to those of Maxcy (2004b), using data from the 1980s and 1990s, do not find support for multi-period contracts for arbitration-eligible players. The variable SWITCH falls just short of statistical significance, but is signed to imply that players who transfer receive not just less pay but also shorter contracts than those players who remain with their clubs. This information combined suggests that transferring players, like the older players in Walters et al's (2017) sample, may also pay a risk premium. It also suggests that transferring players represent, on average, a higher level of risk for clubs than do their current players. There may well be a further extension of Akerlof's (1981) theory of lemons implied here. The prevalence of top players being offered higher-valued contracts by their current clubs contradicts the popular notion of instability (especially along market size directions) caused by the transfers of free agent players. Of course, one of the limitations of this small data set is that a large market effects, or any club-fixed effects, are difficult to test (as Krautmann (2017) could do). Further research with a more comprehensive data set may be illuminating along these lines.

In regard to other further research, detailed contract data is available for all MLB players from 2009 forward, thus the data set can clearly be expanded to a panel of several years and include pitchers. Two more considerations are important in regard to MLB. First, the collective bargaining agreement (CBA), since 2003, has included a penalty that imposes a proportional tax on club payrolls exceeding a set limit.[10] This may have altered contracting behavior of MLB clubs. In order to avoid a luxury tax penalty, clubs may be more likely to back-load and even offer longer terms of contract payouts. This practice appears to have increased in the competitive balance tax era. For example, Albert Pujols signed a 10-year contract with the Los Angeles Angels in 2012 which will pay him a total of $240 million through 2021. Pujols will be 41 years old in the contract's final year, and well past the prime age of most ballplayers. In addition, Pujols' contract is back-loaded, as he received $12 million in the contract's first period (2012) and his payout increases in $1 million annual increments. He will not reach his largest annual salary of $30 million until the last year (2021) of the contract. Pujols' contract is extraordinary in term and value, and has drawn much criticism from the media. Nonetheless, multi-period contracts that specify variable rather than a fixed annual salary, both back-loaded as was Pujols', and (though less common) frontloaded, are increasingly common. More research into the risk tradeoffs involved here may be instructive.

Second, more comparisons to European soccer are likely relevant. MLB players proceed through three stages of negotiation market power. These stages, determined by collective bargaining, are identified by Maxcy (2004a) and Walters et al (2017) as critical determinants of contract length. Players in European soccer leagues, however, proceed directly to free market negotiations. Clubs in this case are potentially subject to more risk, as players with much less experience have full market power. The previous research addressed above (e.g. Frick, 2011) observes a greater prevalence of strategic behavior in the contract year for soccer than for baseball. A comparison of the determinants of multi-period contracts across open and closed leagues is potentially of great interest.

There are some additional research opportunities that may arise from the analysis of the full contract data. Agent effects may be apparent, as the *Baseball Prospectus* contract data lists each player's agent. Additionally, it is curious that injury days show no effect on contract terms. The DL data breaks DL spells according to the types of injuries a player has sustained. More rigorous analysis may determine whether certain types of injuries, say chronic as opposed to random, imply greater productive uncertainty and impose greater term and salary penalties. There are likely additional avenues for exploration, and the expansion to other sports and sports leagues for comparisons to baseball and soccer would also be of great value.

NOTES

1. This contrasts with professional athletes in most individual sports, like golf and tennis, who are typically remunerated *ex post* based on their performance, for example finishing a tournament. However, star athletes in individual sports, including the aforementioned and also runners and triathletes, often do receive *ex ante* payments simply for their agreed participation in a race or tournament (an appearance fee).
2. There is a separate, though related, literature that considers the effects of contest structure on incentives and efforts. Most of this literature, see for example Ehrenberg and Bognanno (1990) on professional golf, considers individual sports.
3. Scroggins' metric, Total Bases, is the sum of bases obtained by a hitter over a period, usually the full regular season (such that a homerun counts as four, a triple as three, a double as two, and a single as one base each). Total Bases is the numerator component of Slugging Average, the calculation of Total Bases per times *At Bat*. Hence, Total Bases is a direct function of playing time, while Slugging Average is not.
4. Extensive use of bonuses may bring about improper incentives for management. Solow and von Allman (2016) offer a thorough explanation of the reasons for these limits, and sport-by-sport variations in bonus rules.
5. Marburger, rather than relying on a single statistic or set of single statistics, calculated a comprehensive 'z score' similar to what has since become vogue in the statistical analysis of baseball performance (Sabermetrics). He developed a simple linear model equal to player's total bases, plus walks, plus hit-by-pitch, plus stolen bases, minus caught stealing per game, relative to the average non-pitcher player.
6. There are many professions, besides professional athletes, that are represented with uniquely skilled workers in this context. Examples include, but are not limited to, software engineers, television writers, research scientists, journalists, and, patently, sports economists.
7. Players switching teams were assumed to be over-represented and a selection problem because contract extensions with the same club were less often reported in the media.
8. Not only are these Sabermetric measures more comprehensive in valuing performance, they are also given increased consideration by MLB decision-makers and are now more accurate as predictors of salaries. For example, Congdon-Hohman and Lanning (2017) examine determinants of MLB salaries using the newer 'Moneyball' metrics and conclude that compensation has adjusted to reflect those values. Lastly, collective bargaining agreements (CBAs) between players' unions and leagues, which determine the framework for all contract negotiations, have been altered in the 2000s.
9. The value of plate appearances has not gone unnoticed but, in the past, it was not included directly in common sources of baseball data. Instead, researchers had to calculate PA as the sum of its several components: At Bats plus Bases-on-Balls plus Intentional Bases-on-Balls plus Hit-by-Pitch plus Sacrifices. So, it was often ignored in favor of less accurate accounts of playing time such as Games or At Bats.
10. The competitive balance tax replaced, with the 2003 CBA, its forerunner called the 'luxury tax'. The luxury tax was not a set threshold, but simply imposed a penalty on the top five spending clubs from 1997 to 2001.

REFERENCES

Akerlof, G. (1981) 'Jobs as dam sites', *Review of Economic Studies*, **48** (1), 37–49.

Alchian, A. and Demsetz, H. (1972) 'Production, information costs, and economic organization', *American Economic Review*, **62** (4), 777–795.

Berri, D. J. and Krautmann, A. C. (2006) 'Shirking on the court: testing for the incentive effects of guaranteed pay', *Economic Inquiry*, **44** (3), 536–546.

Buraimo, B., Frick, B., Hickfang, M., and Simmons, R. (2015) 'The economics of long-term contracts in the footballers' labour market', *Scottish Journal of Political Economy*, **62** (1), 8–24.

Cantor, R. (1988) 'Work effort and contract length', *Economica*, **55**, 343–353.

Congdon-Hohman, J. M. and Lanning, J. A. (2017) 'Beyond moneyball: changing compensation in MLB', *Journal of Sports Economics*.

Ehrenberg, R. G. and Bognanno, M. L. (1990) 'Do tournaments have incentive effects?', *Journal of Political Economy*, **98** (6), 1307–1324.

Feess, E., Gerfin, M., and Muelhueusser, G. (2010) 'The incentive effects of long-term contracts on performance: evidence from a natural experiment in European soccer'. Unpublished working paper University of Bern. Available at http://staff.vwi.unibe.ch/gerfin/downloads/moralhazard_draft_mg_030210.pdf.

Fort, R. (1992) 'A pay and performance omnibus: is the field of dreams barren?', in Paul Sommers (ed.), *Diamonds are Forever: The Business of Baseball*, Washington, DC: Brookings Institution, pp. 134–162.

Frick, B. (2011) 'Performance, salaries, and contract length: empirical evidence from German soccer', *International Journal of Sport Finance*, **6** (2), 87–118.

Hadley, L. and Gustafson, E. (1991) 'Major League Baseball salaries: the impacts of arbitration and free agency', *Journal of Sport Management*, **5**, 111–127.

Hakes, J. K. and Turner, C. (2008) 'Long-term contracts in Major League Baseball', *SSRN Working Paper*. Available at https://papers.ssrn.com/sol3/papers.cfm?abstract_id=1309944.

Hart, O. and Holmstrom, B. (1987) 'The theory of contracts', in T. F. Bewley (ed.), *Advances in Economic Theory Fifth World Congress*, Cambridge UK: Cambridge University Press, pp. 71–156.

Heckman, J. (1976) 'The common structure of statistical models of truncation, sample selection, and limited dependent variables and a simple estimator for such models', *Annals of Economic and Social Measurement*, **5**, 475–492.

Kahn, L. (1993) 'Free agency, long-term contracts and compensation in Major League Baseball: estimates from panel data', *Review of Economics and Statistics*, **75** (1), 157–164.

Krautmann, A. C. (2017) 'Risk-averse team owners and players' salaries in Major League Baseball', *Journal of Sports Economics*, **18** (1), 19–33.

Krautmann, A. C. (1990) 'Shirking or stochastic productivity in Major League Baseball?', *Southern Economic Journal*, **57** (1), 961–968.

Krautmann, A. C. (1993) 'Shirking or stochastic productivity in Major League Baseball: reply', *Southern Economic Journal*, **60** (2), 241–243.

Krautmann, A. C. and Donley, T. D. (2009) 'Shirking in Major League Baseball revisited', *Journal of Sports Economics*, **10** (3), 292–304.

Krautmann, A. C. and Oppenheimer, M. (2002) 'Contract length and the return to performance in Major League Baseball', *Journal of Sports Economics*, **3**, 6–17.

Krautmann, A. C. and Solow, J. L. (2009) 'The dynamics of performance over the duration of Major League Baseball long-term contracts', *Journal of Sports Economics*, **10** (1), 6–22.

Krautmann, A. C. and Solow, J. L. (2015) '(Ma)Lingering on the disabled list', *Contemporary Economic Policy*, **33** (4), 689–697.

Lehn, K. (1982) 'Property rights, risk sharing, and player disability in Major League Baseball', *Journal of Law and Economics*, **25** (2), 343–366.

Marburger, D. R. (2003) 'Does the assignment of property rights encourage or discourage shirking? Evidence from Major League Baseball', *Journal of Sports Economics*, **4** (1), 19–34.

Maxcy, J. G. (1996) 'Efficient contract choice in the market for uniquely skilled labor', Dissertation, Department of Economics, Washington State University.

Maxcy, J. (1997) 'Do long-term contracts influence performance in Major League Baseball?', in W. Hendricks (ed.), *Advances in the Economics of Sport*, Greenwich, CT: JAI Press Inc, pp. 157–176.

Maxcy, J. G. (2004a) 'Contract length as risk management when labor is not homogeneous', *Labour: Review of Labour Economics and Industrial Relations*, **18** (2), 177–189.

Maxcy, J. (2004b) 'Motivating long-term employment contracts: risk management in Major League Baseball', *Managerial and Decision Economics*, **25** (2), 109–120.

Maxcy, J., Fort, R. and Krautmann, T. (2002) 'The effectiveness of incentive mechanisms in Major League Baseball', *Journal of Sports Economics*, **3** (3), 246–255.

O'Neill, H. M. (2014) 'Do hitters boost their performance during their contract years?', *Baseball Research Journal*, **43** (2), 78–85.

Rossi, G. (2012) 'Contract duration and football player performance: the empirical evidence of Serie A', Athens: ATINER'S Conference Paper Series, No: SPO2012-0203.

Scroggins, J. (1993) 'Shirking or stochastic productivity in Major League Baseball: comment', *Southern Economic Journal*, **60** (3), 239–240.

Scully, G. (1974) 'Pay and performance in Major League Baseball', *American Economic Review*, **64** (4), 915–930.

Scully, G. (1989) *The Business of Major League Baseball*, Chicago, IL: University of Chicago Press.

Solow, J. and von Allmen, P. (2016) 'Performance expectations, contracts, and job security', in M. Barry, J. Skinner, and T. Engelberg (eds), *Research Handbook of Employment Relations in Sport*, Cheltenham, UK and Northampton, MA, USA: Edward Elgar Publishing, pp. 46–68.

Sommers, P. and Quinton, N. (1982) 'Pay and performance in Major League Baseball: the case of the first family of free agents', *Journal of Human Resources*, **17**, 426–436.

Stiroh, K. J. (2007) 'Playing for keeps: pay and performance in the NBA', *Economic Inquiry*, **45** (1), 145–161.

Walters, S. J. K., Von Allmen, P. and Krautmann, A. (2017) 'Risk aversion and wages: evidence from the baseball labor market', *Atlantic Economic Journal*, **45** (3), 385–397.

PART III

Teamwork, and the impacts of management

6. Impacts of co-worker heterogeneity on team performance

Robert Simmons

6.1 INTRODUCTION

A growing labour and personnel economics literature has addressed the effects of co-worker heterogeneity on labour market outcomes. For example, Glitz (2017) finds that networks of former co-workers help raise re-employment probabilities for workers who were laid off after substantial plant closures in Germany. Parrotta et al. (2014) show that workforce diversity in educational outcomes raised firm value-added in Denmark. However, diversity in ethnicity and demographics had negative effects on firm productivity. It appeared that communication and integration costs attached to more culturally and demographically diverse workforces more than offset any benefits from creativity and knowledge spillovers.

Trax et al. (2015) modelled total factor productivity in German establishments and found that the percentage of a firm's foreign workers had no effect on productivity. But they did find evidence of productivity gains from an increased degree of fractionalization of groups of foreigners into different nationalities. Having foreigners diversified into many different backgrounds appeared to help establishments raise their productivity levels. These gains were more pronounced in manufacturing than in services. Using a field experiment on call centres, De Grip and Sauermann (2012) found that an increase in the share of peer workers who had received randomly assigned training raised performance levels of workers who had not received training. This training externality could take the form of knowledge spillovers or social pressure, but De Grip and Sauermann were unable to distinguish these two effects.

Call centres operate without team production but are amenable to controlled field experiments as worker tasks are clearly defined with clean measurements of worker performance. Precise separation of workers into treatment and control groups can be achieved. But by construction, teamwork is absent in call centres and we would expect co-worker spillovers to be more important in settings where teamwork is necessary for production.

This is where sports data can be helpful. Following Kahn (2000), team sports offer precise measurement of firm (team) outcomes and increasingly detailed evaluation of worker (player) productivity. In addition, some confounding effects are reduced. Roster sizes are typically fixed, so labour demand effects are absent. League structures have low variation, especially in North American leagues, so entry and exit of firms (teams) can be safely put to one side. Rules governing player labour markets do vary (salary caps, bargaining agreements, player trading rules) and rule changes offer potential sources of variation in team and player outcomes.

Understanding how co-worker heterogeneity affects team performance (if at all) is important for stakeholders in the sports industry. For clubs themselves, performances might be raised by better appreciation of how teammate effects raise team productivity, with the proviso that sports leagues necessarily have both winners and losers and are essentially zero-sum. For leagues, understanding the impacts of player heterogeneity could influence the design of rules that affect players and teams. For example, at the time of writing, the Chinese soccer league is proposing to allow teams to field a maximum of three foreign players, rather than four as previously. If this restriction raises the share of Chinese players on Chinese teams, and also reduces team diversity by nationality, what will this change do to player, team and league outcomes?

The remainder of this chapter is in six sections. Section 6.2 reviews the effects of productivity spillovers on player and team performance, focusing on baseball and basketball. Section 6.3 examines effects of talent disparity on team performance, with examples from baseball and soccer. Cultural diversity is discussed in section 6.4. Spillovers generated by player migration are the subject of section 6.5. Another source of player heterogeneity is salary dispersion and there is a considerable literature on the effects of pay dispersion on team performance. This literature is reviewed in section 6.6. Section 6.7 concludes.

6.2   PRODUCTIVITY SPILLOVERS

Any benefits to teams from co-worker heterogeneity will tend to come from productivity spillovers. In principle, the duellist format of Major League Baseball (MLB), with a hitter facing a pitcher in a given play, might rule out teammate spillovers. Gould and Winter (2009) argue that teammate spillovers do exist within MLB. They find that hitter batting average increases with teammate batting performance but falls with improved pitching performance. Batting was measured by batting average, while pitching was measured by earned run average, which depends on fielding as well as pitching, but the authors claim that their results are robust to alternative performance metrics. Pitchers do better when fellow pitchers perform better but there was no significant effect of a team's batting performance on pitching performance. Gould and Winter argue that these results are rational responses to baseball's production technology. A behavioural model would predict that players should vary their effort levels in the same direction regardless of teammates' role.

Using annual player performance data the model estimated by Gould and Winter is:

$$\text{Performance}_{it} = \beta_0 + \beta_1 \text{ Teammate pitching ERA} + \beta_2 \text{ Teammate}$$
batting average $+ \beta_3$ Controls (Division quality, Manager quality,
Ball Park effects) + Player fixed effects + error $\qquad$ (6.1)

That β_2 is found to be significantly positive for hitters seems intuitively reasonable: a rising tide lifts all boats. Batters who hit in front of other top-class hitters in the batting order will tend to receive easier pitches, as the pitcher will not want to risk a walk that brings a star hitter to the plate. If teammate pitchers perform less well (i.e. give up more runs) then hitters have to increase their effort to score more runs to compensate for a weaker defense. Gould and Winter argue that their finding of $\beta_1 > 0$ shows that hitters and pitchers are substitutes in production. For pitchers, Gould and Winter find that $\beta_1 > 0$, so worse teammate pitching performance leads to lower object pitcher performance. Here, a falling tide apparently lowers all boats. But pitchers themselves have defined roles, split into starters, relievers and closers. Relievers take over when a starting pitcher gets tired or is showing poor form. Closers have the specific role of securing ('saving') a win at the end of a game. Gould and Winter do not account for these different roles on the team.

Although Gould and Winter claim that their spillover effects are driven by production technology, it is hard to rule out peer effects and incentive effects driven by player contract structures. Baseball players are broadly placed into three categories: drafted players on rookie contracts, usually with earnings below marginal revenue product; players eligible for salary arbitration; and free agents. Teams select a number of players under these three categories subject to a fixed roster size, and players under each contract type face different performance incentives. Again, a more granular analysis than seasonal is required to properly assess the incentive effects of contracts and payment types.

A useful research project would be to revisit baseball spillover effects using game level or even play-by-play data. Bryson and Papps (2017) link hitter complementarities to performance-related pay schemes. Conversion of hitter complementarities into positive spillovers that raise team performance requires that hitter pay is determined at least partly by *team* output rather than *individual* output. It is notable that in most team sports, any performance-related component of player compensation is dominated by team outcomes over individual outcomes, since the latter could deliver perverse incentives with excessively selfish player behaviour. Dominance of team bonuses over individual bonuses occurs in American football and soccer as well as baseball.

A play level analysis of teammate spillovers is offered by Arcidiacono et al. (2017). Their starting point is that basketball players are heterogeneous in both their own productivity and in their ability to raise the performances of teammates. This follows research into leadership where workers who are the most productive themselves are also the ones who make other workers more productive (Goodall, 2009). The headline result in Arcidiacono et al. (2017) is that a one standard deviation increase in spillover effect of one player raises team performance by 63 percent as much as a one standard deviation rise in own productivity. Hence, spillovers are important but not as much as direct performance by a player. The econometric identification needed to obtain this result comes from variations in teammate composition across plays. Using play-by-play data from 2006 to 2009 the authors distinguish abilities to (i) score, (ii) help others score, and (iii) stop opponents from scoring. Their principal measure is expected points per possession, defined as the probability of scoring points times expected points conditional on scoring. From a multinomial logit production function and for each player, the authors obtain an offensive intercept, an offensive slope and defensive intercept. The offensive slope is an estimate of productivity spillover. Adding a one standard deviation to each of these three estimates raises point differential per possession by 0.027 (offensive intercept), 0.017 (offensive spillover) and 0.021 (defensive intercept). The model recognizes that adding a good scorer will necessarily reduce opportunities for other players to score.

Although Arcidiacono et al. (2017) find strong, robust evidence that teammate spillovers raise team performance, they also find that these interactions do not affect player salaries over the 2007 to 2010 seasons where performances are lagged by up to four seasons. The salary model includes offensive intercept, offensive slope, defensive slope, experience, experience squared and position dummies. Experience squared and offensive slope each deliver insignificant coefficients. Hence, there is no effect on salary of the ability of players to raise the productivity of teammates. There are reduced incentives for players to invest efforts to help raise teammate productivity. Since teammate spillovers affect team performance but not player salaries, this suggests a source of allocative inefficiency in the basketball players' labour market that merits further research, in particular to reveal why this misalignment of spillover effects exists and whether it persists over time.

6.3   HETEROGENEOUS ABILITY AND TEAM PERFORMANCE

Papps et al. (2011) pose a basic question for team executives to consider. Which is preferred: even levels of player ability, or high levels of talent dispersion with one star and several mediocre players? This question was answered using a long span of MLB data over 1920 to 2009. The authors find evidence of non-linearity in the relationship between heterogeneous ability and team success. Their curve relating team output to skill dispersion has an inverted U-shape. That is, teams with a middling distribution of OPS (on base percentage plus slugging) of hitters and ERA (earned run average) of pitchers tend to win more games than teams with very low or very high skill spreads. This result is robust to inclusion of team fixed effects and endogeneity of talent dispersion. Possible mechanisms by which talent disparity can affect team performance are teammate cooperation, player learning, emulation of peers and coaching effects. The paper was unable to distinguish between these mechanisms, and to do so is an extremely difficult research exercise. The main result that too much heterogeneity in worker ability can damage team (firm) performance echoes findings of Hamilton et al. (2003) on teamwork among garment factory workers.

Greater heterogeneity in player ability can increase team performance by reducing the gap between players' potential performance and their willingness to supply this potential. Also, better hitters can transfer skills or training techniques to less experienced or lower performing hitters – an emulation effect. Alternatively, greater within-team heterogeneity can reduce team performance since opposing teams can set batting lineups that expose weaknesses in opponent team pitching. Heterogeneity facilitates interdependence between hitting and opponent pitching strategies. For example, with heterogeneous hitters, an opponent pitcher can reserve his most effective pitches for the best hitters. Papps et al. (2011) propose an optimal level of heterogeneity. At high levels of heterogeneity, pitchers can exploit the weaknesses of the least-performing hitters. For low levels of heterogeneity, players do not benefit from knowledge spillovers offered by experienced and talented peers.

The model for estimation in Papps et al. (2011) is:

$$\text{Win percent} = \beta_0 + \beta_1 \text{OPS} + \beta_2 \text{ERA} + \beta_3 \text{OPSCOV} + \beta_4 \text{OPSCOV}^2$$
$$+ \beta_5 \text{ERACOV} + \beta_6 \text{ERACOV}^2 + \text{Controls} + \text{error} \qquad (6.2)$$

In this equation, OPSCOV and ERACOV are coefficients of variation of OPS and ERA, respectively. Equation 6.2 was estimated by OLS and Instrumental Variables (IV), where the instrument for the coefficient of variation terms was team coefficient of variation minus coefficient of variation that excludes players who left the club through retirement or free agency. The authors argue that OLS estimation understates the true effect of team inequality on team performance (presumably through measurement error). In the preferred IV results, for the OPS coefficient of variation terms, the level has a significant positive coefficient while the squared term has a negative coefficient. For the ERA coefficient of variation, the level has a significant negative coefficient (recall that higher ERA means worse pitching performance) while the squared term has a significant positive coefficient. For both OPS and ERA, turning points are within sample. Indeed, it is interesting that most teams had inequality measures in hitting and pitching performances that were above optimal values from the estimates. Most teams in most seasons would have benefited from reduced skill dispersion, at least as indicated by ex post performance statistics. Of course, as is typical in sports studies of team production functions, observed player performance is really being used as a proxy for both ability and effort since we cannot observe or measure either of these inputs directly.

The relationship between talent disparity and soccer team performance is analysed for the German Bundesliga by Franck and Nüesch (2010). In a given league match, a Bundesliga team nominates 11 starting players plus seven other players from which three can be used as substitutes. The first team squad (ignoring reserve and youth players) will have around 25 players. Franck and Nüesch suggest that there will be teammate complementarities among the matchday squad of 18 players but there will be substitution effects within the broader squad.

Franck and Nüesch set up a two-step procedure to compute talent measures for each player over six seasons of data. First, they compute individual productivity as the weighted sum of performance statistics that affect winning. These performance measures comprise goals, assists, pass success rate, cross success rate, dribbling success rate, shots on target, red cards, yellow cards, clearances, blocks and interceptions (as one category) and saves per shot by goalkeepers. A composite individual productivity is the sum of performance statistic multiplied by its weight. Then in the second stage, individual 'permanent' productivity is modelled as a function of team fixed effects and average productivity of teammates. The player fixed effects from this second stage are the talent proxies. As a robustness check, Franck and Nüesch use expert ratings from *Kicker* magazine as a performance measure and, interestingly, find that these are better predictors of team success than the detailed performance metrics. Use of *Kicker* ratings does not affect the main results, however.

Franck and Nüesch find that, at the game level, increased talent disparity reduces the probability of a team winning, holding average ability constant. Hence, a team would prefer a uniform distribution of good talent to a matchday squad with some very good and some poor players. Of course, a uniform distribution of star talent would be better still but not all teams can realistically aspire to this selection due to budget restrictions and player labour supply decisions.

For the squad as a whole, Franck and Nüesch model team final, end-of-season standings. They find that increased squad talent disparity raises team performance. The follow-up question for further research is to identify the fringe players who are counted in the broader squad but make relatively few matchday appearances. What happens to these players? Are they: injured so unavailable, used as backups for starter injury or loss of form, surplus to requirements in the opinion of the head coach, or are they allowed to leave 'on loan' to gain playing time and experience with other clubs? Are fringe players young or old or a mix of ages? The fringe players not normally in matchday squads will have less playing time to reveal their abilities, by construction, and, where these abilities are observed to some extent, we would expect greater variation than from more consistent starters. The precise sources and effects of roster heterogeneity need to be better understood.

6.4   CULTURAL DIVERSITY

According to Lazear (1999), there are potential benefits from having culturally diverse work teams. However, these benefits need to be sufficiently large to offset the additional assimilation costs to the firm. The more disjointed the skill sets of sub-groups within teams or firms, the greater the benefits of diversity. Cultural diversity brings with it greater collective knowledge and expands the firm's skill set. But if the skill and knowledge sets of cultural groups overlap, then the gains from cultural diversity are reduced. As an example of successful diversity, Hamilton et al. (2004) use data from a California garment maker to find that work teams of sewers that had more skill diversity were more productive. A rationale for this finding is learning by lower-skill workers from higher-skill workers.

The top sports leagues recruit players globally. MLB features hitters and pitchers from the Dominican Republic and Japan. Chinese players appear in the National Basketball Association (NBA). The five major European soccer leagues (England, France, Germany, Italy and Spain) all have high shares of foreign-born players in their teams. Player heterogeneity brings benefits to teams in terms of different playing styles and 'creative problem solving', following Lazear (1999). But heterogeneity also brings problems of language barriers, communication and coordination among players and assimilation of foreign players. Empirical evidence is needed to assess the net impact of cultural diversity on team performances.

The UEFA Champions League brings together the best performing teams from each European soccer league under UEFA jurisdiction in one prestigious and lucrative tournament. Ingersoll et al. (forthcoming) model cultural diversity as 'linguistic distance', a concept that has been much used in trade analyses. Essentially, Spain and Portugal are closer together in language than Spain and Germany. Linguistic distance is computed externally using an Automated Similarity Judgement Program. On this basis, Deportivo la Coruna (2004) had the least diverse measure, being comprised of a squad that was almost entirely Spanish. The German team Wolfsburg (2009) had a wide mix of player nationalities and very few German players and so had the most diverse team.

For teams competing in the UEFA Champions League between 2003 and 2012, Ingersoll et al. find that more heterogeneous teams outperform less diverse teams. A one standard deviation rise in linguistic distance leads to a doubling of goal difference over the tournament. In a model of team performance in the Champions League with controls for team roster market values[1] and with team fixed effects, linguistic distance had a significant and positive coefficient. However, richer teams have broader hiring networks to obtain talent globally so teams' linguistic distance is likely to be endogenous. Ingersoll et al. use instrumental variables estimation to deal with this problem. Their main equation, estimated for team-seasons, is:

$$\text{Goal difference} = \beta_0 + \beta_1 \text{ Average market value} + \beta_2$$
$$\text{Linguistic distance} + \text{error} \qquad (6.3)$$

Average market value is average player value over the roster.[2] This average value is instrumented by changes in the country stock market index. Linguistic distance is instrumented by non-EU domestic quotas. Each competitor in the Champions League nominates a 25-man squad to UEFA, although extra players under 21 years old can be brought in at will. Each EU country has different rules regarding work permits for non-EU players. For example, in Italy five non-EU players are allowed on the roster with three permitted in any matchday squad. Spain allows three 'licensed' and three fielded non-EU players. France stipulates four non-EU players

Personnel economics in sports

Table 6.1   *Structural equation estimates by Ingersoll et al. (forthcoming)*

Variable	Goal Difference	Average Value	Linguistic Distance
Linguistic distance	0.009**	0.035***	
Average value	0.781***		−22.27***
Lagged national stock market value		0.005***	
Domestic quota			−6.41***

in any team roster. These quota variations deliver econometric identification. The domestic quota variable used is then the number of domestic players required to be represented in a given playing squad and this varies across countries and over time. The estimates of the structural equation model in Ingersoll et al. are shown in Table 6.1.

In the IV estimation, an Angrist-Pischke F test rejects weak instruments. The instruments themselves deliver significant and plausible effects with higher stock prices raising average market values of teams and stricter domestic quotas reducing linguistic distance. The key result is that greater linguistic distance (more diversity in language) raises teams' average goal difference through the Champions League tournament. That means greater net goals in both group stage and over the tournament as a whole. As predicted, the IV coefficient on linguistic distance in the goal difference equation is lower than the ordinary least squares (OLS) coefficient (0.014) but is statistically significant at the 5 percent level.

It would be a worthwhile research exercise to apply the approach of Ingersoll et al. to domestic soccer leagues but to reinforce the analysis with alternative measures of cultural diversity. An alternative instrument for average market value of players would be size of sale of domestic television rights in a given country.

In the National Hockey League (NHL), teams are set up in groups, termed 'lines'. Due to the intensity of skating and the physical demands on players, teams rotate lines very frequently. One line will come off the ice to be replaced by a different set of players. Only the goalkeeper keeps his position on the ice. The NHL admits many players from outside North America, principally from Scandinavian and Eastern European countries where ice hockey is played. Kahane et al. (2013) model the effects of diversity through nationality on NHL team performances over the 2001–2002 to 2007–2008 seasons but excluding 2004–2005, which was cancelled due to a player lockout. Two measures of diversity are employed. The first is a Herfindahl-Hirschman index (HHI) derived from shares of players in five main groups: North American, Czech Republic and Slovak

Republic, Sweden, Finland, and Russia. This index was dominated by the North American group, which had a 67 per share over the sample period. Recall that the index is the sum of the squared group shares. Kahane et al. deal with North American dominance by including a variable, relative European share, defined as the share of a team's players from outside North America scaled by the league average of this measure. In the model, variations in HHI capture changes in concentration within the European group after controlling for shares of European players on team rosters.

In models of win percent and team points, both HHI and relative European share deliver significant and positive coefficients. These results are robust to alternative measures of team performance (points as well as win percent) and to inclusion of team fixed effects. A team with a greater share of European players is estimated to have better performance than a team with a smaller share of Europeans, assuming they have the same levels of group concentration. For two teams with the same European share, the team with higher HHI (more group concentration) performs better. The recipe for success in the NHL is to hire large numbers of mostly homogeneous European players, i.e. from the same country. This was the policy successfully adopted by the Detroit Red Wings over the 2000s, which recruited large numbers of Swedish players.

Kahane et al. (2013) also model effects of HHI and relative European share on productivity measures at the individual player level. They find no effect of either diversity measure on North American player performances. Instead, they find positive effects of each diversity measure on European player productivity (points and assists but not goals; significant at 10 percent level only).

The evidence presented by Kahane et al. suggests two beneficial effects to NHL teams from adding more European players. First, in the sample considered, European players were more skilled and more productive than North American counterparts. Second, adding more European players raised the productivity of existing European players. Specifying the precise mechanisms behind these results is a task for further research. Critical to team success is the capability to recruit skilled migrant players and to assimilate these effectively into team rosters. What are the relevant human resource management practices that facilitate successful integration of foreign players into teams dominated by domestic players?

6.5   BENEFITS FROM PLAYER MIGRATION

Three notable papers identify the benefits to teams from having immigrant players by comparing performances in different competitions, one at the club level and the other at the national level. Each of these papers points to productivity spillovers from importing foreign talent into sports leagues.

The first paper on player migration effects is Alvarez et al. (2011) on European basketball. They consider whether countries with more foreign players in leagues do better in important national team tournaments including European and World Championships and the Olympic Games.

Alvarez et al. regress national team ranking in a given competition on a set of control variables and numbers of foreign basketball players in a national league. The probability of tournament qualification is instrumented by the number of places available in a given tournament divided by the number of eligible countries in a Heckman selection model. The selection model is found to be appropriate in the model of World tournament rankings as the instrument was positively and significantly related to probability of qualification; and the inverse Mills ratio also has a positive and significant coefficient. However, the instrument has an insignificant coefficient in the European tournament ranking model.

A greater number of foreign players in a national league leads to statistically significant improvement in tournament rankings in the European competition (at one percent level) and in the World tournament (at 10 percent level). Alvarez et al. (2011) conclude that foreign spillovers mattered for performance of the top teams in European and World basketball championships. They conjecture that the more highly skilled indigenous players would benefit more from spillovers brought in by imported foreign talent.

Berlinschi et al. (2013) study the effect of footballer migration to foreign clubs on origin (sending) national team performance. They conjecture that migration to foreign clubs allows players to improve their skills through training and development (learning and emulation). Moreover, their theoretical model predicts that the positive impact of player migration on national team performance increases with the difference in quality between foreign and home country clubs. The migration of national team players then improves national team performance more for countries with lower quality clubs and domestic leagues such as African nations.

Berlinschi et al. used FIFA points and FIFA rankings as alternative measures of national team performance where the former was a three-year weighted average. League strength was measured by UEFA rankings. A migration index is computed that weights each migrant player by the strength of the league and the division of the host club to which they move. Hence, a move to Greece has a lower weight in the migration index than a move to Germany. The migration index is the weighted number of national team squad players in foreign clubs. Berlinschi et al. find that the coefficients on the migration index are positive and significant in OLS estimation of FIFA points and FIFA rankings. Moreover, the migration index still has a positive and significant effect on national team performance when it is instrumented by dummy variables for past and current colonial links (e.g. French colonies in Africa) and for former communist countries. Overall, Berlinschi et al. conclude that footballer migration has a positive and significant effect on national team performance. This evidence is contrary to fan and media perceptions that limiting foreign migration might give more playing opportunities at the top level and improve the performance of a national team.

An analysis along similar lines to Berlinschi et al. (2013) is offered by Ichniowski and Preston (2014) in a working paper. Their research question is whether the talent of an individual's co-workers explains differences in rates of human capital accumulation 'on the job'. The analysis of Ichniowski and Preston suggests that football player performance improves more after a player joins an elite team than when he is a member of a lower level team. The treatment here is the exposure of migrant players to better players at elite clubs. The response is the change in national team performance after this exposure.

In a famous paper, Mas and Moretti (2009) show how lower quality checkout workers improved their performance when higher quality checkout workers came on shift. Crucially, the arrival of these superior operators was observable to the lower quality workers. Hence, the rise in productivity brought about by the lower quality workers could be attributed to monitoring and supervision rather than learning. In the football setting of Ichniowski and Preston, the source of productivity improvement is different. Players from inferior leagues are hired by teams in high-level leagues because of their potential. These players already have ability and show signs of future quality improvement. Of course, it is not known how such players will assimilate and integrate into better teams, similar to the migrant hockey players in Kahane et al. (2013), so hiring players from low-quality leagues is a risky proposition. On average, these migrant players do deliver productivity improvements for themselves and for their teams and this quality improvement persists after transfers have occurred. Such productivity improvement represents a genuine increase in human capital. There are also secondary peer effects at the national team level, since non-elite players improve while working with elite players in their teams.

The empirical model in Ichniowski and Preston (2014) uses a national team panel data set over 1990 to 2010, comprising 101 national soccer teams. The dependent variables were FIFA rankings, FIFA points and ELO points and rankings. The focus independent variable was PCTELITE, the percentage of a given national team's roster who were members of elite clubs in that season. Elite meant belonging to one of Europe's top five leagues (top divisions in England, France, Germany, Italy or Spain) or being a member of the top 50 clubs in the standings in the Champions League and Europa League. Control variables included average age of team and its square, national GDP per capita and average life expectancy of the object country.

Ichniowski and Preston find that a one standard deviation increase in PCTELITE is associated with a rise in national team ELO points by 45. If the model is restricted to a threshold percentage of common players on national team roster between years then the effect of PCTELITE on team performance is also positive and significant.

Players can join elite teams but subsequently make few appearances. Ichniowski and Preston offer a revised measure of PCTELITE, defined as the number of player-games during a national team's year made up by elite club players. This modified measure has a positive and significant effect on team performances. The model is further refined to consider changes in national team roster places from three groups of players: (i) in the top five leagues and in the Champions League; (ii) in the top five leagues but not in the Champions League; and (iii) not in the top five leagues but in the Champions League. Moving through these three groups, Ichniowski and Preston find declining impacts on national team performance measured as differences in ELO rankings. The impact of each group is positive and significant indicating robustness of results.

In a final refinement, Ichniowski and Preston compare the contribution of 'about to be first time elite players' to improvements in the contribution of the same players when they are 'first time elite players' one year ahead. Specifically, they define four groups of players with relevant PCTELITE coefficients in parentheses:

A. First time elite club players in time t who were contributing to national teams in $t+1$ (β_A)
B. Players who were in a national team but not an elite club in t but will be in an elite team at $t+1$; these were 'about to be first time elite players' (β_B)
C. Veterans on national teams and elite teams (β_C)
D. New elite players who are also new to the national team (β_D).

Ichinowski and Preston estimate β_B at 112.6 and β_A at 67.1 in a model of ELO rankings. This result is consistent with the conjecture that when elite clubs recruit players without previous elite club experience then on average they are selecting better players, a reassuringly rational outcome. These players contribute even more to national team performances in years after which they are members of elite clubs than in earlier years, even though they were already high performers in their origin (non-elite) clubs.

Taken together, the three papers surveyed in this section provide convincing evidence of productivity spillovers from migrant players. Of course, a team consisting only of players from the club's proximate region can nevertheless perform well despite deliberately restricting its hiring pool. Athletic Bilbao, in Spain's La Liga, has maintained high domestic league positions and entry into UEFA competitions despite deliberately restricting its hiring pool. Bilbao's development model is to train young players from the local region (or acquire local players from other clubs), bring them forward quickly into the first team and renew the process with the help of some lucrative transfer fees (e.g. Javi Martinez to Bayern Munich, Anders Herrera to Manchester United). But it is hard to see La Liga thriving as a whole in Champions League and revenue performances if all of its teams pursued a locals-only recruitment strategy, which would surely be summarily dismissed anyway by Barcelona and Real Madrid with their more outward market orientation.

The analysis of Ichniowski and Preston can be built upon in a number of ways. First, some national team games are friendlies in which the head coach can experiment by trying out new players. Competition games (e.g. World Cup qualifiers and World Cup finals) need to be differentiated from friendlies. The analysis could then shift to game-level rather than through FIFA or ELO rankings or points. Second, there are different work permit rules in different countries. England requires that a non-EU player must already be a recently appearing national team player, and that national team must be sufficiently high in FIFA rankings. Such rules do not apply in the other major European leagues. Exploiting national variation in work permit rules would aid econometric identification in assessing the impacts of player migration on national team performance. Third, the volatility and inconsistency of migrant players' performance in elite clubs need to be considered. Are migrant players able to perform consistently well at the top level and then generate useful productivity spillovers from sustained club performance?

6.6   PAY DISPERSION AND TEAM PERFORMANCE

All professional sports teams have pay structures and these are generally not uniform. Starting with Bloom (1999) and Depken (2000) on MLB, scholars have posed the question of whether greater pay dispersion among players increases or reduces team performance, controlling for total team payroll. Depken concludes that greater pay disparity, measured by a HHI, is detrimental to team performance over the 1985 to 1998 seasons, and several other studies since then have given further support to this result (see Table 6.2).

Table 6.2   A selection of pay dispersion-team performance econometric
           results

Study	League	Sample Period	Notes
Positive relationship			
Hill et al. (2017)	MLB	Not specified	Alignment of resource and pay dispersion
Simmons and Berri (2011)	NBA	1990 to 2008	Conditional and residual pay inequality; Gini coefficients
Frick et al. (2003)	NBA, NHL	1985 to 2001	
Bucciol et al. (2014)	Italy Serie A	2009/10 and 2010/11	Game level where dependent variable is win dummy. Pay dispersion over whole team roster
Zero relationship			
Avrutin and Sommers (2007)	MLB	2001 to 2005	
Tao et al. (2016)	MLB	1985 to 2013	Zero effect when payroll is scaled by league average; negative effect when payroll is not scaled
Katayama and Nuch (2011)	NBA	2002 to 2006	Game level. Robust zero effect for three different team constructs ranging from matchday squad to whole roster
Berri and Jewell (2004)	NBA	1996 to 2002	Model player turnover. Sample period has sharp increase in pay dispersion for most teams
Caruso et al. (2016)	Italy Serie A	2001 to 2015	Insignificant coefficients on Gini and Shannon measures but negative coefficient on Simpson inequality measure
Yamamura (2015)	Japan football	1993 to 2006	Zero for 1993 to 2006 and for dynamic fixed effects model; negative and significant for 1993 to 2001 and for static fixed effects model
Negative relationship			
Bloom (1999)	MLB	1985 to 1993	Gini coefficient
Depken (2000)	MLB	1985 to 1998	Herfindahl-Hirschman index

Table 6.2   (continued)

Study	League	Sample Period	Notes
Debrock et al. (2004)	MLB	1985 to 1998	Use conditional and residual inequality via Hirschman-Herfindahl indices
Jane (2010)	MLB	1998 to 2007	
Annala and Winfree (2011)	MLB	1985 to 2004	
Wiseman and Chatterjee (2007)	MLB	1985 to 2002	
Breunig et al. (2014)	MLB	1985 to 2010	Game level
Frick et al. (2003)	MLB, NFL	1985 to 2001	
Kahane (2012)	NHL	2001 to 2008 excluding 2004/05	Regular season and playoff performance. Uses residual salary dispersion based on standard deviation and interquartile range. Finds negative, significant coefficients in several specifications
Depken and Lureman (2017)	NHL	2000 to 2012	Herfindahl-Hirschman index; negative relationship only when team points and goals against are used as performance measures, not for goals scored
Bucciol et al. (2014)	Italy Serie A	2009/10 and 2010/11	Game level where dependent variable is win dummy. Pay dispersion over matchday squad
Coates et al. (2016)	MLS	2005 to 2013	Gini and coefficient of variation with level and squared terms considered jointly

Depken contrasts two theories of how pay dispersion amongst workers might affect organizational performance. Narrow salary dispersion might promote team morale and cohesion and hence greater effort by players leading to improved performance (Levine, 1991). Alternatively, narrow pay dispersion might increase workers' 'damage potential' where some workers become disaffected and shirk or even practice sabotage to undermine their teammates (Ramaswamy and Rowthorn, 1991). The latter argument seems hard to justify in team sports because players are selected into starting squads by team coaches and managers, and disruptive players can be jet-tisoned by various means. In MLB, players who damage their teammates' productivity can be reassigned to the minor leagues, traded, or just let go. Any sabotage activity would be observable to team management and action would surely be taken, albeit sometimes with a lag.

Several studies have revisited Depken's analysis both for MLB and for other leagues, with mixed results. Tao et al. (2016) stay with MLB, considering the period 1985 to 2013. Part of their study is a replication of Depken (2000) for a longer and updated sample period. For their own analysis, tournament theory was contrasted with team cohesiveness arguments. From tournament theory, wider pay disparities can raise a player's effort level as that player aspires to take on the role of one of the top earners in the franchise. This theory has been applied in various papers to individual sports (e.g. Sunde (2009) for tennis and Ehrenberg and Bognanno (1990) for golf). The extension of tournament theory to team sports is not straightforward as team cohesion has to be maintained to some extent; teammates need to interact with each other successfully in a well-performing team and managers need to guard against players' excessively selfish behaviour.

The empirical model in Tao et al. (2016) for team j at time t in MLB is:

$$WPC_{jt} = \gamma_0 + \gamma_1 \, WPC_{jt-1} + \gamma_2 \, Dispersion_{jt} + \gamma_3 \, Payroll_{jt} + \\ \text{Controls + Team fixed effects + error} \qquad (6.4)$$

Under the team cohesiveness argument, players are disincentivized by large wage dispersions due to adverse perceptions of pay inequality. Tao et al. take the team roster to be comprised of the top 25 players in the team by salary rank order (as opposed to number of appearances). They do not distinguish between free agents, arbitration eligible players and early career players on reserve clause contracts. The latter group tends to consist of drafted players who generally have pay determined by union rates and who are well known to suffer from monopsony exploitation (Humphreys and Pyun, 2017). The pay dispersion measure is a Gini coefficient, but results are also shown for a HHI. Control variables include team manager quality, league dummy, average pay in MLB, market size and tenure in the city.

A lagged dependent variable is used to capture persistence of win percent. This will necessarily be endogenous in a panel data set, so Tao et al. apply the Arellano-Bond GMM procedure to deal with this problem. The authors have two main empirical results. First, increased pay disper-sion has a negative effect on team performance when the payroll control is the log team average payroll. But a second result is that increased pay dispersion has no effect on team performance if the payroll control is team payroll divided by MLB average for teams in a given season. This suggests that the negative association between team pay dispersion and team performance is not robust.

In Depken (2000) and Tao et al. (2016), total payroll is a proxy for team quality even though in North American player labour markets, monopsony power of teams against players under restrictive contracts means the link between pay and marginal revenue product is severed. Hill et al. (2017) apply a managerial resource-based theory of the firm and model 'resource value' of teams as sum of player contributions to team performance. The player contributions are measured by a Bill James formula that combines marginal products of offense and defense. Resource dispersion is then the Gini coefficient for dispersion of individual contributions to team performances. This is contrasted with pay dispersion, measured by Gini coefficient of players' total pay. Hill et al. hypothesize that teams with greater congruence or fit of resource dispersion and pay dispersion will perform better than teams with less congruence. They also hypothesize that the relationships between resource value and team performance and between total pay and team performance are both stronger when congruence between resource and pay dispersion is high. Congruence between resource and pay dispersions is computed as one minus the absolute difference between resource dispersion and pay dispersion.

Each of these hypotheses is supported by Hill et al.'s empirical estimates. Teams whose congruence rises as a result of a one standard deviation shift in pay disparity are predicted to win one more game in a regular season. For teams with higher resource values, a one standard deviation rise in congruence generates two more wins. Overall, a one standard deviation shift in pay disparity is found to be capable of generating three more wins per season. The authors conclude that 'resource decisions need to be supported by tightly aligned salary and resource dispersions'. Hence, adding a star free agent to an MLB team roster on a large salary need not undermine team cohesion provided that expected player performance is actually delivered. Team managers need to be able to demonstrate to playing staff that the addition of a star player adds value to the franchise.

Simmons and Berri (2011) derive a conditional measure of pay inequality for NBA teams over the period 1990 to 2008. This measure was obtained from a log salary model of players where previous season performance measures were regressors. The performance metrics included points per game, rebounds, blocks, assists and minutes played. Age, age squared, team win percent and year dummies were also included as controls. The team Gini coefficient of predicted salaries from this regression was used as an 'expected' or even 'justified' measure of pay inequality. The Gini coefficient of residual salary is interpreted as a measure of 'unexpected' salary dispersion. In a fixed effects model of team win percent, the coefficient on expected pay dispersion is positive and significant while the coefficient on unexpected pay dispersion is not significant.

Simmons and Berri also model the effects of pay dispersion on player productivity. The preferred composite productivity measure is *ADJP48*, where weights in each performance component are taken from a regression of team wins on player performance statistics. Expected pay dispersion has a positive and significant effect on *ADJP48* while unexpected pay dispersion has an insignificant effect. Use of an alternative productivity measure delivers similar findings. The results on effects of pay dispersion on team performance and individual productivity are therefore consistent and are also compatible with the findings of Hill et al. (2017) for MLB. However, Simmons and Berri do not test directly for alignment of productivity dispersion with pay dispersion in the NBA, and that remains a task for further research.

A considerable number of studies have investigated the relationship between pay dispersion and team performance, with coverage extending to soccer as well as major North American leagues. Their results are summarised in Table 6.2. Around one half of the studies surveyed are on MLB. Of these, most point to negative effects of pay dispersion on team performance, in the spirit of Bloom (1999) and Depken (2000). As noted above, the effects of pay dispersion in Tao et al. (2016) depend on whether or not total team payroll is scaled by league average to control for salary inflation over time. One question not addressed in the reported studies is whether teammate effects of pay dispersion apply to the whole roster or to the playing role. Do hitters compare themselves to fellow hitters or are they concerned about their position within the whole franchise salary structure? Also, since only free agents have salaries determined on a competitive market via bilateral bargaining, should the effects of salary dispersion be restricted by contract type? If team performance does respond negatively to wage disparity then perhaps teams should respond by altering the mix of contract types on their rosters, i.e. fewer free agents and more reserve clause players. However, the analysis of Hill et al. (2017) points in a different direction and emphasizes the need for performance disparity of players to be matched to wage disparity. This leaves open the possibility that hiring expensive free agents might be beneficial to team performance. These questions of how the pay dispersion/team performance relationships are moderated by player role and contract type within the franchise are areas where further research is needed.

Looking outside MLB, it appears that empirical results on pay dispersion effects on individual and team performance are far from robust. In Bucciol et al.'s (2014) study of Italy Serie A, the sign of pay dispersion coefficient changes when they move from matchday playing squad to whole team roster. Results vary by specification of playing squad, choice of dispersion measure, sample period, econometric estimation method and league. This suggests than future scholars wishing to tackle the relationship between pay disparity and team performance should work hard to establish robustness of their results. An encompassing approach would be welcome, where different playing squad definitions, alternative dispersion measures and different estimation methods all feature. Comparisons of results across leagues should be performed, although European soccer is limited by a lack of information on player salaries. A comprehensive, consistent database of player salaries has been provided by *Gazzetta dello Sport* since 2008, and a comparable data set has only recently (2014) emerged for the German Bundesliga.[3]

Most importantly, the correlations between pay disparity and team performance discovered so far tend to suffer from a crucial econometric identification problem since omitted variables will necessarily be correlated with the error term. Unfortunately, it is difficult to find a clean natural experiment to generate distinct treatment and control groups and then apply a difference-in-difference analysis to obtain an average treatment of treated effect of pay disparity on team performance. Some researchers have examined changes in collective bargaining agreements in North American sports (Berri and Jewell, 2004; Depken and Lureman, 2017; Simmons and Berri, 2011) but these are problematic in that changes affect all teams at the same time. Searching for misalignments between resource disparity and pay disparity, as proposed by Hill et al. (2017), is a useful, intermediate step to understanding how resource and pay disparities map into individual and team performances. Future work should also focus more extensively on the team-selection effects of pay disparity on team performance, as imposed by coaches' decisions, and the corresponding impacts on player morale and motivation. Here, matchday-level analysis could be helpful. One way of modelling exogenous changes in player selection is to consider player absences due to random injuries as opposed to deselection through loss of form.

6.7 CONCLUSIONS

The dominant theme of this chapter has been that co-worker heterogeneity in professional sports teams can foster productivity spillovers. These spillovers have been found to be statistically and economically relevant in a wide range of sports including baseball, basketball, ice hockey, and soccer. In soccer in particular, productivity spillovers are facilitated by player migration. Specifically, the research surveyed in section 6.3 shows that national team performances are enhanced when players migrate from lower-status to higher-status teams and leagues. An important policy conclusion that follows from this work is that quota restrictions on numbers of foreign players in domestic leagues will have adverse rather than beneficial impacts on national team performance and will hence be counterproductive. For example, this does not bode well for current proposals in China to restrict numbers of foreign players appearing in teams in the Chinese Super League.

Although this chapter has uncovered a substantial volume of research on co-worker effects on team performance, much more work remains to be done. In particular, further research is needed to:

- apply more granular, high frequency data to identify magnitudes and sources of productivity spillovers;
- examine whether teammate productivity spillovers are fully reflected in player salaries, and if not, why not (Arcidiacono et al., 2017);
- examine which particular channels of player migration contribute successfully to individual and team performance;
- distinguish more precisely between migration effects on productivity through human capital enhancement, on the one hand, and peer and monitoring effects, on the other;
- demonstrate whether migration effects on national team performances carry over to clubs and leagues as a whole, using a fully developed welfare analysis;
- reconcile the conflicting results on effects of pay disparity on team performance, both across and within leagues;
- assess the effects of congruence of resource disparity and pay disparity on team performance, following Hill et al. (2017).

NOTES

1. Compiled by experts from http://www.transfermarkt.de.
2. Note that the market value assessed by http://www.transfermarkt.de is an amalgam of player salary and potential transfer fee, most of which goes to the selling club in the event of a player trade.
3. See http://www.fussball-geld.de.

REFERENCES

Alvarez, J. C., David Forrest, Ismael Sanz, and Juan de Dios Tena (2011) 'Impact of importing foreign talent on performance levels of local co-workers', *Labour Economics*, **18** (3), 287–296.

Annala, Christopher N. and Jason Winfree (2011) 'Salary distribution and team performance in Major League Baseball', *Sport Management Review*, **14** (2), 167–175.

Arcidiacono, Peter, Josh Kinsler, and Joseph Price (2017) 'Productivity spillovers in team production: evidence from professional basketball', *Journal of Labor Economics*, **35** (1), 191–225.

Avrutin, Brandon M. and Paul M. Sommers (2007) 'Work incentives and salary distributions in Major League Baseball', *Atlantic Economic Journal*, **35**, 509–510.

Berlinschi, Ruxanda, Jeroen Schokkaert, and Johan Swinnen (2013) 'When drains and gains collide: migration and international football performance', *Labour Economics*, **21** (2), 1–14.

Berri, David J. and R. Todd Jewell (2004) 'Wage inequality and firm performance: professional basketball's natural experiment', *Atlantic Economic Journal*, **32**, 130–139.

Bloom, Matt (1999) 'The performance effects of pay dispersion on individuals and organizations', *Academy of Management Journal*, **42** (1), 25–40.

Breunig, Robert, Bronwyn Garret-Ruba, Mathieu Jardin, and Yvon Rocaboy (2014) 'Wage dispersion and team performance: a theoretical model and evidence from baseball', *Applied Economics*, **46** (3), 271–281.

Bryson, Alex and Kerry L. Papps (2017) 'Spillovers and team incentives', IZA Discussion Paper.

Bucciol, Alessandro, Nicolai J. Foss, and Marco Piovesan (2014) 'Pay dispersion and performance in teams', *PlosOne*.

Caruso, Raul, Carlo Bellavite Pellegrini, and Marco Di Domizio (2016) 'Does diversity in the payroll affect soccer teams' performance? Evidence from the Italian Serie A', MPRA Working Paper.

Coates, Dennis, Bernd Frick, and R. Todd Jewell (2016) 'Superstar salaries and soccer success: the impact of designated players in Major League Soccer', *Journal of Sports Economics*, **17** (7), 716–735.

Debrock, Lawrence, Wallace Hendricks, and Roger Koenker (2004) 'Pay and performance: the impact of salary distribution on firm level outcomes in baseball', *Journal of Sports Economics*, **5** (3), 243–261.

De Grip, Andries and Jan Sauermann (2012) 'The effects of training on own and co-worker productivity', *Economic Journal*, **122**, 376–399.

Depken, Craig A. (2000) 'Wage dispersion and team productivity: evidence from Major League Baseball', *Economics Letters*, **67**, 87–92.

Depken, Craig A. and Jeff Lureman (2017) 'Wage disparity, team performance and the 2005 NHL collective bargaining agreement', *Contemporary Economic Policy*.

Ehrenberg, Ronald G. and Michael L. Bognanno (1990) 'Do tournaments have incentive effects?', *Journal of Political Economy*, **98** (6), 1307–1324.

Franck, Egon and Stephan Nüesch (2010) 'The effect of talent disparity on team production in soccer', *Journal of Economic Psychology*, **31** (2), 218–229.

Frick, Bernd, Joachim Prinz, and Karina Winkelmann (2003) 'Pay inequalities and team performance: empirical evidence from the North American major leagues', *International Journal of Manpower*, **24** (4), 472–488.

Glitz, Albrecht (2017) 'Coworker networks in the labour market', *Labour Economics*, **44** (1), 218–230.

Goodall, Amanda H. (2009) 'Highly cited leaders and the performance of research universities', *Research Policy*, **38** (7), 1079–1092.

Gould, Eric D. and Eyal Winter (2009) 'Interactions between workers and the technology of production: evidence from professional baseball', *Review of Economics and Statistics*, **91** (1), 188–200.

Hamilton, Barton H., Jack A. Nickerson, and Hideo Owan (2003) 'Team incentives and worker heterogeneity: an empirical analysis of teams on productivity and participation', *Journal of Political Economy*, **111** (3), 465–497.

Hamilton, Barton H., Jack A. Nickerson, and Hideo Owan (2004) 'Diversity and productivity in production teams', Social Science Research Network Working Paper.

Hill, Aaron D., Federico Aime, and Jason W. Ridge (2017) 'The performance implications of resource and pay dispersion: the case of Major League Baseball', *Strategic Management Journal*, **38** (9), 1935–1947.

Humphreys, Brad R. and Hyunwoong Pyun (2017) 'Monopsony exploitation in professional sport: evidence from Major League Baseball position players, 2000–2011', *Managerial and Decision Economics*, **38** (5), 676–688.

Ichniowski, Casey and Anne Preston (2014) 'Do star performers produce more stars? Peer effects and learning in elite teams', *National Bureau of Economic Research Working Paper* 20478.

Ingersoll, Keith, Edmund Maesky, and Sebastian M. Saiegh (forthcoming) 'Heterogeneity and team performance: evaluating the effect of cultural diversity in the world's top soccer league', *Journal of Sports Analytics.*

Jane, Wen-Jhan (2010) 'Raising salary or redistributing it?: A panel analysis of Major League Baseball', *Economics Letters*, **107** (2), 297–299.

Kahane, Leo H. (2012) 'Salary dispersion and team production: evidence from the National Hockey League', in Stephen Shmanske and Leo H. Kahane (eds), *The Oxford Handbook of Sports Economics*, Vol. 2, Oxford: Oxford University Press.

Kahane, Leo H., Neil Longley, and Robert Simmons (2013) 'The effects of co-worker heterogeneity on firm-level output: assessing the impacts of cultural and language diversity in the National Hockey League', *Review of Economics and Statistics*, **95** (1), 302–314.

Kahn, Lawrence M. (2000) 'Sports as a labor market laboratory', *Journal of Economic Perspectives*, **14** (3), 75–94.

Katayama, Hajine and Hudan Nuch (2011) 'A game-level analysis of salary dispersion and team performance in the National Basketball Association', *Applied Economics*, **43** (10), 1193–1207.

Lazear, Edward (1999) 'Globalisation and the market for team-mates', *Economic Journal*, **109**, C15–C40.

Levine, David (1991) 'Cohesiveness, productivity and wage dispersion', *Journal of Economic Behavior and Organization*, **15**, 237–255.

Mas, Alexandre and Enrico Moretti (2009) 'Peers at work', *American Economic Review*, **99** (1), 112–145.

Papps, Kerry L., Alex Bryson, and Rafael Gomez (2011) 'Heterogeneous worker ability and team-based production: evidence from Major League Baseball, 1920–2008', *Labour Economics*, **18** (3), 310–319.

Parrotta, Pierpaolo, Dario Pozzoli, and Mariolo Pytlikova (2014) 'Labor diversity and firm productivity', *European Economic Review*, **66** (1), 144–179.

Ramaswamy, Ramana and Robert E. Rowthorn (1991) 'Efficiency wages and wage dispersion', *Economica*, **58**, 501–514.

Simmons, Rob and David J. Berri (2011) 'Mixing the princes and the paupers: pay and performance in the National Basketball Association', *Labour Economics*, **18** (3), 381–388.

Sunde, Uwe (2009) 'Heterogeneity and performance in tournaments: a test for incentive effects using professional tennis data', *Applied Economics*, **41** (25), 3199–3208.

Tao, Yu-Li, Hwei-Lin Chuang, and Eric S. Lin (2016) 'Compensation and performance in Major League Baseball: evidence from salary dispersion and team performance', *International Review of Economics & Finance*, **43** (2), 151–159.

Trax, Michaela, Stephan Brunow, and Jens Suedekum (2015) 'Cultural diversity and plant-level productivity', *Regional Science and Urban Economics*, **53**, 85–96.

Wiseman, Frederick and Sangit Chatterjee (2007) 'Team payroll and team performance in Major League Baseball: 1985–2002', *Economics Bulletin*, **1**, 1–10.

Yamamura, Eiji (2015) 'Wage disparity and team performance in the process of industry development: evidence from Japan's professional football league', *Journal of Sports Economics*, **16** (2), 214–223.

7. Pay dispersion and productivity in sports

Leo Kahane

7.1 INTRODUCTION

One of the topics of personnel economics concerns the impact of wage or salary dispersion on the productivity of workers. At the center of this issue are essentially worker incentives and how greater dispersion may affect effort. Two key models have been put forth by the theoretical literature: the 'fairness' or 'cohesiveness' model and the 'tournament' model. In the fairness model (Akerlof and Yellen, 1988, 1990; Lazear, 1989; Levine, 1991) it is argued that a more compressed payroll structure will lead to greater output. The concept here is that if workers doing similar tasks receive significantly different compensation this may be viewed by low-wage workers as being unfair. As Akerlof and Yellen (1990) write, 'The motivation for the fair wage-effort hypothesis is a simple observation concerning human behavior: when people do not get what they deserve, they try to get even' (p. 256). Thus a wide dispersion in wages may lead to discord and a lack of cohesiveness (perhaps even sabotage) in the work place and negatively impact firm output. This effect would be particularly strong in production environments that entail a great deal of cooperation among workers.[1]

The tournament model (Lazear and Rosen, 1981; Rosen, 1986; Lazear, 1989) stands in stark contrast to the fairness hypothesis. As Lazear (1989) writes, 'The desire for similar treatment is frequently articulated as an attempt to preserve worker unity, to maintain morale, and to create a cooperative work environment. But it is far from obvious that pay equality has these effects. The morale of high-quality workers is likely to be adversely affected by pay that regresses toward the mean' (pp. 561–562). The tournament model describes a compensation structure where top-ranked workers (in terms of production) are compensated at a significantly higher rate of pay than the lowest-ranked workers, thus producing a wide dispersion of wages within the firm. The idea here is that, with this type of payment scheme, low-ranked workers will be incentivized to increase their efforts, move up in the ranks and, in doing so, significantly increase their wages.

In addition, high-ranked workers are incentivized to maintain a high effort so as to not move down in the rankings and suffer significant wage reductions. This kind of 'competition' for rankings results in increased effort and output by the firm.

Given the clear differences between the fairness and tournament models, empirical analyses are needed to see which hypothesis is supported. While some research has been produced (discussed in greater detail in the next section), progress has been slow as the data needed to conduct such analyses (e.g. employee wages and skills, firm outputs, etc.) are generally difficult to obtain. There is one industry, however, where the lack of data is not a problem, namely that of professional sports. Sports markets produce highly accurate, easily obtained data for teams and players, thus making such markets a good testing ground for the two models.[2] The aim of this chapter is to briefly outline the key findings from the sports economics literature regarding tests of the fairness vs. tournament models.

The remainder of this chapter is organized as follows. Section 7.2 provides a brief discussion of the theoretical predictions stemming from the two models. Section 7.3 follows with a short discussion of how the models have been tested in more traditional settings. Section 7.4 presents a lengthy review of the tests of the tournament vs. fairness models, particularly in sports markets. Section 7.5 provides an empirical example of how the two models fare in the case of the National Hockey League. Finally, section 7.6 contains some concluding remarks.

7.2 TESTABLE HYPOTHESES FROM THE TOURNAMENT AND FAIRNESS MODELS[3]

A. Tournament Model

In work environments where employee monitoring is costly and shirking is possible, a tournament-style compensation scheme may be an effective way to increase effort and output.

The papers by Lazear and Rosen (1981), Rosen (1986) and McGlaughlin (1988) put forth four key predictions for the tournament model:[4]

- There will be a positive relationship between pay dispersion and firm performance.
- There will be a convex relationship between pay and contestant ranking within a firm.
- As the number of contestants in a tournament increases, the dispersion in pay will be greater.

- As market demand volatility increases, so will the degree of pay dispersion.

The first item in this list, discussed earlier, simply says that greater pay dispersion will motivate workers to increase effort in an attempt to win a greater 'prize', and this in turn increases firm output. The second item essentially notes that there will be a non-linear payout for higher ranked contestants (i.e. workers within a firm). That is, the 'prize' for moving up the rankings gets increasingly higher. This provides motivation for those who have moved up in rankings to continue to increase effort to move up even more.[5] The third and fourth items are simply cases where the probability that a contestant is able to move up in rank is reduced, thus requiring ever greater prizes to induce increased effort.

B. Fairness Model

In a later paper by Lazear (1989) he points out the possibility that wage *compression* may be optimal in some cases. He writes, 'If harmony is important, pay compression is optimal on strict efficiency grounds. Thus the ability to sabotage one's rival provides an efficiency argument for equitable treatment within a firm' (p. 579). This concept of 'sabotage' is reflected in Akerlof and Yellen (1990) as they refer to workers 'getting even' (as quoted earlier) when they feel they are not getting what they deserve. The authors employ ideas from equity theory, social psychology and social exchange theory to develop their 'fair wage-effort' hypothesis. According to this hypothesis, workers decrease effort when they perceive they are not being paid some notion of a 'fair' wage. Akerlof and Yellen (1990, p. 255) propose the following relationship between effort (e), wages (w), and the perceived fair wage (w^*):

$$e = \min(w/w^*, 1) \qquad (7.1)$$

where the perceived fair wage comes from some relevant comparison group and 1 represents 'normal effort'. To the extent that w falls short of w^* workers will begin to withdraw effort. If it is the case that lost productivity due to workers withdrawing effort is significant, employers may benefit (in terms of efficiency) by narrowing the difference between w and w^*. That is, wage compression may be optimal.

Levine (1991, p. 249) builds a simple model where intra-firm wage differences affect the 'cohesiveness' of workers. He models firm output (net of fixed costs and intermediate inputs) as:

$$q = C\left(\frac{w_L}{w_H}\right) f(H, L) \tag{7.2}$$

where q is output, H and L denote 'high productivity' and 'low productivity' worker types, C represents 'cohesion' of worker groups, and w_L and w_H are wages paid to worker types L and H, respectively, with the assumption that $w_L < w_H$. Levine assumes that output is an increasing function of C, and that C increases as the ratio of w_L to w_H increases. His model thus predicts that as wages within work groups become more dispersed (widening the gap between w_L and w_H), output suffers, all else equal. Like Akerlof and Yellen (1990), this would mean that payroll compression may increase efficiency and output.

7.3 EMPIRICAL TESTS FROM NON-SPORTS MARKETS[6, 7]

Given that the tournament and the fairness models predict opposite effects from pay compression, empirical analysis is needed to explore these hypotheses. One of the earliest papers to test the effects of pay compression is by Leonard (1990). Working with a sample of 439 large US corporations for 1981 and 1985, he finds no statistically significant relationship between pay equity or the steepness of pay differences for executives and firm performance. He does, however, find that pay differences increase significantly as one moves up the management hierarchy, which is consistent with one of the tournament model's predictions.

Cowherd and Levine (1992) work with data on 102 'business units' from 41 corporations headquartered in North America and Europe. The authors examine the effects of hourly pay dispersion on perceived product quality, their measure of firm performance. They find a positive, significant relationship between pay equity and product quality, thus supporting the benefits of salary compression.

Papers by Main et al. (1993) and Eriksson (1999) consider the effects of executive pay dispersion and firm performance. Main et al. (1993) work with data from over 200 firms and 2,000 executives for a five-year period for the years 1980 to 1984. Their results lend support to the tournament model. Eriksson (1999) works with information for 2,600 executives in 210 Danish firms over a four-year period from 1992 to 1995. He writes, 'In summary, I conclude that almost all of my findings are consistent with tournament models' (p. 279). However, with regard to the specific prediction that greater pay dispersion leads to better firm performance, he finds only weak support.

Two research papers have examined the effects of pay inequality on satisfaction and performance in academia. Pfeffer and Langton (1993) use data from over 17,000 individuals in more than 600 academic departments. They find that, 'the greater the degree of wage dispersion within academic departments, the lower is individual faculty members' satisfaction and research productivity and the less likely it is that faculty members will collaborate on research' (p. 382). Later, Card et al. (2012) also find that within-department pay inequality affects the satisfaction of individuals in those departments. Working with data for employees of the University of California they find an asymmetric effect of pay inequality. Those individuals who were paid below the median value of their peers reported being less satisfied with their jobs. However, individuals paid above the median of their peers did not report higher satisfaction. To the extent that worker satisfaction affects productivity, both of these papers provide some support for the fairness hypothesis.

In both Akerlof and Yellen (1990) and Levine (1991), pay inequality is a relative measure that involves some reference group. This brings up the issue of what the relevant comparison group should be. Papers by Winter-Ebmer and Zweimüller (1999) and Heyman (2005) address this issue by considering the effects of pay dispersion *conditioned* on the skills/ attributes of workers. The basic approach in these papers has two steps. First, individual workers' wages are estimated as a function of observable skills and attributes. Second, the residuals from the estimated wage equation are used to create dispersion measures that then appear as regressors in a firm performance estimation. Winter-Ebmer and Zweimüller (1999) work with Austrian data for 130 firms covering the period 1975 to 1991. Due to a lack of data on direct firm performance the authors use 'standardized wages', a measure of the overall wages within a firm, which the authors argue is a reasonable proxy for worker productivity and firm performance. They find that for 'white-collar' workers there is a hump-shaped relationship between wage dispersion and productivity: greater salary dispersion initially increases worker productivity, but continued increases in dispersion eventually reduce productivity. As for 'blue-collar' workers, their productivity generally rises as wage dispersion increases.[8]

Heyman (2005) also employs the two-step procedure described above.[9] He uses a large, employer-employee matched data set for Swedish firms from the 1990s. He finds positive, robust effects of conditional wage dispersion on profits and average pay for white-collar workers. He similarly finds a robust, positive effect of conditional wage dispersion for executives. Heyman also finds a positive relationship between demand volatility and conditional pay dispersion. These results are in agreement with the tournament model.[10]

7.4 EMPIRICAL TESTS FROM SPORTS MARKETS

The empirical tests of the tournament vs. fairness models in more traditional markets have produced mixed results. The greatest challenge to these tests is finding the necessary data on firms and employees. Given this problem, researchers have turned to sports markets to test the two models. The appeal of using sports markets data is stated clearly by Kahn (2000, p. 75):

> Professional sports offers a unique opportunity for labor market research. There is no research setting other than sports where we know the name, face, and life history of every production worker and supervisor in the industry. Total compensation packages and performance statistics for each individual are widely available, and we have a complete data set of worker-employer matches over the career of each production worker and supervisor in the industry. These statistics are much more detailed and accurate than typical microdata samples such as the Census or the Current Population Survey. Moreover, professional sports leagues have experienced major changes in labor market rules and structure – like the advent of new leagues or rules about free agency – creating interesting natural experiments that offer opportunities for analysis.

Research using sports markets data to test the tournament vs. fairness models have produced numerous publications. Before summarizing the key findings of these papers we will begin by discussing the general approach used in the bulk of this research.[11]

A. Empirical Specification

The basic approach in testing the tournament vs. fairness models in sports begins with some sort of performance model, for example:

$$P = f(X, Z; \sigma) \tag{7.3}$$

where P is a measure of performance (e.g. winning percent), X is a vector of player/contestant inputs, Z contains team-level inputs where applicable (e.g. coaching quality) and σ is a measure of pay dispersion within the team or across contestants. All else equal, a positive relationship between P and σ would lend support to the tournament model. A negative relationship would support the fairness model. As far as player input measures for individual sports is concerned, a contestant's prior performance (earlier in the season or perhaps over their career leading up to the current contest) is typically employed. For team sports, the extant literature has typically used one of two approaches. One has been to use team-averaged skill vectors.

For example, if we consider ice hockey, we could compute a team's career points (goals plus assists) scored per game, as one input measure. This is typically done by computing the average career points scored per game across all players on a team up to, but not including, the current season.[12] This approach can be used for other measures (e.g. penalty minutes, plus/minus values, etc.) and combined to form the vector X.

A second approach to capturing player inputs in team sports has been to use relative team payrolls for the current season. That is, we can compute team i's relative payroll in year t, as the ratio of its team payroll to the average payroll across the league in year t,

$$Relative\ Payroll_{it} = \frac{Payroll_{it}}{Average\ Payroll_t} \qquad (7.4)$$

The underlying assumption in using relative payrolls is that if the market for players' skills is highly competitive, then a team's relative payroll should serve as a good proxy for the vector X.[13] The typical specification includes both relative payroll and its squared value in order to allow for diminishing returns to players' skills.

In terms of coaching skills, several measures are commonly used. Examples include career winning percentage, years coaching, whether or not the coach played as a professional in the sport and the number of championships won.[14] Other team-level measures have included league dummies (e.g. American League vs. National League in Major League Baseball), market size and tenure of the team in their current city.

Lastly, regarding within-team measures of pay dispersion, several have been employed. This includes Gini coefficients, Herfindahl-Hirschman indices, variances, standard deviations, coefficients of variation and interquartile ranges. Individual sports (e.g. tennis tournaments or foot races) typically use a measure of prize spreads. Most team research employs panel data with two-way fixed- or random-effects estimation methodologies.

B. Survey of Research[15]

The tests of the tournament and fairness models in sports have been carried out for both individual sports (e.g. golf, foot racing and auto racing)[16] and team sports (e.g. baseball, basketball, ice hockey, football and soccer). In the case of individual sports, the empirical tests center on whether the tournament model has support (i.e. whether the impact of σ in the above performance equation is significant and positive). Tests on team sports (where cohesion may be important and/or sabotage is possible) typically test the tournament model *against* the fairness model (i.e. whether σ is significant and either positive or negative). Table 7.1 presents a summary of the findings from the sports economics papers discussed below.

One of the earliest tests of the tournament model can be found in two papers by Ehrenberg and Bognanno (1990a, 1990b). The authors collect data on professional golf tournaments (from the US Professional Golf Association in the first paper and the Men's European Golf Association in the second). They then regress a golfer's score on total prize money, controlling for other factors (e.g. difficulty of the course, the weather, the golfer's skills and the quality of their opponents). They find robust support that as the prize money increases, final round scores improve, thus supporting the tournament model.[17, 18]

The Becker and Huselid (1992) paper is another of the early papers to test the tournament model on an individual sport. Working with auto racing data from 1990 and 1991 from the National Association for Stock Car Auto Racing (NASCAR) and the International Motor Sports Association (IMSA) the authors study the impact of variation in the prize 'spread' on driver performance. They find that as the spread increases, so does performance, but with diminishing effects.[19] They also find that risky behavior (measured as the number of caution flags in a race) increases as the prize spread increases.[20]

Two papers examining foot racing come to different results. Lynch and Zax (2000) employ data for both men and women from the USA Track and Field Road Running Information Center for road races during 1994, which took place in the US and abroad. Their key findings are that race times improve as the prize money increases. However, they also find that when they control for runner ability the incentive effect erodes. Thus, they do not find support for the tournament effect in so far as increased individual effort is concerned. Maloney and McCormick (2000), however, do find support for the tournament model. Using data from 115 open invitational foot races over the years 1987 to 1991, they uncover two effects from increased prizes and prize spread. First, like Lynch and Zax, they find that higher prizes attract more highly skilled participants. Second, increasing the spread of the prize encourages runners to try harder. They note that, 'This second effect is detected across the entire sample and for individuals measured against their own average performance' (p. 99). In addition, Maloney and McCormick find that women have a higher elasticity with regard to both entry decisions and performance effects than do men. Lastly, they note that as the prize structure becomes more concentrated, runners exhibit greater effort.

Another individual sport studied has been tennis. Gilsdorf and

Table 7.1 Survey of previous sports economics literature

Sport or League	Author(s)	Seasons/Period Covered	Measure(s) of Dispersion/Incentive	Performance Measure(s)	Key Findings/Support	Notes
MLB	Bloom (1999)	1985 to 1993	Gini, CV, internal ranking	Individual and team performance	Greater pay dispersion decreases individual and team performance.	Finds an asymmetric affect on individual performance.
	Depken (2000)	1985 to 1998	HHI	Winning percentage	Greater pay dispersion decreases team performance.	
	Frick et al. (2003)	1985 to 2001	Gini	Winning percentage	Greater pay dispersion decreases team performance.	
	DeBrock et al. (2004)	1985 to 1998	HHI; conditional HHI	Winning percentage and others	Unconditional dispersion reduces performance. Conditional dispersion is less important.	
CPBL	San and Jane (2008)	1990 to 2000	Adjusted HHI	Winning percentage	Greater pay dispersion decreases team performance.	Uses an HHI index that includes both intra- and inter-team pay dispersion.

NPB	Jane et al. (2011)	1996 to 2008	Gini, HHI, CV	Winning percentage and others	Greater pay dispersion increases team performance.	Uses fixed-effects, random-effects and quantile regression.
NBA	Frick et al. (2003)	1990–91 to 2000–01	Gini	Winning percentage	Positive, significant relationship between dispersion and performance.	
	Berri and Jewell (2004)	1996–97 to 2001–02	Changes in standardized HHI	Changes in winning percentage	No relationship between pay dispersion and performance.	
	Katayama and Nuch (2011)	2002–02 to 2006–07	Weighted CV, Gini and HHI	Ratio of teams' scores in an individual game	No relationship between pay dispersion and performance.	Uses a GMM estimator for potential endogeneity.
NHL	Gomez (2002)	1993–94 to 1997–98	Gini	Winning percentage	No dispersion effects when team fixed effects are included.	
	Frick et al. (2003)	1988–89, 1993–94 and 1995–96 to 2000–01	Gini	Winning percentage	No dispersion effects on performance.	
	Kahane (2012)	2001–02 to 2007–08 (excluding the lockout season 2004–05)	Conditional SD, conditional IQR (interquartile range)	Winning %, points %, goal differentials; making playoffs	Negative, significant relationship between pay dispersion and team performance.	Fixed effects used for winning percentage. Random effects probit used for making playoffs.

Table 7.1 (continued)

Sport or League	Author(s)	Seasons/Period Covered	Measure(s) of Dispersion/ Incentive	Performance Measure(s)	Key Findings/ Support	Notes
NFL	Frick et al. (2003)	1988, 1993 and 1995 to 2000	Gini	Winning percentage	No relationship between pay dispersion and performance.	
	Mondello and Maxcy (2009)	2000 to 2007	CV	Winning percentage; team revenues	Negative effect of dispersion on winning percentage. Positive effect on team revenues.	
Golf	Ehrenberg and Bognanno (1990a, 1990b)	PGA, 1984; European Men's PGA, 1987	Total prize money	Final tournament score	Tournament model supported. Larger prizes tend to produce better performance.	Performance increases tend to be in final rounds, not in earlier rounds.
Foot Racing	Lynch and Zax (2000)	1994, in US and abroad	Difference in prize by finishing one rank lower than pre-race ranking	Time (in seconds) to finish a race	Performance increases as the prize increases. This effect erodes when runner ability is controlled for.	Larger prizes entice better runners to enter races.

	Study	Data	Independent variable	Dependent variable	Findings	
	Maloney and McCormick (2000)	1987 to 1991 in US	Log of average prize; prize spread	Log of time per mile	Larger prizes entice more entrants. Larger spreads incite greater effort.	Women respond more to both incentives than men.
Auto Racing	Becker and Huselid (1992)	1990 NASCAR; 1990, 1991 IMSA	'Spread' in prize money	Rank; miles per hour	Tournament model supported.	Incentive effects diminish with increasing spread. Risky behavior increases with spread.
Tennis	Gilsdorf and Sukhatyme (2008)	2004 Women's Tennis Association matches	Prize differences between rounds	Probability of winning a match	As the prize difference increases, the probability that the favorite wins increases.	
	Sunde (2009)	1990 to 2002 Association of Tennis Professionals matches	Heterogeneity of players' skills	Games won per match/set	Greater heterogeneity in contestants' skills leads to reduced efforts.	
Bundesliga Soccer	Franck and Nüesch (2011)	1995–96 to 2006–07	Gini and CV and their squared values	Winning percentage; league standing	Dispersion has a U-shaped effect on performance.	Also find that hierarchical pay structures affect playing style.

Table 7.1 (continued)

Sport or League	Author(s)	Seasons/Period Covered	Measure(s) of Dispersion/ Incentive	Performance Measure(s)	Key Findings/ Support	Notes
MLS	Coates et al. (2016)	2005 to 2013	Gini and CV and their squared values	Log of points	Support for the fairness-cohesiveness model.	

Notes: MLB = Major League Baseball, CPBL = Chinese Professional Baseball League, NPB = Nippon Professional Baseball, NBA = National Basketball Association, NHL = National Hockey League, NFL = National Football League, PGA = Professional Golfers' Association, NASCAR = the National Association for Stock Car Auto Racing, IMSA = International Motor Sports Association, MLS = Major League Soccer.

Sukhatme (2008) work with data on 58 tournaments (2,098 individual matches) from the Women's Tennis Association. Given the elimination, tournament-style, play, Gilsdorm and Sukhatme employ a probit estimation methodology to examine the effects that increased prize money has on the probability of advancing through tournaments. The tournaments studied have the features of non-linear payouts (with greater prize spreads for higher levels of attainment in the tournament) and pay being a function of relative (as opposed to absolute) performance – hallmarks of the tournament model. Gilsdorf and Sukhatme include career win differentials on given court surfaces, previous head-to-head results and differences in player rankings as control variables. The results of their probit estimation show that as prizes increase, the favored player in a match has a greater probability of winning, in line with Rosen's (1986) predictions for elimination tournaments.

Sunde (2009) also employs data from professional tennis. He works with data from the Association of Tennis Professionals (ATP) 'Grand Slam' and 'Master Series' tournaments for males spanning the years 1990 to 2002. One distinguishing factor of Sunde's paper is that he explores the idea of contestant heterogeneity. One of the predictions stemming from the tournament model is that if there is *ex ante* significant heterogeneity between contestants then this may result in an overall *lower* effort. The idea here is that if an underdog in a tournament is considerably less skilled than the favorite, then this may discourage effort on the part of the underdog as they face a seemingly impossible task of winning. In addition, the favorite may also reduce their effort if, by knowing their advantage over the underdog, they can do so without significantly jeopardizing their probability of winning. This aspect of tournament theory has been little studied. Using the difference between contestants' ATP rankings *prior* to the match, Sunde finds that there is evidence that contestant heterogeneity does have an impact on effort exerted. Specifically, he finds that, 'for the same level of heterogeneity, underdogs do significantly better than favorites, implying that a negative incentive effect moderates the positive effect of a stronger ability on favorites' performance relative to underdogs' (p. 3205).

As noted earlier, research on individual sports generally investigates whether there is support for the tournament model. In the case of team sports, the concepts of team cohesion and cooperation among teammates become perhaps important for production and thus the tournament model is tested against the fairness model. Even within the realm of team sports, the impact of pay dispersion on productivity may differ substantially depending on the degree of reliance a player has on their teammates for doing their own job. For example, basketball and ice hockey have a tremendous amount of teammate interaction and as such may witness a stronger impact from pay dispersion than, say, baseball, where a player's individual performance is much less dependent on the performance of teammates. We begin with the latter sport.

Major League Baseball (MLB) is perhaps the most studied team sport when it comes to the effects of pay dispersion. An early paper by Bloom (1999) uses data from MLB covering the seasons 1985 to 1993 and looks at two ways in which pay dispersion may impact performance: at the individual levels and at the team level. Employing various measures of within-team pay dispersion measures (including Gini coefficients, coefficients of variation and other relative measures) he finds robust support for the fairness model for team production. That is, as pay dispersion increases, all else being equal, team performance decreases. In addition, Bloom (1999) finds that there is an asymmetric effect of pay dispersion on individual performance; he writes, 'Greater dispersion is negatively related to the performance of those lower in a dispersion and positively related to those higher in the dispersion' (p. 32). Follow-up work by Depken (2000) and Frick et al. (2003) confirm Bloom (1999) with regard to team performance: greater dispersion reduces team performance, all else being equal.

DeBrock et al. (2004) differs from the earlier MLB papers in one significant way. Their dataset contains MLB data for 1985 to 1998 and begins in a similar way to the work noted above by regressing team performance measures on a measure of pay dispersion (the Herfindahl-Hirschman index, or HHI) and other controls. They generally find a negative and significant coefficient for the measure of pay dispersion, which is consistent with the fairness model and the papers noted above. However, the authors note that it may be the case that this *unconditional* negative relationship may be picking up a technological aspect of production, rather than a fairness concept. That is, the authors write, 'one could argue that the proper technology involved in winning baseball games requires a relatively equal set of talented players on the roster and hence a relatively flat salary profile' (p. 248). DeBrock et al. then present a *conditional*, two-step approach. First, they estimate an individual player wage regression and compute expected wages and the associated regression residuals. Second, they use the expected wages and residuals from the first step to produce team-level average expected wages, the team-level dispersion of those expected wages and the team-level dispersion of the residuals. These measures are then included in team performance regressions.[21] The results of these *conditional* regressions show that workers of similar skill level are important for winning and that the importance of wage 'fairness' is decreased.

Several other papers have been published that examine baseball in countries other than the US. San and Jane (2008) study the effects of pay dispersion on performance in the Chinese Professional Baseball League (CPBL).

Using data for 364 CPBL players from seven teams for the period 1990 to 2000 they construct an 'adjusted HHI' measure that attempts to capture intra- *and* inter-team wage dispersion. They find modest support for the fairness model.[22] Jane et al. (2011) study Japan's Nippon Professional Baseball (NPB) League for the period 1996 to 2008. Contrary to the other papers on baseball discussed earlier, this paper finds support for the tournament model with increased wage dispersion increasing performance.

Berri and Jewell (2004) investigate the impact of changes in pay dispersion on changes in winning percentage in the National Basketball Association (NBA). They work with data following the implementation of the 1995 collective bargaining agreement (CBA), specifically using data from the 1996–1997 to 2001–2002 seasons. They employ a relative dispersion measure defined as team HHI divided by the league average HHI. Among their control variables is a measure of 'roster stability', a novel measure designed to capture team 'chemistry'. Fixed-effects regressions produce no significant relationship between changes in pay dispersion and changes in winning percentage.[23] In contrast to their findings, Frick et al. (2003) find a positive, significant relationship between pay dispersion (as measured by the intra-team Gini coefficient) and performance when analyzing NBA data from 1990–1991 to 2000–2001. The study by Katayama and Nuch (2011) is perhaps the most comprehensive study of this issue for the NBA. They work with five seasons' worth of NBA data (2002–2003 to 2006–2007) and add to the extant literature in three key ways. First, they analyze both individual game outcomes and season outcomes. Second, they address possible endogeneity problems by employing a Generalized Method of Moments (GMM) estimation methodology. Third, they consider three subsets of players: players playing in a given (current) game, players that played in more than half their team's games in a season, and lastly, all players on a team. The results of their GMM analysis show no causal link between their three measures of pay dispersion and team performance.

The National Hockey League (NHL) has also been a testing ground for the fairness vs. tournament models. Gomez (2002) works with data from the 1993–1994 to 1997–1998 seasons and finds, at first, a positive relationship between salary inequality and team performance. However, when he includes team fixed effects the relationship disappears. Frick et al. (2003) come to a similar finding when using data from the 1980s to 2000.[24] Kahane (2012) takes a different approach and considers the relationship between *conditional* dispersion measures and team performance in the NHL. Similar to DeBrock et al. (2004), this paper uses a two-step procedure. In the first step, an individual player salary regression is carried out and the residuals from this regression are used to compute measures of intra-team pay dispersion. The second step is to then use these conditional dispersion measures as regressors in various team performance regressions (both regular season and post-season). Kahane (2012) finds robust support for the fairness model with 16 of the 24 regressions producing negative, significant coefficients for the conditional dispersion measures.[25]

Regarding the National Football League (NFL), there are relatively few papers that have studied the effects of pay dispersion on performance. Frick et al. (2003) find no significant relationship for data from the late 1980s to 2000. Mondello and Maxcy (2009) however find different results. Working with NFL team data from 2000 to 2007, they find that increases in pay dispersion lead to reduced team winning. However, they also find that when team revenue is used as the dependent variable, pay dispersion has a positive, significant impact. They offer the following reasoning: 'An explanation is that fans respond to the acquisitions of high salaried superstars by purchasing more season tickets, premium seating, luxury suite rentals etc.' (p. 121).

Compared to other team sports, soccer appears to be the least researched with regard to the effects of pay dispersion on performance. Franck and Nüesch (2011) use data from the first German soccer league (the Bundesliga) for the seasons 1995–1996 to 2006–2007. A key focus of their paper is to explore the possible non-linear effects of pay dispersion on both performance and style of play. They employ an instrumental variables approach with team fixed effects and allow pay dispersion (as measured by the Gini coefficient and the coefficient of variation) to enter the regression with linear and squared values. They find that the effects of pay dispersion have a U shape and they note, 'our results imply that teams do better by either deciding for a steep hierarchical pay structure or for a rather egalitarian one. However, to be "stuck in the middle" is detrimental for sporting success' (p. 3043). They also find that teams that choose a more hierarchical pay structure have a different style of play, particularly one that is more individualistic (with more 'dribbling and runs'). Lastly, Coates et al. (2016) explore pay dispersion effects on performance using data from Major League Soccer (MLS), the North American professional soccer league. The authors exploit a 2007 rule change where teams were allowed to exceed their payroll caps to sign a marquee, 'designated player' (the first being David Beckham, who was signed by Los Angeles Galaxy in 2007). This rule change increased the possible payroll dispersion of teams in the years that followed. Using data from the 2005 to 2013 seasons they estimate a fixed-effects regression and, like Franck and Nüesch (2011), allow their measures for dispersion (Gini and coefficient of variation) to enter the regression as a quadratic. The results of their regressions lend some weak support to the non-linear relationship between team performance and pay dispersion. Their analysis of the regression results is that the fairness model is supported.[26]

7.5 PAY DISPERSION AND PERFORMANCE IN THE NHL PRE- AND POST-LOCKOUT[27]

As an illustration of the concepts discussed above, this section presents an example of a test of the fairness model vs. the tournament model for the NHL. The data employed are from the 2001–2002 to 2006–2007 seasons, excluding the 2004–2005 season which was lost due to a lockout by the owners. Studying this period is desirable as the changes to the financial structure of the NHL post-lockout were significant and led to a dramatic effect on team payrolls, particularly their dispersion. The empirical approach utilized in the regression analysis is to use *conditional* payroll dispersion, similar to that used by DeBrock et al. (2004) and Kahane (2012). We begin with a brief description of the factors leading up to the lockout and the financial changes implemented post-lockout.

A. Financial Strife and the 2004–2005 Lockout

Following months of unsuccessful negotiations, NHL Commissioner Gary Bettman announced on February 16, 2005 that the 2004–2005 NHL season had been cancelled. The announcement marked the first time a major North American sports league had cancelled an entire season due to a dispute between owners and players.[28]

The root cause of the dispute had to do with the escalation of player salaries. Following the filing for bankruptcy by two NHL teams (the Buffalo Sabres and the Ottawa Senators) in 2003, Commissioner Bettman noted, 'We need to change our economic system because no matter how quickly our revenues have grown, no matter how strong our following is, the economics of this game – because of the escalation of player salaries – doesn't work for a number of our clubs'.[29] Backing up this claim by Bettman was the 'Levitt Report', commissioned by the NHL and produced by Arthur Levitt, former Chairman of the Securities Exchange Commission.[30] Levitt reviewed the financial data for the combined 30 teams in the NHL for the 2002–2003 season and concluded that the league suffered approximately $273 million in losses on about $2 billion in revenues. He found that of the 30 NHL teams, 19 had losses that season (with four losing more than $30 million).

On July 22, 2005 the owners and players signed a new collective bargaining agreement ending the 310-day lockout. The details of the agreement contained some drastic changes to player salaries and payrolls. These included an immediate 24 percent reduction in current player salaries, a team payroll cap of $39 million and a payroll *floor* of $21.5 million. In addition, individual player salaries were capped at no more than 20 percent of a team's payroll (equal to $7.8 million for the 2005–2006 season). The news was not bad for all players, however, as the new minimum player salary would be *increased* from $175,000 to $450,000 for the 2005–2006 season. The impact of the new payroll cap and floor values was felt by many of the teams. A review of 2003–2004 payroll data shows that 13 teams would not have been in compliance with the new payroll rules, with nine being above the cap (even after the 24 percent rollback of player salaries), and four being below the minimum.[31] The end result was that the payroll cap and floor was binding at both ends of the payroll spectrum and this led to a significant reduction in payroll dispersion both between and within teams. Figure 7.1 presents graphical evidence of the league-wide compression of between-team payrolls. The figure shows kernel density graphs for team payrolls for three seasons prior to the lockout and three seasons after the lockout.

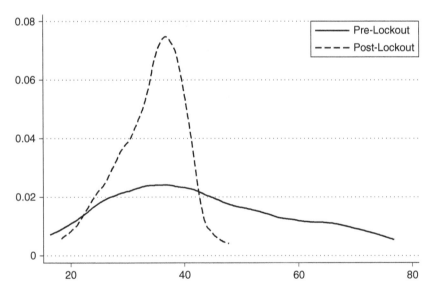

Figure 7.1 *Kernel density graphs of team payrolls pre-lockout (2001–2002 to 2003–2004) and post-lockout (2005–2006 to 2007–2008) (millions of 2007 dollars)*

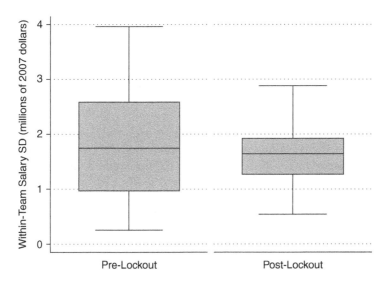

Figure 7.2   *Box-plots for within-team salary standard deviation,*
                 pre-lockout (2001–2002 to 2003–2004) and post-lockout
                 (2005–2006 to 2007–2008)

The capping of individual player salaries combined with an increase in the minimum salary also compressed within-team pay dispersion. This reduction is evident in Figure 7.2, which shows boxplots of within-team salary standard deviations for the three seasons before and after the lockout.

B. Estimation Approach

The financial changes brought about by the 2005 CBA in the NHL (particularly with regard to within-team pay dispersion) provide for an ideal setting for testing the fairness model vs. the tournament model. As noted earlier, the financial changes in the new CBA brought about a significant change in pay dispersion and thus this should help with identifying any impact of within-team pay dispersion on productivity. The six seasons of data discussed earlier will be used in two ways. First, the entire period will be employed to consider the impact of changes in within-team pay dispersion on team productivity. Second, if within-team dispersion is truly an important factor in determining productivity then its importance should be more prominent in the pre-lockout period, when team pay was less constrained, than in the post-lockout period. Thus, regressions analysis will be conducted separately on the two periods to see whether there is such a difference. We begin with the general model specification.

Following Kahane (2012), the model used to estimate team production is,

$$P_{jt} = \beta_o + \beta_1 X_{jt} + \beta_2 Z_{jt} + \beta_3 \sigma_{jt} + \gamma_j + v_{jt} \qquad (7.5)$$

where P_{jt} is a production measure for team j in season t. There are three different production measures employed: regular season percent points (*Points %*),[32] the natural log of the ratio of goals scored ('goals for') to goals given up ('goals against') (*ln(GF/GA)*) and a dummy variable indicating whether the team made the playoffs that season (*Playoffs*). Production inputs are captured by X_{jt}. As noted earlier, the sports economics literature has employed two basic approaches to including inputs: team-averaged skill vectors and relative payrolls. The approach used here is the latter, thus *Relative Payroll* and *Relative Payroll²* are used in the production regressions.[33] The expectations are that the coefficient to *Relative Payroll* should be positive and the coefficient to *Relative Payroll²* should be negative, implying that output increases with greater payroll, but with diminishing returns. Other team-level, non-player inputs are represented by Z_{jt}. In this category two measures are included. First, coaching quality measured as career winning percentage up to, but not including the current season (*Coach Career Win %*), is part of Z_{jt}. Second, in order to capture the potential impact of relatively new players, whose career statistics may not yet represent the talent they possess, the variable *Top Draft Picks* is included. This variable is equal to the number of top (first-round) draft picks that are currently playing on the team.[34] A positively coefficient is expected for this measure.

The next variable appearing in the production equation is σ_{jt}, the measure of within-team salary dispersion. As noted earlier, the *conditional* approach is employed in the analysis. What this means is that the measure σ_{jt} measures within-team salary dispersion net of individual salary differences due to individual skill differences. Thus, to compute σ_{jt} the first step is to estimate an individual salary equation and then use this estimation to produce salary residuals. These salary residuals are then used to compute within-team dispersion measures.[35] The two dispersion measures employed in this analysis are the within-team residual standard deviation (*Residual SD*) and the within-team residual interquartile range (*Residual IQR*). If the coefficient to either of these measures is positive, then this would lend support to the tournament model. If it is negative, then this would give support to the fairness model.

Lastly, two other variables are included. The variable γ_j represents an individual team fixed effect to control for team-specific, time invariant

Table 7.2   *Summary statistics*

Variable	Mean	Std. Dev.	Min	Max
Points %	0.543	0.091	0.329	0.756
ln(GF/GA)	0.002	0.186	−0.467	0.420
Playoffs	0.533	0.500	0	1
Relative Payroll	1.000	0.281	0.390	1.739
Relative Payroll^2	1.079	0.606	0.152	3.023
Coach Career Win %	0.533	0.074	0.302	0.800
Residual SD	1.054	0.428	0.337	2.686
Residual IQR	1.009	0.356	0.327	2.064
Top Draft Picks	0.261	0.489	0	2

factors that may affect production. Also included is a dummy variable, *Post Lockout*, equal to 1 if the observation is from the post-lockout period, and equals zero otherwise. This variable is included to take into account some of the rule changes that were put into place with the 2005 CBA that could have an impact on team production.[36] Summary statistics for the dependent variables and covariates appears in Table 7.2.

C. Results

Regression results for the production function described above appear in Tables 7.3 and 7.4. The total number of observations is 180 (30 teams × 6 seasons) for the full sample. All regressions that have *Points %* or *ln(GF/ GA)* as the dependent variables are estimated with fixed effects, and regressions with the dummy dependent variable *Playoffs* employ a probit estimation procedure with random effects. All regressions report robust standard errors.

Table 7.3 contains a total of six regressions for the full sample, three using *Residual SD* as the conditional pay dispersion measure and three using *Residual IQR*. Several results are consistent for all six regressions. The coefficients to *Payroll* and *Payroll²* have the predicted sign pattern (positive and negative, respectively) in all regressions. *Payroll* is significant in all regressions, but *Payroll²* is only significant in regression (6). Thus, there is clear evidence that teams with relatively greater payrolls win more, but there is only weak evidence that the effect of relative payrolls diminishes. The variable *Top Draft Picks* is positive and significant in all regressions and suggests that teams with a stock of highly talented, relatively new professionals tend to produce more, all else equal. The two measures *Coach Career Win %* and *Post Lockout* are not significant in

Table 7.3 Full-sample regression results

VARIABLES	(1) Points %	(2) ln(GF/GA)	(3) Playoffs	(4) Points %	(5) ln(GF/GA)	(6) Playoffs
Relative Payroll	0.328**	0.765**	6.739***	0.277*	0.664*	6.640***
	(0.160)	(0.334)	(2.600)	(0.162)	(0.332)	(2.446)
Relative Payroll^2	−0.0845	−0.215	−2.038	−0.0655	−0.179	−2.110*
	(0.0741)	(0.161)	(1.241)	(0.0788)	(0.168)	(1.245)
Coach Career Win %	0.0410	0.0938	1.249	0.0497	0.111	1.529
	(0.0982)	(0.191)	(1.374)	(0.107)	(0.200)	(1.369)
Residual SD	−0.0533**	−0.105**	−0.823*			
	(0.0260)	(0.0434)	(0.425)			
Post Lockout	0.00503	−0.0557	−0.388	0.00723	−0.0513	−0.419
	(0.0164)	(0.0340)	(0.281)	(0.0170)	(0.0348)	(0.297)
Top Draft Picks	0.0567***	0.145***	0.608*	0.0537***	0.139***	0.605*
	(0.0124)	(0.0274)	(0.326)	(0.0127)	(0.0268)	(0.350)
Residual IQR				−0.062***	−0.120***	−0.950***
				(0.0210)	(0.0331)	(0.369)
Constant	0.323***	−0.480***	−4.215***	0.355***	−0.418***	−4.077***
	(0.0618)	(0.140)	(1.239)	(0.0691)	(0.147)	(1.274)
Observations	180	180	180	180	180	180
R-squared	0.189	0.211		0.212	0.234	

Notes: Robust standard errors in parentheses.
*** p<0.01, ** p<0.05, * p<0.1.

any of the regressions. Finally, turning to our measures of conditional pay dispersion – the focus of this model – we see that all six estimated coefficients are negative and significant. While the units of these variables are somewhat difficult to interpret, there is clear support for the fairness model in that greater, within-team conditional dispersion of pay is associated with poorer team performance.[37] For example, working with the results from regression (1), a one-unit increase in *Residual SD* would reduce a team's *Points %* by approximately 5.3 percentage points.

Table 7.4 contains two sets of output. The first, A, contains six regressions for sub-periods (pre- and post-lockout) when using *Residual SD* as our dispersion measure. The second, B, is the same except it uses *Residual IQR*. In both A and B, regressions (1), (3) and (5) are the pre-lockout regressions and (2), (4) and (6) show post-lockout regressions. Focusing on Table 7.4A, some interesting patterns emerge for the estimated coefficients to *Payroll* and *Payroll²*. For regressions (1), (3) and (5) – the pre-lockout period – the pattern is the expected one: positive for *Payroll* and negative for *Payroll²*, with the former significant in all three regressions and the latter significant in (1) and (3). However, neither *Payroll* nor *Payroll²* is significant in the post-lock-out regressions (2), (4) and (6). These results seem to indicate that payroll differences were important in determining performance in the pre-lockout period when payrolls were unrestricted. Later, when payrolls were forced into a compressed band by the cap and floor, team payroll differences became less of a driver of performance. As for the dispersion measure *Residual SD*, this should be more important in the pre-lockout period when within-team individual pay was less constrained than in the post-lockout period when the individual player maximum and minimum values of pay were pushed closer together. This pattern is not evident in Table 7.4A. It is, however, present in Table 7.4B when *Residual IQR* is used. Lastly, regarding the variable *Top Draft Picks*, it is generally positive and significant in the regressions shown in Tables 7.4A and 7.4B. *Coach Career Win %* is generally not significant, with the exception of regression (5) in both tables where it is positive and significant.

In the 18 regressions presented in Tables 7.3, 7.4A and 7.4B, all 18 estimated coefficients to the dispersion measures are negative and 12 of the 18 are statistically significant. Taken as a whole, this provides strong support for the fairness model where greater within-team, conditional pay dispersion is associated with lower team performance.

Table 7.4 *Regression results by pre- and post-lockout periods*

A. Regressions using residual SD

VARIABLES	(1) Pre-Lockout Points %	(2) Post-Lockout Points %	(3) Pre-Lockout ln(GF/GA)	(4) Post-Lockout ln(GF/GA)	(5) Pre-Lockout Playoffs	(6) Post-Lockout Playoffs
Relative Payroll	0.475**	-0.299	0.981**	-0.111	6.063**	5.392
	(0.199)	(0.930)	(0.419)	(1.196)	(2.887)	(15.37)
Relative Payroll^2	-0.139*	0.212	-0.297*	0.218	-1.832	-0.787
	(0.0721)	(0.474)	(0.168)	(0.616)	(1.269)	(7.920)
Coach Career Win %	-0.0607	-0.203	0.0128	-0.359	3.994**	-3.030
	(0.149)	(0.199)	(0.321)	(0.375)	(1.929)	(3.866)
Residual SD	-0.0615*	-0.0688*	-0.0652	-0.142**	-0.614	-1.248
	(0.0333)	(0.0404)	(0.0648)	(0.0564)	(0.445)	(0.761)
Top Draft Picks	-0.0104	0.0666***	0.0434	0.155***	1.415***	0.147
	(0.0156)	(0.0198)	(0.0321)	(0.0445)	(0.528)	(0.410)
Constant	0.313**	0.791*	-0.586*	0.168	-5.583***	-1.634
	(0.147)	(0.439)	(0.303)	(0.602)	(1.774)	(6.526)
Observations	90	90	90	90	90	90
R-squared	0.134	0.111	0.154	0.183		

B. Regressions using residual IQR

VARIABLES	(1) Pre-Lockout Points %	(2) Post-Lockout Points %	(3) Pre-Lockout ln(GF/GA)	(4) Post-Lockout ln(GF/GA)	(5) Pre-Lockout Playoffs	(6) Post-Lockout Playoffs
Relative Payroll	0.276	-0.184	0.675	0.172	6.338**	5.608
	(0.228)	(0.975)	(0.419)	(1.332)	(3.044)	(15.37)
Relative Payroll^2	-0.0262	0.106	-0.0927	-0.0203	-1.562	-1.655
	(0.0879)	(0.475)	(0.173)	(0.651)	(1.411)	(7.844)
Coach Career Win %	0.0578	-0.124	0.221	-0.213	5.072**	-1.712
	(0.121)	(0.220)	(0.227)	(0.366)	(2.545)	(3.725)
Residual IQR	-0.113***	-0.0200	-0.209***	-0.0580	-1.831***	-0.521
	(0.0252)	(0.0337)	(0.0481)	(0.0486)	(0.549)	(0.713)
Top Draft Picks	0.0424*	0.0549**	0.147***	0.130**	1.776***	-0.00779
	(0.0246)	(0.0263)	(0.0401)	(0.0602)	(0.691)	(0.394)
Constant	0.363**	0.698	-0.494*	-0.0258	-5.509**	-2.368
	(0.133)	(0.439)	(0.248)	(0.611)	(2.155)	(6.222)
Observations	90	90	90	90	90	90
R-squared	0.353	0.048	0.373	0.100		

Notes: Robust standard errors in parentheses.
*** $p<0.01$, ** $p<0.05$, * $p<0.1$.

7.6   CONCLUDING THOUGHTS

Following the development of the theoretical literature of the tournament and fairness models in the 1980s and 1990s there have been dozens of papers published testing these models using data from sports markets. The appeal for using sports data is that these markets produce the kind of information needed to carefully measure inputs, outputs and payments to workers. Table 7.1 presented a survey of 23 sports papers that test the two models. A pattern emerges from this table in terms of support for the tournament or fairness model and sport type. Sixteen of the papers included come from team sports (baseball, basketball, hockey, football and soccer) and seven come from individual sports (golf, foot racing, tennis and auto racing). Eight of the 16 team sports papers show support for the fairness model (with two supporting the tournament and six others either finding no support for either model or a more complex finding). As for the seven individual sports papers, five find support for the tournament model (with two finding no relationship between effort and pay dispersion). This quasi 'meta analysis' of the sports literature suggests that research on team sports, where cooperation and cohesion tend to be more important, generally finds that pay compression is beneficial to output. The opposite seems to be the case for individual sports. This general conclusion is in line with Lazear (1989), who writes, 'If harmony is important, pay compression is optimal on strict efficiency grounds. Thus the ability to sabotage one's rivals provides an efficiency argument for equitable treatment within the firm' (p. 579). The possibility of sabotage exists in team sports, but not so in individual sports.

As for directions for future research on the effects of pay dispersion in sports markets, a few ideas come to mind. First, the use of *conditional* pay dispersion has only been studied in a few sports papers. Expansion of this approach to other team sports would be a worthwhile endeavor. Second, expanding data sets to encompass periods where key changes in compensation have been implemented (e.g. the introduction of, or changes to, payroll caps/floors) would provide for greater variation in pay dispersion and hence increase the likelihood of identifying any effects of pay dispersion on effort and production. Third, greater exploration of the potential non-linear effects of pay dispersion on performance could be explored and possibly lead to some sort of 'optimal dispersion' concept. Finally, other concepts of player heterogeneity can possibly be incorporated into models of team production along with pay dispersion to produce a more comprehensive study of inputs, pay and output.[38]

NOTES

1. Milgrom (1988) and Milgrom and Roberts (1990) offer another mechanism by which widely dispersed payrolls (i.e. tournament-style compensation schemes) may reduce production. Specifically, they discuss the possibility of counter-productive rent-seeking activity. That is, workers may employ non-productive activities with a goal towards winning favor from managers in the form of wage increases or promotions. Compressed wage structures may lessen this possibility.

2. Kahn's (2000) article titled, 'The sports business as a labor market laboratory', provides an excellent description of how sports markets have been used as a means for studying a wide variety of labor economics topics.

3. This discussion draws heavily from Heyman (2005), which provides an excellent summary of the key propositions of the tournament model.

4. See Predergast (1999) for an overview of the literature devoted to incentives in contracts.

5. The prize for the top-ranked finisher will be substantially greater than all other prizes at lower ranks since contestants can see that there is no remaining incentive to increase effort once the top rank is achieved.

6. Given that the primary function of this chapter is to discuss papers testing the tournament vs. fairness models in sports markets, the discussion regarding non-sports markets research on this topic will be brief. The reader is, once again, directed to Prendergast (1999) and Heyman (2005) for a richer discussion of non-sports tests of these hypotheses.

7. This chapter does not contain a discussion of the experimental research designed to test the tournament model. See Bull et al. (1987) and Schotter and Weigelt (1992) for examples of this type of research.

8. Lallemand, Plasman and Rycx (2004) use 1995 survey data from the Belgian private sector to assess the effects of salary dispersion on profits per employee. Their findings are similar to those of Winter-Ebmer and Zweimüller (1999).

9. Heyman (2005) also estimates results using non-conditional measures of dispersion.

10. Heyman (2005) also finds a *negative* relationship between the number of managers (or 'contestants') and pay dispersion. This is contrary to the third bullet point in section 7.2 above regarding predictions from the tournament model.

11. Much of the following discussion draws from Kahane (2012).

12. Excluding the current season lessens the likelihood of endogeneity problems. In addition, these team-averaged skill vectors are often computed as a weighted average where the chosen weights are frequently a measure of a player's playing time (e.g. time on the ice for hockey) in the current season.

13. In addition to its simplicity, another advantage of using team relative payroll is that it may capture certain player skills that are difficult to measure. For example, a particular player may be valued for their team leadership and mentoring skills. Such skills are typically not found in sports data, but may be reflected in a player's pay.

14. As with the player skill variables, coaching skill measures typically do not include the current season values.

15. As with any survey of a literature, there are space constraints and as such not every relevant paper can be included in this section.

16. While foot racing and auto racing do, in some circumstances, have a team element to them, they are considered individual sports for the purposes of this discussion.

17. They do not find support that greater prize money influences earlier round scores.

18. Orzag (1994), in a similar study using 1992 Professional Golf Association (PGA) data, fails to find support for the tournament model.

19. The authors postulate that this may be due to the limitations of the drivers' automobiles.

20. There have been several other papers examining the effects of the payout structure in NASCAR. For example, O'Roark et al. (2012) describe how changes to the points system and how racers may qualify for the 'Chase for the Championship' at the end of the season may generate a 'mixed tournament' environment. That is, earlier in the

season some drivers will have secured a slot in the 'Chase' (essentially a slot in the play-offs) and hence they will be less willing to take on risky behavior in races taking place before the Chase begins. Those drivers who are eliminated from the Chase early on will be more likely to use more risky tactics in pre-Chase races since winning these earlier races increases their income. The authors find support for this hypothesis by studying the occurrence of wrecks in races.

21. Other controls are also included, as in their unconditional regressions.
22. Their analysis relies on a very small sample size (n = 59).
23. The title of the Berri and Jewell (2004) paper makes reference to a 'natural experiment'. This presumably refers to the fact that, following the passage of the 1995 CBA, changes were made to the economics of teams' payrolls (e.g. an increased team payroll cap) which had an impact on team pay dispersion. Oddly, the period they employ in their regression analysis only includes seasons that *followed* the new CBA. By not including the earlier seasons, they exclude a significant amount of variation in team pay dispersion that would be exhibited in a 'before and after' CBA analysis. I presume their decision to exclude the earlier seasons was due to data limitations.
24. Their NHL data cover the seasons 1988–1989, 1993–1994 and the period 1995–1996 to 2000–2001.
25. For the other eight regressions, seven had negative signs but were not significant and one had a positive, significant sign.
26. Coates et al. (2016) find that when the Gini coefficient is the measure of dispersion, neither its coefficient nor that of its squared value are individually significant, but they are jointly significant. The sign pattern for these two covariates is positive for the linear term and negative for the squared term, implying a hump-shape. When the CV measure is used the linear term is individually significant, the squared term is not, but they are jointly significant. The sign pattern on these measures, however, is reversed, implying a U-shaped relationship. The authors note (pp. 727–728) that regardless of the measure, given the *observed* ranges for the Gini and the CV measures, teams would find themselves on the negatively sloped portion of the 'hump' or the 'U'. Tests for whether in fact the quadratic terms are necessary (e.g. a RESET test) were not discussed in the paper.
27. This section draws heavily from Kahane (2012).
28. See Kahane (2006) for more details on the 2004–2005 NHL lockout.
29. From, USATODAY.com: 'Sabres file for bankruptcy protection' (http://usatoday30. usatoday.com/sports/hockey/nhl/sabres/2003-01-13-sabres-bankruptcy_x.htm).
30. The report can be found at http://www2.nhl.com/images/levittreport.pdf.
31. See Kahane (2006) p. 114 and Table 6 for more details.
32. In the NHL, a team receives two points for a win. The variable *Points %* is computed by dividing the total points a team earned in the regular season by the 164 possible points (82 games x 2 points per game) in a regular season.
33. In a similar analysis Kahane (2012) employs both team-averaged skill vectors and relative payrolls. The regression results are qualitatively similar, with the within-R^2 measures being slightly greater for the regressions using relative payrolls. To conserve space, only relative payrolls are used in the current analysis. In addition, Kahane (2012) included a measure of goalie quality (regular season save percentage) as an additional team input. The coefficient to goalie save percentage was not significant in any of the regressions. For this reason, this variable is excluded from the current analysis.
34. As noted in Kahane (2012), top draft picks are computed using the draft years 1994 to 2000 and include only players who have played at least half the team's games in the current season and who have not been traded more than once since they began their professional career.
35. The individual player salary regression is excluded from this study to conserve space. The individual salary regression model and results are available in Kahane (2012).
36. Individual season dummies were also included. None of these dummies were significant in any of the regressions and as such they were dropped.

37. It should be noted that regressions using *non-conditional*, within-team pay dispersion measures did not produce significant coefficients.
38. For example, Kahane et al. (2013) study the effect of cultural and language diversity on production in the NHL. The idea of player skill heterogeneity is discussed in DeBrock et al. (2004).

REFERENCES

Akerlof, George A. and Janet L. Yellen (1988) 'Fairness and unemployment', *American Economic Review*, **78**, 44–49.

Akerlof, George A. and Janet L. Yellen (1990) 'The fair wage-effort hypothesis and unemployment', *Quarterly Journal of Economics*, **105**, 255–283.

Becker, Brian E. and Mark A. Huselid (1992) 'The incentive effects of tournament compensation systems', *Administrative Science Quarterly*, **37**, 336–350.

Berri, David J. and R. Todd Jewell (2004) 'Wage inequality and firm performance: professional basketball's natural experiment', *Atlantic Economic Journal*, **32**, 130–139.

Bloom, Matt (1999) 'The performance effects of pay dispersion on individuals and organizations', *Academy of Management Journal*, **42**, 25–40.

Bull, Clive, Andrew Schotter and Keith Weigelt (1987) 'Tournaments and piece rates: an experimental study', *Journal of Political Economy*, **95**, 1–33.

Card, David, Alexandre Mas, Enrico Moretti and Emanuel Saez (2012) 'Inequality at work: the effect of peer salaries on job satisfaction', *American Economic Review*, **102**, 2981–3003.

Coates, Dennis, Bernd Frick and Todd Jewell (2016) 'Superstar salaries and soccer success: the impact of the designated player in major league soccer', *Journal of Sports Economics*, **17**, 716–735.

Cowherd, Douglas M. and David I. Levine (1992) 'Product quality and pay equity between lower-level employees and top management: an investigation of distributive justice theory', *Administrative Science Quarterly*, **37**, 302–320.

DeBrock, Lawrence, Wallace Hendricks and Roger Koenker (2004) 'Pay and performance: the impact of salary distribution on firm level outcomes in baseball', *Journal of Sports Economics*, **5**, 243–261.

Depken, Craig A. (2000) 'Wage disparity and team productivity: evidence from Major League Baseball', *Economic Letters*, **67**, 87–92.

Ehrenberg, Ronald G. and Michael L. Bognanno (1990a) 'Do tournaments have incentive effects?, *Journal of Political Economy*, **98**, 1307–1324.

Ehrenberg, Ronald G. and Michael L. Bognanno (1990b) 'The incentive effects of tournaments revisited: evidence from the European PGA Tour', *Industrial and Labor Relations Review*, **43**, 74S–88S.

Eriksson, Tor (1999) 'Executive compensation and tournament theory: empirical tests on Danish data', *Journal of Labor Economics*, **17**, 262–280.

Franck, Egon and Stephan Nüesch (2011) 'The effect of wage dispersion on team outcome and the way team outcome is produced', *Applied Economics*, **43**, 3037–3049.

Frick, Bernd, Joachim Prinz and Karina Winkelmann (2003) 'Pay inequalities and team performance: empirical evidence from the North American major leagues', *International Journal of Manpower*, **24**, 472–488.

Gilsdorf, Keith F. and Vasant A. Sukhatme (2008) 'Tournament incentives and match outcomes in women's professional tennis', *Applied Economics*, **40**, 2405–2412.

Gomez, Rafael (2002) 'Salary compression and team performance: evidence from the National Hockey League', *Zeitschrift für Betriebswirtschaf: Ergänzungsheft 'Sportökonomie'*, **72**, 203–220.

Heyman, Fredrik (2005) 'Pay inequality and firm performance: evidence from matched employer-employee data', *Applied Economics*, **37**, 1313–1327.

Jane, Wen-Jhan, Yi-Pei Ou and Shen-Tung Chen (2011) 'The effects of equities on team performance for winners and losers in Nippon Professional Baseball: a quantile analysis', *Giornale degli Economisti e Annali di Economia*, **70**, 117–138.

Kahane, Leo H. (2006) 'The economics of the National Hockey League', in Plácido Rodríguez, Stefan Késenne and Jaume García Villar (eds), *Sports Economics After 50 Years: Essays in Honor of the Golden Anniversary of Simon Rottenberg*, Oviedo, Spain: Universidad de Oviedo, pp. 107–124.

Kahane, Leo H. (2012) 'Salary dispersion and team production: evidence from the National Hockey League', in Leo H. Kahane and Stephen Shmanske (eds), *The Oxford Handbook of Sports Economics. Volume 2. Economics Through Sports*, Oxford and New York: Oxford University Press, pp. 153–171.

Kahane, Leo H., Neil Longley and Rob Simmons (2013) 'The effects of coworker heterogeneity on firm-level output: assessing the impacts of cultural and language diversity in the National Hockey League', *Review of Economics and Statistics*, **95**, 302–314.

Kahn, Lawrence (2000) 'The sports business as a labor market laboratory', *Journal of Economic Perspectives*, **14**, 75–94.

Katayama, Hajime and Hudan Nuch (2011) 'A game-level analysis of salary dispersion and team performance in the National Basketball Association', *Applied Economics*, **43**, 1193–1207.

Lallemand, Thierry, Robert Plassman and François Rycx (2004) 'Intra-firm wage dispersion and firm performance: evidence from linked employer-employee data', *Kyklos*, **57**, 533–558.

Lazear, Edward P. (1989) 'Pay equality and industrial politics', *Journal of Political Economy*, **97**, 561–580.

Lazear, Edward P. and Sherwin Rosen (1981) 'Rank-order tournaments as optimum labor contracts', *Journal of Political Economy*, **89**, 841–864.

Leonard, Jonathan S. (1990) 'Executive pay and firm performance', *Industrial and Labor Relations Review*, **43**, 13–29.

Levine, David I. (1991) 'Cohesiveness, productivity and wage dispersion', *Journal of Economic Behavior and Organization*, **15**, 237–255.

Lynch, James G. and Jeffrey S. Zax (2000) 'The rewards to running: prize structure and performance in professional road racing', *Journal of Sports Economics*, **1**, 323–340.

Main, Brian G. M., Charles A. O'Reilly and James Wade (1993) 'Top executive pay: tournament or teamwork?', *Journal of Labor Economics*, **11**, 606–628.

Maloney, Michael T. and Robert E. McCormick (2000) 'The response of workers to wages in tournaments: evidence from foot races', *Journal of Sports Economics*, **1**, 99–123.

McGlaughlin, Kenneth J. (1988) 'Aspects of tournament models: a survey', *Journal of Labor Economics*, **15**, 403–430.

Milgrom, Paul R. (1988) 'Employment contract, influence activities, and efficient organisation design', *Journal of Political Economy*, **96**, 42–60.

Milgrom, Paul and John Roberts (1990) 'The efficiency of equity in organisational decision processes', *American Economic Review: Papers and Proceedings*, **80**, 154–159.

Mondello, Mike and Joel Maxcy (2009) 'The impact of salary dispersion and performance bonuses in NFL organizations', *Management Decision*, **47**, 110–123.

O'Roark, J. Brian, William C. Wood and Benjamin Demblowski (2012) 'Tournament chasing NASCAR style: driver incentives in stock car racing's playoff season', *Eastern Economic Journal*, **38**, 1–17.

Orszag, Jonathan M. (1994) 'A new look at incentive effects and golf tournaments', *Economics Letters*, **46**, 77–88.

Pfeffer, Jeffrey and Nancy Langton (1993) 'The effect of wage dispersion on satisfaction, productivity, and working collaboratively: evidence from college and university faculty', *Administrative Science Quarterly*, **38**, 382–407.

Prendergast, Canice (1999) 'The provision of incentives in firms', *Journal of Economic Literature*, **37**, 7–63.

Rosen, Sherwin (1986) 'Prizes and incentives in elimination tournaments', *American Economic Review*, **76**, 701–715.

San, Gee and Wen-Jhan Jane (2008) 'Wage dispersion and team performance: evidence from the small size professional baseball league in Taiwan', *Applied Economic Letters*, **15**, 883–886.

Schotter, Andrew and Keith Weigelt (1992) 'Asymmetric tournaments, equal opportunity laws, and affirmative action: some experimental results', *Quarterly Journal of Economics*, **107**, 511–540.

Sunde, Uwe (2009) 'Heterogeneity and performance in tournaments: a test of incentive effects using professional tennis data', *Applied Economics*, **41**, 3199–3208.

Winter-Ebmer, Rudolf and Josef Zweimüller (1999) 'Intra-firm wage dispersion and firm performance', *Kyklos*, **52**, 555–572.

8. Magicians, scapegoats and firefighters: the peculiar role of head coaches in professional soccer

Bernd Frick

8.1 MOTIVATION

Evaluating the performance of CEOs has always been – and continues to be – a challenge for shareholders, analysts and management scholars. Irrespective of the large amount of market- and accounting-based figures that are typically available to stakeholders as well as researchers, it remains notoriously difficult to identify the causal impact of leaders on firm performance. Using a large sample of some 3,300 CEO dismissals in the period 1993 to 2009, Jenter and Kanaan (2015) show that CEOs are often fired after bad firm performance caused by factors beyond their control, suggesting that even corporate boards fail in filtering out exogenous industry and market shocks from firm performance before deciding on CEO retention.[1]

Following the seminal publications by Grusky (1963, 1964) and Gamson and Scotch (1964), the team sports industry is now widely accepted as a 'laboratory' to study the impact of leaders on the performance of the organizations for which they are responsible: 'Professional sports offer a unique opportunity for labor market research. There is no other research setting than sports where we know the name, face, and life history of every production worker and supervisor in the industry. Total compensation packages and performance statistics for each individual are widely available, and we have a complete data set of worker-employer matches over the career of each production worker and supervisor in the industry' (Kahn, 2000: 75).

Soccer head coaches have roles that resemble that of CEOs.[2] They propose hiring and firing decisions to the board of directors (most often through a Director of Football) and they impose team playing strategies and make tactical adjustments within games. Head coaches have important motivational roles to try to raise individual player and team performance. Coaches take credit from fans and media when results are good, i.e. the team wins games, but also take the blame when games are lost. Unlike conventional businesses, football clubs share a number of commonalities such as, for example, a clearly defined production process of weekly matches, similar organizational structures and the constant pursuit of sporting success. This, in turn, implies that the performance of football clubs is more precisely attributable to managerial performance than are either market- or accounting-based measures of organizational performance in more heterogeneous industries such as, for example, automobiles, chemicals or banks and insurance companies.[3]

The reminder of the chapter is organized as follows: Using data from the last 20 seasons of German top division football, section 8.2 demonstrates that – as expected – sequences of poor results very often leads to head coach dismissals. Section 8.3 summarizes a representative sample of studies on the causes and consequences of head coach dismissals in different soccer leagues from all over the world. Section 8.4 discusses a number of reasons why poor performance may or may not lead to head coach dismissal. Sections 8.5 and 8.6 conclude with a summary and some implications for club managers as well as for future research.

8.2   THE ANTECEDENTS OF HEAD COACH DISMISSALS IN PROFESSIONAL SOCCER

In the last 20 seasons, 131 managers in the German Bundesliga lost their job due to dismissal. It is shown in Table 8.1 that at the time of dismissal

Table 8.1   Points per game by different types of head coaches in the German Bundesliga, 1997/1998 to 2016/2017

Head Coach Type	All Observations		Observations where Games ≥ 2		Observations where Games ≥ 3	
	Points Mean	N	Points Mean	N	Points Mean	N
Dismissed	0.94	131	0.94	131	0.95	130
Substitute	1.23	189	1.25	171	1.26	159
Permanent	1.48	229	1.48	229	1.48	229
Total	1.27	549	1.27	521	1.28	518
F-Value	45.39***		F=54.44***		F=57.33***	

Notes: *p < 0.10, **p < 0.05, ***p < 0.01. Data compiled from pre- and post-season special issues of soccer magazine *Kicker*.

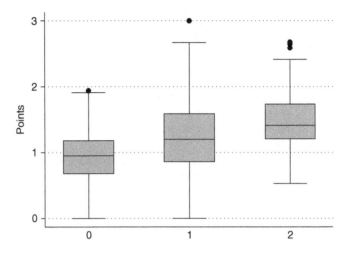

Figure 8.1   Points per game realized by dismissed coaches (0), substitute coaches (1) and permanent coaches (2) in the German Bundesliga, 1997/1998 to 2016/2017

these coaches had accumulated 0.94 points per match,[4] suggesting that their teams had performed poorly thus far. With less than one point per match, a team will be relegated to the second division at the end of the season. Therefore, it is not surprising to see that the clubs' managing directors are often quick in firing their head coach. It also appears that substitute coaches – very often recruited from the club's youth academy and temporarily promoted until a new head coach has been found and signed – are more successful than their unfortunate predecessors (with 1.23 points per match) as are the permanent coaches (i.e. those who manage to survive an entire season) with 1.48 points.[5]

However, as the boxplot reveals, some clubs even fire their head coach when his performance is better than that of the average permanent coach, while at the same time some of the head coaches who survive an entire season accumulate fewer points per game than their colleagues who lose their jobs (see Figure 8.1).

Due to the statistically significant impact of team wage bills on team performance (see e.g. Szymanski, 2000, Simmons and Forrest, 2004, Frick, 2013) it is plausible to assume that teams that perform worse than expected (i.e. accumulate fewer points than anticipated by their respective management and their fans) are more likely to dismiss their head coach than teams that perform better than expected by their stakeholders. Using the market value of each of the 18 teams in the German Bundesliga at the

Table 8.2   Impact of player market values on realized points, 2005/2006 to
2016/2017

Dependent Variable	Realized Points
Log Average Player Value	10.38***
	(2.467)
Year Dummies	included
Constant	41.51***
	(2.283)
N of Observations	216
N of Teams	35
R^2 *within*	10.7
R^2 *between*	74.6
R^2 *overall*	52.1

Notes: Standard errors (clustered at team id) in parentheses.
* $p < 0.10$, ** $p < 0.05$, *** $p < 0.01$.

start of the 2005/2006 to 2016/2017 seasons[6] as a measure of expectations,
it appears from Table 8.2 that a one-standard deviation increase in the log
average player value relative to the league average in that particular season
is associated with 10 additional points at the end of the season. Thus, the
teams' performance can indeed be predicted with some accuracy.

Figure 8.2 contains a plot of realized versus predicted points using
the estimation presented in Table 8.2. Teams above the regression line
performed better than expected, while those below the regression line
performed worse.

Finally, Figure 8.3 reveals that the difference between expected and
realized points is a good predictor for head coach dismissals, because
the number of dismissals increases from rank to rank, i.e. the more a
team is behind expectations, the more likely its management is to fire the
incumbent head coach.

8.3   HEAD COACH DISMISSALS IN PROFESSIONAL
SOCCER

Identifying the impact of head coach dismissals on subsequent team
performance is difficult for a number of reasons. First, teams in European
soccer play a balanced schedule, i.e. they face each opponent – 19 in the
English Premier League and 17 in the German Bundesliga – twice during
a season, suggesting that the old and the new coach play against different

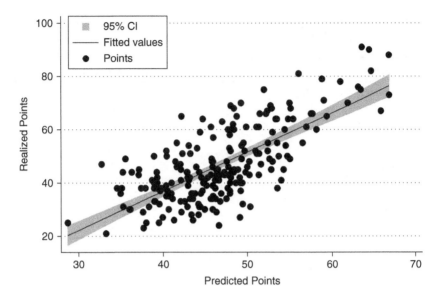

Figure 8.2   Realized versus predicted points

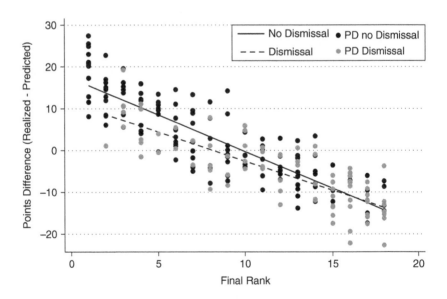

Figure 8.3   Points differential and dismissals

teams that are most likely of different quality. Thus, when comparing team performance prior to and after a dismissal, these differences need to be controlled. Most of the studies following this approach (see Tables 8.3 and 8.4 below) find that team performance does not always improve under a new head coach, and even deteriorates in a considerable number of cases, suggesting that head coach dismissals occur too often.

Second, it is difficult to determine what the performance of the team would have been if its management had not dismissed and replaced its head coach. What is required, therefore, is a control group of teams that retained their head coach while performing similarly during the period under investigation to the teams that fired their head coach. The construction of such a control group can be difficult and its composition is likely to affect the results obtained. Since the probability of a dismissal increases rapidly following a longer streak of poor results (usually four or five lost matches in a row), it is often difficult to find enough observations to construct a control group satisfying the condition of not having fired its head coach. Most of the studies following this approach (see Table 8.3 below) find that firing the head coach is neither efficient nor effective: team performance in the control group typically improves faster than in the treatment group, i.e. teams retaining their head coach recover more rapidly from a performance dip than teams replacing their head coach. Even worse:

> When forced resignations are successful, this success does not seem to exceed the success that might have been achieved by not sacking the manager. When forced resignations are unsuccessful, the failure exceeds that which would have to be incurred when the manager would not have been sacked. (Bruinshoofd and ter Weel, 2003: 244)

Thus, the expected payoff of dismissals is less than that of not forcing the head coach to leave.

Third, a more recent strand of literature (e.g. Van Ours and Van Tuijl, 2016; Pieper et al., 2014) uses bookmakers' betting odds as a proxy for performance expectations and finds that in, for example, the German Bundesliga, a one-standard-deviation increase of the number of points expected in the previous five matches increases the likelihood of being sacked by around 50 percent (depending on the estimation procedure used).

Summarizing, these three methodologically different approaches reach a similar, yet disappointing conclusion: On average, replacing an unsuccessful head coach with a new one because 'new brooms sweep clean' (Höffler and Sliwka, 2003) is clearly unsubstantiated.

Table 8.3   Summary of selected studies using match data

Author(s) and Year of Publication	League(s) and Time Period Covered	Estimation	Main Findings
Audas, Dobson and Goddard (1997)	42,624 matches played in Divisions 1 to 4 in England, 1972/1973 to 1992/1993	Descriptive Statistics	Comparing the win ratios of teams terminating their head coach with teams retaining the coach, it appears that replacing the manager is associated with a poorer performance.
Audas, Dobson and Goddard (2002)	All 113,768 fixtures played in Divisions 1 to 4 in England, 1972/1973 to 1999/2000	Ordered Probit	Controlling for mean-reversion, teams that changed managers within-season subsequently tended to perform worse than those that did not (e.g. in 1999/2000, home win probability decreases under new coach from 0.463 to 0.425).
Tena and Forrest (2007)	1,050 fixtures in Spanish 'Primera Division', 2002/2003 to 2004/2005 (first three rounds of each season excluded)	Ordered Probit	Appointment of a new manager is associated with a statistically significant increase in home wins (+0.8 in the first seven matches) while having no effect in away games.
Wirl and Sagmeister (2008)	1,979 league and cup matches involving Division 1 teams in Austria, 1994/1995 to 2003/2004	Ordered Probit	Coach change increases the probability of a home win and reduces the probability of an away win. However, neither of the two effects is statistically significant.
De Paola and Scoppa (2012)	4,042 matches played in Italian 'Serie A', 1997/1998 to 2008/2009	Ordered Probit and Poisson; Matching estimator	Coach change has in no specifications a statistically significant impact on the number of points per match, the number of goals scored or the number of goals conceded.
Flores, Forrest and Tena (2012)	7,000 matches played in the top division in Argentina, 1986/1987 to 2005/2006 (first four rounds of each season excluded)	Ordered Probit	Change of head coach is followed by a deterioration in team performance. While this effect is insignificant for home games, it is statistically significant from the very first match under the new coach in away games.

Table 8.3   (continued)

Author(s) and Year of Publication	League(s) and Time Period Covered	Estimation	Main Findings
Pieper, Nüesch and Franck (2014)	5,562 team-match-observations from German 'Bundesliga', 1998/1999 to 2007/2008	RE and FE models, FE Logit	An increase of one standard deviation in the number of points expected in the previous five matches (as estimated from betting odds) reduces the probability of a head coach dismissal by more than 70 percent.
Madum (2016)	3,762 matches played in the Danish 'Superligaen', 1995/1996 to 2013/2014	Ordered Probit OLS and Matching estimation	Following a dismissal, teams win about 0.5 points more per home match. Teams that have not dismissed their head coach would not have done better if they had. Thus, teams seem to behave optimally as they only dismiss the coach when they benefit from doing so.
Lago-Penas (2011)	2,878 matches from 1st and 2nd divisions in Spain, 1997/1998 to 2006/2007	Anova and OLS	Team performance increases by about 20 percent under the new head coach. This effect, however, is short-lived and decreases rapidly after the fourth week under the auspices of the new coach.
Mühlheusser, Schneemann and Sliwka (2016)	4,896 fixtures in German 'Bundesliga', 1994/1995 to 2009/2010	Ordered Probit	Arrival of a new head coach is associated with an additional 0.35 points per game compared to a team that retained its manager if players' individual skills are homogeneous. This effect decreases over time and is stronger in away games.
Detotto, Paolini and Tena (forthcoming)	3,303 fixtures from Italian 'Serie A' (2000/2001 to 2009/2010, first four rounds excluded)	Random Effects and Bivariate Ordered Probit Model	Controlling for past results, it appears that regardless of the econometric specification, replacing the head coach has no statistically significant effect on team performance, neither in home nor in away matches.

Table 8.4   Summary of selected studies using team and head coach data

Author(s) and Year of Publication	League(s) and Time Period Covered	Estimation	Main Findings
Bruinshoofd and ter Weel (2003)	45 head coach sackings in Dutch 'Eredivisie', 1988/1989 to 2000/2001	DiD estimation	Head coach dismissals are neither effective nor efficient. Effectiveness requires that a team's performance improves under a new coach. Efficiency requires that the effect of a dismissal could not have been achieved at lower cost by taking measures other than sacking the head coach. Teams that allow their manager to stay during a period of performance deterioration recover better and faster than those that sack their manager.
Koning (2003)	28 head coach changes in Dutch 'Eredivisie', 1993/1994 to 1997/1998	Rank Model	Controlling for selectivity (teams do not face the same opponents before and after a coach is fired) it appears that appointing a new head coach in the middle of the season has no statistically significant impact on the team's performance. Home advantage decreases in 10 and team quality (i.e. goal difference) in 11 out of 28 cases.
Frick and Simmons (2008)	398 team season observations from German 'Bundesliga', 1981/1982 to 2002/2003	Stochastic Frontier Model	Relative spending on playing talent and on head coach talent combine effectively to reduce technical ineffciency and improve league performance. Teams that fire their head coach suffer from increased technical inefficiency.
Barros, Frick and Passos (2009)	398 team-season-observations from German 'Bundesliga', 1981/1982 to 2002/2003	Mixed Logit Model	Salary of head coach as well as team wage bill have statistically significant positive impact on dismissal probability. Head coach experience and head coach career win percentage both reduce the probability of a separation (be it voluntary or involuntary).
Balduck, Buelens and Philippaerts (2010)	72 cases of coach turnover in the 1st, 2nd and 3rd Divisions in Belgium, 1998/1999 to 2002/2003	DiD estimation	Performance in the last four games before the dismissal and in the first four matches under the new head coach was identical. Moreover, performance of teams in the control group recovered faster to mean performance.

Table 8.4   (continued)

Author(s) and Year of Publication	League(s) and Time Period Covered	Estimation	Main Findings
Balduck, Prinzie and Buelens (2010)	45 within-season changes of head coach in 1st Division in Belgium, 1998/1999 to 2004/2005	Rank model (as in Koning 2003)	Using the same methodology as Koning (2003) it appears that 36 teams improved their quality after head coach turnover. This improvement was statistically significant only for eight teams (at $p < .05$) and five teams (at $p < .10$) respectively.
Frick, Barros and Prinz (2010)	398 team season observations from German 'Bundesliga', 1981/1982 to 2002/2003	Hazard Models for Repeated Events	Coaches of more expensive teams tend to be fired earlier, i.e. expectations of management and fans are apparently higher than in teams that spend less money for their players. Coaches with a higher career win percentage tend to survive longer. Sporting performance has a negative impact on the hazard rate.
Wagner (2010)	256 forced separations in the German 'Bundesliga', 1963/1964 to 2002/2003	DiD estimation	Teams that replaced their coach perform significantly better in the first four matches under the new coach than teams in a closely matched control group (winning on average an additional 0.2 points). This effect is significantly stronger under the 3 point (as compared to the 2 point) rule.
Ter Weel (2011)	81 forced and 103 voluntary head coach resignations of teams playing in Dutch 'Eredivisie', 1986/1987 to 2003/2004	DiD and 2SLS estimation	Manager turnover is not followed by significant improvements in team performance. Moreover, manager experience does not predict turnover. Remaining contract length reduces the likelihood of a dismissal while the number of players signed during their spell with the current club increases dismissal probability.
Van Ours and Van Tuijl (2016)	252 team season observations, Dutch 'Eredivisie', 2000/2001 to 2013/2014	Matching estimator	The number of points achieved as well as the 'cumulative surprise' (i.e. the number of excess points) in the last four/five/six matches reduce the probability of head coach dismissal significantly.

Table 8.5   Summary of selected studies on head coach characteristics and
*   performance[7]*

Author(s) and Year of Publication	League(s) and Time Period Covered	Estimation	Main Findings
Bachan, Reilly and Witt (2008)	626–736 head coach-season observations (spells at risk) in English Divisions 1, 2 and 3 in seasons 2001/2002 to 2003/2004	Kaplan-Meier and Maximum Likelihood Estimation	League position and attendance have a statistically significant effect on an individual manager's exit (with the former being far more important than the latter). Manager characteristics (age, experience, nationality, length of service) were completely irrelevant.
D'Addona and Kind (2014)	2,376 turnovers of head coaches in the four professional English leagues in seasons 1949/1950 to 2007/2008	Logit and Duration Models	Sensitivity of firing decisions on the outcome of recent matches has steadily increased during the six decades covered in the study. While in the 1950s a manager from the bottom performance quintile faced a 21 percent probability of being fired, a similar manager in the 2000s was sacked with a probability of 65 percent. Moreover, the probability of being sacked is higher for older and less experienced managers.
Mühlheusser, Schneemann, Sliwka and Wallmeier (forthcoming)	103 head coaches (with 44 movers) at 29 clubs in seasons 1993/1994 to 2013/2014 (764 coach-team-observations)	Fixed Effects	Teams employing a manager from the top 20 percent of the ability distribution gain on average 0.3 points per game more than those employing a manger from the bottom 20 percent of that distribution (enough to bring a team from the relegation zone to Champions League qualification). The slope of the manager rank is about 50 percent of the slope of the team (i.e. players) rank, suggesting that it is easier (and cheaper) to replace the manager than to replace the whole squad. Former professional players perform worse as head coaches than former non-professionals.

8.4 WHY DO SOME POORLY PERFORMING TEAMS RETAIN THEIR HEAD COACH WHILE THE MAJORITY DO NOT?

Since the early studies by Grusky (1963, 1964) and Gamson and Scotch (1964) the literature distinguishes three different explanations for head coach dismissals. The 'common sense' model rests on the assumption that signing a new head coach might produce a 'healthy shock effect', leading to improved team performance. This shock effect, in turn, can be attributed to increased competition among players (those who have not been selected by the old coach now have an incentive to demonstrate to the new one that they should be nominated for the starting squad, or at least should receive more minutes on the pitch) or to better strategies and tactics employed by the newcomer. The 'scapegoat' explanation emphasizes that the team's management dismisses a head coach not necessarily because it is convinced that a new coach would do a better job, but to demonstrate that they are taking concrete action to remedy an undesirable situation. In such a 'crisis situation', it is far easier to exchange the coach than to replace the entire squad of players. Finally, the 'vicious circle' explanation argues that firing the head coach is likely to exacerbate an already difficult situation by producing additional disruptive effects on the organization, such as declining fan support and poor morale and low team stability among players.

So far, the evidence does not allow distinguishing between these three explanations because there is evidence supporting each of them: anecdotal as well as econometric evidence is compatible with the common sense, the scapegoat and the vicious circle explanations to roughly the same extent.

Moreover, some poorly performing teams might hesitate to dismiss their head coach not only because they are afraid to be trapped in a vicious circle, but because they cannot afford to sack him. In line with this argument, some of the studies quoted above find that the remaining contract length of a head coach serves as an insurance policy. Since the dismissed coach remains on the club's payroll until his contract expires or until he signs with another club, it may simply be too expensive to fire a (presumably) unsuccessful coach. Moreover, a rational management will fire a head coach only if suitable candidates are available. Thus, if the pool of (potential) candidates is depleted, firing is not a viable strategy. Finally, where the head coach was given the opportunity to assemble a new squad before the start of the season, he might also be given more time to help the squad to develop the 'automatisms' required to be successful on the pitch. Players arriving shortly before the start of a season may not yet be familiar with the tactics and the playing style of their new team and may, therefore, perform worse than initially expected.

8.5 IMPLICATIONS

What are the implications for managers as well as researchers? For the former, the recommendation is obvious: since even an extended streak of poor results comes to an end, it is likely to pay to retain the head coach instead of sacking him. Supporting the incumbent coach even after a number of lost matches is not only the cheaper alternative, but is also likely to avoid additional disruptions to the organization that are undeniably associated with the arrival of a new coach (admittedly, these disruptions might be welcomed by some managers as they expect them to induce players to expend more effort to recommend themselves to the new coach[8]). Moreover, one-year contracts combined with large bonus payments in the case of a particularly good performance are not only cost-saving devices (i.e. firing the head coach is cheaper in the case where he is on a one-year, as opposed to a two- or even three-year, contract) but are also likely to induce self-selection among potential candidates.

The implications for organizational economists in general and sports economists in particular are less straightforward. Ideally, one would follow the route suggested by Nobel Laureate Herbert Simon in one of his seminal publications:

> What is needed is empirical research and experimentation to determine the relative desirability of alternative administrative arrangements ... First, it is necessary that the objectives of the administrative organization under study be defined in concrete terms so that results, expressed in terms of these objectives, may be accurately measured. Second, it is necessary that sufficient experimental control be exercised. (Simon, 1958: 42)

Clearly, this research design is difficult – if not impossible – to implement. What can and should be done instead is to take into account changes in the composition of the pool of unemployed head coaches and analyze the impact these changes have on the firing behavior of poorly performing clubs. Most likely, a poorly performing coach will be retained by his current team if the available alternatives are considered worse by the team's management. If, on the other hand, a coach with a good reputation is available on short notice – because he has been fired previously – this is likely to affect the decisions of other poorly performing clubs' managers. Although plausible from a theoretical perspective, it is certainly difficult to demarcate the pool of candidates that are considered alternatives to the incumbent coach. The size as well as the composition of this pool is likely to be affected by a particular club's reputation (highly reputed coaches will prefer unemployment to working for a club at the bottom of the league especially when they are still on their old club's payroll for another one or two seasons) as well as its ability to pay (even clubs with a long tradition and loyal fans might lack the means to sign a new head coach while still having to pay another person). Finally, changes in the composition of the squad need to be taken into account when estimating the probability of head coach dismissals. If the head coach has been responsible for the composition of the squad (either alone or in cooperation with the club's director of football) the probability of dismissal is likely to be different than when somebody else (e.g. the previous head coach) can be held accountable.

8.6 SUMMARY

Why, then, do teams fire their head coach in light of the evidence presented above? The most plausible answer to this question has been provided by Audas et al. (2002: 465), who argue that the decision to change the manager represents:

> A gamble on achieving a favorable 'draw' from a distribution of possible outcomes with a higher variance. Even though the mean effect is negative, the higher variance might increase the probability of achieving the required improvement in performance. If changing the manager does cause performance to decline further, this is unfortunate, but relegation is likely anyway if no change is made. But if a fortunate replacement appointment is made, inspiring a sufficiently large short-term improvement, the gamble will have paid off.

NOTES

1. The more recent and more convincing literature on the impact of 'leaders' on firm performance uses changes in stock prices following sudden and unexpected deaths as a difficult to manipulate measure of the CEO's value to shareholders (e.g. Hayes and Schaefer, 1999; Johnson et al., 1985; Nguyen and Nielsen, 2010, 2014; Quigley et al., forthcoming).
2. To avoid confusion, I emphasize that the terms 'soccer' and 'football' will be used as synonyms throughout the chapter.
3. The concentration on European soccer leagues does not imply that comparable evidence is not available for other team sports such as, e.g., the NBA (Goodall et al., 2011) or Formula 1 (Goodall and Pogrebna, 2015).
4. In European football, each team plays each opponent twice during a season, once at home and once on the opponent's ground. A win gives three points, a draw one point and a loss zero points.
5. Although the number of events decreases from 189 to 171 and 159 respectively, excluding substitute coaches with less than two or three games (so-called 'caretaker coaches') leaves the findings virtually unaffected.
6. See http://www.transfermarkt.de.
7. Dawson et al. (2000), as well as Dawson and Dobson (2002), were among the first to estimate coaching efficiency in English Association Football. Their main result is that mean efficiency depends to a large extent on the choice of the estimation procedure

(mean efficiency can be as low as 0.549 and as high as 0.841) and that the observable variation in efficiency can be explained by certain head coach characteristics, such as previous experience as manager.

8. This effect, however, is likely to occur only in homogeneous teams, i.e. in squads where the weakest four among the top 11 players and the strongest four contenders are close together in terms of their most recent performance (Mühlheusser et al., 2016).

REFERENCES

Audas, R., S. Dobson and J. Goddard (1997) 'Team performance and managerial change in the English football league', *Economic Affairs*, **17**, 30–36.

Audas, R., S. Dobson and J. Goddard (2002) 'The impact of managerial change on team performance in professional sports', *Journal of Economics and Business*, **54**, 633–650.

Bachan, R., B. Reilly and R. Witt (2008) 'The hazard of being an English football league manager: empirical estimates for three recent league seasons', *Journal of the Operational Research Society*, **59**, 884–891.

Balduck, A.-L., M. Buelens and R. Philippaerts (2010) 'Short-term effects of mid-season head coach turnover on team performance in soccer', *Research Quarterly for Exercise and Sport*, **81** (3), 379–383.

Balduck, A.-L., A. Prinzie and M. Buelens (2010) 'The effectiveness of coach turnover and the effect on home team advantage, team quality and team ranking', *Journal of Applied Statistics*, **37** (4), 679–689.

Barros, C. P., B. Frick and J. Passos (2009) 'Coaching for survival: the hazards of head coach careers in the German Bundesliga', *Applied Economics*, **41** (11), 3303–3311.

Bruinshoofd, A. and B. ter Weel (2003) 'Manager to go? Performance dips reconsidered with evidence from Dutch football', *European Journal of Operational Research*, **148** (2), 233–246.

D'Addona, S. and A. Kind (2014) 'Forced manager turnovers in English soccer leagues: a long-term perspective', *Journal of Sports Economics*, **15** (2), 150–179.

Dawson, P. and S. Dobson (2002) 'Managerial efficiency and human capital: an application to English association football', *Managerial and Decision Economics*, **23**, 471–486.

Dawson, P., S. Dobson and B. Gerrard (2000) 'Estimating coaching efficiency in professional team sports: evidence from English association football', *Scottish Journal of Political Economy*, **47**, 399–421.

De Paola, M. and V. Scoppa (2012) 'The effects of managerial turnover: evidence from coach dismissals in Italian soccer teams', *Journal of Sports Economics*, **13** (2), 152–168.

Detotto, C., D. Paolini and J. D. Tena (forthcoming) 'Do managerial skills matter? An analysis of the impact of managerial features on performance for Italian football', *Journal of the Operational Research Society*.

Flores, R., D. Forrest and J. D. Tena (2012) 'Decision taking under pressure: evidence on football manager dismissals in Argentina and their consequences', *European Journal of Operational Research*, **222**, 653–662.

Frick, B. (2013) 'Team wage bills and sporting performance: evidence from (major and minor) European soccer leagues', in P. Rodriguez, S. Késenne and J. Garcia (eds), *The Econometrics of Sports*, Cheltenham, UK and Northampton, MA, USA: Edward Elgar Publishing, pp. 63–80.

Frick, B. and R. Simmons (2008) 'The impact of managerial quality on organizational performance: evidence from German soccer', *Managerial and Decision Economics*, **29**, 593–600.

Frick, B., C. P. Barros and J. Prinz (2010) 'Analyzing head coach dismissals in the German "Bundesliga" with a mixed logit approach', *European Journal of Operational Research*, **200** (1), 151–159.

Gamson, W. A. and N. A. Scotch (1964) 'Scapegoating in baseball', *American Journal of Sociology*, **70**, 69–72.

Goodall, A. H. and G. Pogrebna (2015) 'Expert leaders in a fast-moving environment', *Leadership Quarterly*, **26**, 123–142.

Goodall, A. H., L. M. Kahn and A. J. Oswald (2011) 'Why do leaders matter? A study of expert knowledge in a superstar environment', *Journal of Economic Behavior & Organization*, **77**, 265–284.

Grusky, O. (1963) 'Managerial succession and organizational effectiveness', *American Journal of Sociology*, **69**, 21–31.

Grusky, O. (1964) 'Reply', *American Journal of Sociology*, **70**, 72–76.

Hayes, R. E. and S. Schaefer (1999) 'How much are differences in managerial abilities worth?', *Journal of Accounting and Economics*, **27**, 125–148.

Höffler, F. and D. Sliwka (2003) 'Do new brooms sweep clean? When and why dismissing a manager increases the subordinates' performance', *European Economic Review*, **47** (5), 877–890.

Jenter, D. and F. Kanaan (2015) 'CEO turnover and relative performance evaluation', *Journal of Finance*, **LXX** (5), 2155–2183.

Johnson, W. B., R. P. Magee, N. J. Nagarajan and H. A. Newman (1985) 'An analysis of the stock price reaction to sudden executive deaths: implications for the managerial labor market', *Journal of Accounting and Economics*, **7**, 151–174.

Kahn, L. (2000) 'The sports business as a labor market laboratory', *Journal of Economic Perspectives*, **14** (3), 75–94.

Koning, R. (2003) 'An econometric evaluation of the effect of firing a coach on team performance', *Applied Economics*, **35**, 555–564.

Lago-Penas, C. (2011) 'Coach mid-season replacement and team performance in professional soccer', *Journal of Human Kinetics*, **28**, 115–122.

Madum, A. (2016) 'Managerial turnover and subsequent firm performance: evidence from Danish soccer teams', *International Journal of Sport Finance*, **11**, 46–62.

Mühlheusser, G., S. Schneemann and D. Sliwka (2016) 'The impact of managerial change on performance: the role of team heterogeneity', *Economic Inquiry*, **54** (2), 1128–1149.

Mühlheusser, G., S. Schneemann, D. Sliwka and N. Wallmeier (forthcoming) 'The contribution of managers to organizational success: evidence from German soccer', *Journal of Sports Economics*.

Nguyen, B. D. and K. M. Nielsen (2010) 'The value of independent directors: evidence from sudden deaths', *Journal of Financial Economics*, **98**, 550–567.

Nguyen, B. D. and K. M. Nielsen (2014) 'What death can tell: are executives paid for their contributions to firm value?', *Management Science*, **60** (12), 2994–3010.

Pieper, J., S. Nüesch and E. Franck (2014) 'How performance expectations affect managerial replacement decisions', *Schmalenbach Business Review*, **66**, 5–23.

Quigley, T. J., C. Crossland and R. J. Campbell (forthcoming) 'Shareholder perceptions of the changing impact of CEOs: market reactions to unexpected CEO deaths, 1950–2009', *Strategic Management Journal*.

Simmons, R. and D. Forrest (2004) 'Buying success: team performance and wage bills in U.S. and European sports leagues', in R. Fort and J. Fizel (eds), *International Sports Economics Comparisons*, Westport, CT: Praeger, pp. 123–140.

Simon, H. A. (1958) *Administrative Behavior*, 2nd edn, New York: Macmillan.

Szymanski, S. (2000) 'A market test for discrimination in the English professional soccer leagues', *Journal of Political Economy*, **108**, 590–603.

Tena, J. D. and D. Forrest (2007) 'Within-season dismissal of football coaches: statistical analysis of causes and consequences', *European Journal of Operational Research*, **181**, 362–373.

Ter Weel, B. (2011) 'Does manager turnover improve firm performance? Evidence from Dutch soccer, 1986–2004', *De Economist*, **159**, 279–303.

Van Ours, J. C. and A. Van Tuijl (2016) 'In-season head-coach dismissals and the performance of professional football teams', *Economic Inquiry*, **54** (1), 591–604.

Wagner, S. (2010) 'Managerial succession and organizational performance – evidence from the German soccer league', *Managerial and Decision Economics*, **31**, 415–430.

Wirl, F. and S. Sagmeister (2008) 'Changing of the guards: new coaches in Austria's Premier Football League', *Empirica*, **35**, 267–278.

Index

ABA *see* American Basketball
    Association (ABA)
Adler, M. 75
AFL *see* American Football League
    (AFL)
age group
    effects for youth players 65
    selection 60
age intervals, negative effects of 61
Akerlof, George A. 138–140
    theory of lemons 98, 106
all-star games 78, 79
alternative performance metrics 114
Alvarez, A. 122
American Basketball Association
    (ABA) 14
American Football League (AFL) 14
annual player performance 114
arbitration
    eligibility 105
    eligible players 106
    panels 88
Arcidiacono, Peter 115
Association of Tennis Professionals
    (ATP) 149
    rankings 149
    World Tour 74
assortative matching 48
athletic skills, transferability of 11
ATP *see* Association of Tennis
    Professionals (ATP)
automatisms 179
average market value 119

BAA *see* Basketball Association of
    America (BAA)
Barcelona 125
bargaining 12
power 28
    see also collective bargaining
        agreements (CBAs)

baseball 18, 93–94, 150–151
    players 114
Basketball Association of America
    (BAA) 14
Battré, M. 80
Beckham, David 152
behavioral economics 29
Bell, Bert 26–27
Berlinschi, Ruxanda 122, 123
Berri, D. J. 32–34, 37–38, 94, 129, 130,
    151
Bettman, Gary 153
Big 4 leagues 19
Bilbao's development model 125
Bloom, Matt 130
Bognanno, M. L. 128, 143
Borland, J. 55
bounded rationality, concept of 29
Brook, Stacey L. 37–38
Bryson, Alex 114–115
Bucciol, Alessandro 130
Buraimo, B. 95
Burke, Brian 34
Büschemann, A. 81

career performance 33
CBAs *see* collective bargaining
    agreements (CBAs)
CEOs
    dismissals of 168
    leadership 10
    performance of 168
'The Chart' 30
Chinese players 113
Chinese Professional Baseball League
    (CPBL) 150–151
Chinese soccer league 113
clubs
    football 169
    foreign 122
    groups of 66

reputation 180–181
specific knowledge 21
coaches in professional soccer 168–169
  head coach dismissals in professional
    soccer 168–178
  implications for managers 180–181
coaching skills 142
cohesiveness model 136–137
collective bargaining agreements
    (CBAs) 15, 82, 107, 130, 154
  European soccer 19
  player drafts 16–17
  player mobility 17–18
  roster size and make-up 16
  team payrolls and individual player
    salaries 18–19
collective judgment, value of 82
common sense' model 179
communication 80
company unions 13
compensation 7–9
  fees 53
  requirements 17
  structure 136
    design of 8
  types of 74
conditional dispersion measures 152
conditional payroll dispersion 140, 153
conditional wage dispersion 140
confidence 80
contract length, determinants of 105,
    106
Cowherd, Douglas M. 139
co-worker heterogeneity on team
    performance 112–113
  benefits from player migration
    121–125
  cultural diversity 118–121
  heterogeneous ability and 116–118
  pay dispersion and team
    performance 125–131
  productivity spillovers 113–116
CPBL *see* Chinese Professional
    Baseball League (CPBL)
cultural diversity 118–121
culture 21, 23, 110

Davis, Anthony 42
DeBrock, Lawrence 150, 151, 153
De Grip, Andries 112

demand volatility 140
dependent variables, summary statistics
    for 157
Depken, Craig A. 125, 127, 130
  analysis of Major League Baseball
    (MLB) 128
designated hitters (DH) 105
designated player 152
Deutscher, C. 81
development 5–7, 21–22
DFB *see* German Soccer Association
    (DFB)
DFL *see* German Soccer League
    (DFL)
DH *see* designated hitters (DH)
difference-in-difference analysis 130
disabled list (DL) 89, 93, 107–108
dismissals, head coach 169
  bonus payments 180
  characteristics and performance 178
  English Premier League 171–172
  in German Bundesliga 169, 171–172
  impact of 171–172
  motivational roles of 168–169
  points differential and dismissals
    171, 172
  points per game 170
  realized vs. predicted points 171, 172
  selected studies using match data
    174–175
  selected studies using team and
    176–177
dispersion
  measures for 152
  of wages 136
distribution of births per month 63
diversity in ethnicity and demographics
    112
DL *see* disabled list (DL)
domestic leagues 19
domestic players 121
domestic soccer leagues 120
domestic television rights 120
Donley, T. D. 94
draft picks 41
  average performance of 38
drafts 26–28
  in baseball and hockey 27
  failed promise of 43
  history of 32

NFL performance by position in 33
over bidding process 27
quarterbacks in 32
rationality 28–29
systems 12, 48
trust the process 34–43
Duncan, Tim 40–41

earned run average (ERA)
coefficient of variation 116
of pitchers 115
earnings function 75
effectiveness of leaders 10
Ehrenberg, R. G. 128, 143
elimination tournaments 149
elite soccer education 49
elite youth academies 50
minimum requirements for 51
under weighted evaluation criteria
for 51
elite youth education 65
ELO, points and rankings 123–125
empirical model 128
empirical tests
from non-sports markets 139–140
from sports markets 141
employer-employee relations 2, 7, 10
radical transformation of 13
in sports 12–13
employment
contracts 8
market in professional sports 10–11
entrepreneurship 55
ERA *see* earned run average (ERA)
Eriksson, Tor 139
estimation, model for 115–116
European professional soccer 19, 47–49
German youth recruitment system
49–54
labor market for young athletes
54–57
matching and determinants of
professional career 57–59
relative age effects 59–66
European youth soccer
reference market for 49
selection process in 48
Europe elite youth education 47
executive pay dispersion 139
experience 76

fairness model 136–139, 141, 149, 159
for team production 150
tests of 142–143
vs. tournament model 151, 155
'fair wage-effort' hypothesis 138
Fenn, Aju 37–38
FIFA 49
law 52, 53
points and rankings 122–123
training compensation fees 53, 54
firm performance 140
firm-specific human capital 7
firm-specific knowledge 7
firm-specific skills 7
firm-specific training 5, 6
football clubs, performance of 169
footballer migration 123
foreign basketball players 122
foreign clubs, footballer migration to
122
foreign players 122
integration of 121
former co-workers 112
franchises, scarcity of 11
Franck, Egon 116–117
free agency 88
institutional change 89
rights 14
free agents
performance 105–108
restricted vs. unrestricted 17
status 101, 105–108
Frick, Bernd 95
Friedman, Milton 28–29

Generalized Method of Moments
(GMM) 151
general skills 7
general training 5
German Bundesliga 95, 116, 170–171,
173
expenses for youth recruitment 52
head coaches dismissals in 169
German establishments 112
German Soccer Association (DFB) 47,
49, 66
youth regulations 53
German Soccer League (DFL) 47
elite youth academies under 50, 51
market evaluation 50

German soccer, youth recruitment system in 47
Germany 47, 61
Gini coefficient 61, 128, 129, 142, 152
　of predicted salaries 129–130
　of residual salary 130
Glitz, Albrecht 112
GMM *see* Generalized Method of Moments (GMM)
Gould, Eric D. 113, 114
'Grand Slam' tournaments 149
Greer, Price, and Berri 36
Griffin, Robert 29–30
groups of clubs 66

Hakes, J. K. 99
Hamilton, B. 118
Hart, O. 96
head coach dismissals 169
　bonus payments 180
　characteristics and performance 178
　English Premier League 171–172
　in German Bundesliga 169, 171–172
　impact of 171–172
　motivational roles of 168–169
　points differential and dismissals 171, 172
　points per game 170
　realized vs. predicted points 171, 172
　selected studies using match data 174–175
　selected studies using team and 176–177
healthy shock effect 179
Heckman, J. 99
　selection model 122
Herfindahl-Hirschman index (HHI) 120–121, 128, 142
　model effects of 121
heterogeneity
　levels of 115
　in player ability 115
heterogeneous ability 116–118
heterogeneous work teams 116–118
Heyman, Fredrik 140
HHI *see* Herfindahl-Hirschman index (HHI)
Hickman, D. 80
hierarchical pay structure 152
higher education 55

Hinkie, Sam 41
hiring 20–21
hitters, positive for 114
Hoang, H. 78
Holmstrom, B. 96
human capital 48, 54, 56
　accumulation 123
　club-specific 58
　firm-specific 7
　soccer-related 47, 55
　soccer-specific 59
　standard/traditional concepts of 81
　team-specific 58
　variables 79

Ichniowski, Casey 123–125
incentives 7–9, 22, 89
　clauses and bonuses 93
　compatible mechanisms 93
individual clubs 19
individual 'permanent' productivity 116–117
individual player salaries 18–19, 155
individual skill differences 156
individual sports 142, 143–144
inequality measures 116
information asymmetries 65
Ingersoll, Keith 119, 120
injuries 56, 59
innovation process 48
instability, popular notion of 106–107
International Motor Sports Association (IMSA) 143
intra-firm wage differences 138
intra-team pay dispersion 151–152
invitational foot races 143

Jewell, R. Todd 151
job separation 58
job shopping 58
Jovanovic, B. 57

Kahane, Leo H. 121, 123, 151–153, 156
Kahn, L. 99, 100–101, 113
Kahn-Maxcy approach 100
Krautmann, A. C. 92, 94, 97, 100–101

labor contracts in sports 90
labor market research 141
Langton, Nancy 140

Lazear, E. 9, 10, 74, 118, 119, 138
leaders
  effectiveness of 10
  impact of 168
leadership skills 79–80
league structures 113
Lehmann and Schulze 79
Levine, David I. 138, 139
linguistic distance 119
  standard deviation rise in 119
long-term contracts
  probability of 99
  in professional sports 97
  as risk allocation 96
lottery picks 41–42
Lucifora, C. 78
lucrative transfer fees 125
Lye, J. 55

Main, Brian G. M. 139
Major League Baseball (MLB) 12,
    14–15, 21, 27, 78, 89, 125, 130, 150
  average for teams 129
  clubs 107
  contracting in 99
  Depken's analysis of 128
  duellist format of 113
  negotiating and contracting process
    in 99
  players 14
    individual performances 91
    salaries and contract length 97
  position players contracts 101
  signings, contact term for 2017 96
  team roster 129
  teams 16
Major League Baseball Players'
    Association (MLBPA) 13, 18
Major League Soccer (MLS) 152
management
  effectiveness of 10
  roles of 9–10, 22–23
managerial performance 169
managerial resource-based theory 129
Marburger, Daniel 94
marginal revenue products (MRPs)
    14, 94
  economic conception of 94
Mas, Alexandre 123
Massey, Cade 30–31, 34

'Master Series' tournaments 149
matching quality, gathering private
    information to assess 58
match-specific productivity 2
Matthew effect 60
Maxcy, Fort, and Krautmann (MFK)
  contribution of 93
  interpretation of strategic behavior
    95
Maxcy, J. 89, 92, 99, 100–101, 105, 106,
    152
  empirical analysis 92
  negotiating and contracting process
    in MLB 99
  theoretical model of contracting
    process 97
Metz, N. 80
MFK *see* Maxcy, Fort, and
    Krautmann (MFK)
migrant hockey players 123
migrant players, productivity spillovers
    from 125
migration index 122
Miller, Marvin 13
Mincer, J. 75
Minnesota Golden Gophers 26
MLB *see* Major League Baseball
    (MLB)
MLBPA *see* Major League Baseball
    Players' Association (MLBPA)
MLS *see* Major League Soccer (MLS)
Mondello, Mike 152
monetary payoffs on performance 80
Moretti, Enrico 123
MRPs *see* marginal revenue products
    (MRPs)
multi-period contracts 88, 90, 95, 96,
    99, 100
  examination of 90
  and incentive issues 90–96
  individual players with 89
  institutional change 89
  in MLB 97
  motivation for 89
  as risk allocation mechanisms
    96–101
multi-term contracts
  risk premium associated with 100
  sample of 100
multi-variate probit models 101–102

narrow salary dispersion 127
NASCAR *see* National Association
    for Stock Car Auto Racing
    (NASCAR)
National Association for Stock Car
    Auto Racing (NASCAR) 143
National Basketball Association
    (NBA) 11, 17, 19, 27, 29, 78, 80,
    90, 117–118
    decision-makers 43
    draft in 35, 37, 43
    draft pick 40
    lottery 41
    lottery pick 38, 39
    productivity 38
    sunk-cost effects in 78
National Basketball League (NBL) 14
National Football League (NFL) 10,
    17, 19, 29, 78, 90, 152
    draft in 43
    draft positions 33
    performance 32, 33
    quarterbacks 34
    replacement players 18
    rosters 16
    teams 26
National Hockey League (NHL) 12,
    17, 19, 21, 27, 78, 120, 151
    analyzing salaries in 81
    beneficial effects to 121
national team performances 124
NBA *see* National Basketball
    Association (NBA)
NBL *see* National Basketball League
    (NBL)
NCAA
    basketball 35–36
    tournament 36
negative relationship 141
new brooms sweep clean 173
NFL *see* National Football League
    (NFL)
NFL Players' Association (NFLPA)
    18
NHL *see* National Hockey League
    (NHL)
Nippon Professional Baseball (NPB)
    145, 148, 151
Noel, Nerlens 42
non-cognitive skills 79

non-linear payouts 138
    features of 149
non-sports markets, empirical tests
        from 139–140
North American leagues 130
    clubs in 73–74
North American sports, collective
        bargaining agreements in 130
NPB *see* Nippon Professional Baseball
    (NPB)
Nüesch, Stephan 116–117

OLS *see* ordinary least squares (OLS)
on-base plus slugging (OPS) 101
on-field performance 98
on-the-job performance 4
Oppenheimer 97, 101
opportunistic behavior 92
OPS *see* on-base plus slugging (OPS)
ordinary least squares (OLS)
    coefficient 120
    determinants of annual salary 103,
        104
    estimation 116
    results for determinants of salary 103
Oyer, Paul 2, 19–20

PA *see* plate appearances (PA)
Papps, Kerry L. 114–116
pay 22
    compression 139
    differences for executives 139
    disparity, team-selection effects of
        130
    dispersion-team performance
        126–127
    equity 139
    schemes 8
    structures 125
pay dispersion 125–131, 136–137
    effects of 130, 150, 152
    empirical tests from non-sports
        markets 139–140
    empirical tests from sports markets
        141–153
    specification 141–142
    survey of research 142–153
    impact of changes in 151
    measure of 150
    non-linear effects of 152

and performance in NHL 153–161
testable hypotheses
  fairness model 138–139
  from tournament model 137–138
pay inequality 140
  asymmetric effect of 140
  effects of 140
  justified measure of 129–130
payrolls 154
  dispersion of teams 152
PCTELITE 123–124
Peeters, T. 82–83
'perfect' assortative matching 58
performance 7–9, 22, 76–77, 89
  actual measure of 89
  bonuses 22
  equation 92
  fluctuations 98
  individual and team 130
  in league games 66
  measures of 81
  monetary payoffs on 80
  on-field 98
  potential variability in 1
  of professional athletes 98
  psychological pressure on 80
performance-related pay schemes
  114–115
performance volatility 81
personnel economics
  applications and implications for
    sport 19–20
  collective bargaining agreements
    15
  employer-employee relationship in
    sports 12–13
  employment market in professional
    sports 10–11
  European soccer 19
  incentives, compensation, and
    performance 7–9
  literatures on 74
  models of 7
  performance, pay, and incentives 22
  player drafts 16–17
  player mobility 17–18
  player-owner relations 13–14
  recruiting and hiring 20–21
  recruiting process 1–5
  rival leagues 14–15

  roles of teammate effects and
    management 22–23
  roster size and make-up 16
  team payrolls and individual player
    salaries 18–19
  training and development 5–7,
    21–22
  work teams and role of management
    9–10
personnel functions 15
pertinent data, availability of 73
Pfeffer, Jeffrey 140
PGA Tour 74
piece-rate compensation scheme 8
pitchers 114
  ERA (earned run average) of 115
'Plan B' free agency system 18
plate appearances (PA) 101
player migration
  benefits from 121–125
  on national team performance 125
player-owner relations 13–15
player productivity 38, 40, 41, 43
  spillovers on 113
players 14
  ability, heterogeneity in 115
  birth rates and representation 64
  compensation 88, 115
  data for 137
  development 21
  distribution of 61, 62
  drafts 16–17
  experts evaluate abilities of 83
  free agency, existence of 88
  individual performances 91
  from inferior leagues 123
  labor services, spot market for 99
  labour markets 113
  marginal productivity 48
  market values 171
  mobility 17–18
  performance and availability 101
  performance disparity of 130
  production 98
  salaries and contract length 97
  salary and economic value 30
  services, market price for 99
  shares of 120–121
  values, 'traditional' drivers of 75
  wage premiums to 99–100

player salaries 97, 98, 115, 154
  differences in 75
  disputes 13
  measures of 81
  penalty 9
  in professional sports 74
  significant rise of 95
  'traditional' drivers of 75
players productivity
  spillovers on 113
player valuation and compensation
    73–74
  distribution of income in
      professional sports 74–75
  future paths 81–83
  novel approaches 79–81
  traditional approaches 75–76
    experience 76
    performance 76–77
    popularity 78–79
    talent 77–78
playing squad 130
playing-time 101
popularity 78–79
  indicators of 78
  network externalities of 75
potential performance, dispersion in 2
precise separation of workers 112
pre-employment screening 4
Preston, Anne 123–125
pricing anomalies 82
principal-agent issues 89
principal-agent problem 92
principal-agent theory 90
Prisinzano, R. 58
prize 138
Pro Bowl 78
productivity/production
  equation 156
  levels of 98
  pay dispersion and *see* pay,
      dispersion and productivity
  risk 97
  spillovers 113–116
  standard deviation in 3
  technologies 9
  uncertainty 98, 99
productivity spillovers 113–116
professional athletes, skill levels and
    performance 98

professional golf tournaments
    143
professional ice hockey 90
professional sports, employment
    market in 10–11
property rights 50, 52–53
Pujols, Albert 107

quality improvement 123
quarterbacks 33, 34
  performance of 34

rationality 28–29
  bounded 29
  drafts 28–29
Real Madrid 125
recruiting 20–21
  process 1–5
regression 157, 158
  line 171
  results by pre- and post-lockout
      periods 159, 160–161
  for sub-periods 159
Regulations on the Status and Transfer
    of Players (RSTP)
  youth regulations 53
relative age effects 59–66
relative payroll 142, 156
reserve clause 12
resource dispersion 129
restricted free agency, requirements
    of 17
reverse-order draft 28, 29
risk allocation
  long-term contract as 96
  mechanisms 96–101
risk-averse worker 96
risk management in professional sports
    88–90, 100
  empirical model 101–102
  multi-period contracts and incentive
      issues 90–96
  multi-period contracts as risk
      allocation mechanisms
      96–101
  results and discussion 103–108
risk reallocation 90
risk-sharing model 89
risky workers 5
  advantage to hiring 5

rival leagues 10–11, 14–15
Rosen, S. 9, 74, 75
  'superstar' approaches of 75

salaries 98
  differences in 75
  disputes 13
  measures of 81
  penalty 9
  in professional sports 74
  significant rise of 95
  'traditional' drivers of 75
San Antonio Spurs 40
Sanderson, A. 75
Sauermann, Jan 112
Savage, L. J. 28–29
scapegoat 179
scarcity of franchises 11
Schaefer, S. 2
Schmidt, S. L. 55
screening
  mechanisms 22
  pre-employment 4
Scroggins, J. 91–92
Seitz, Peter 18
selection bias 99
shirking 90, 97
  costs of 95
  evidence of 91, 94
  literature on 90
  in principal-agent models 90
  problems 93
  tests in baseball 94
  tests of 94–95
signaling, concept of 2
Simmons, Ben 42
Simmons, R. 32–34, 78, 129, 130
skills
  athletic 11
  coaching 142
  firm-specific 7
  general 7
  'laboratory' tests 66
  leadership 79–80
  non-cognitive 79
  sport-related 21–22
soccer
  European professional 19, 47–49
  European youth 48, 49
  German 47

players 61, 62, 64
  youth *see* youth soccer
soccer players
  birth rates and representation 64
  distribution of 61, 62
soccer-related human capital 47
social cohesiveness of workgroup
  6
social exchange theory 138
social psychology 138
solidarism mechanism 53
Spence, M. 2
sport-related skills 21–22
sports
  applications and implications for
    19–23
  clubs 21
  economics literature 144–148
  personnel decisions in 15–19
  personnel economics *see* personnel
    economics
  professional 10–15
sports markets 137
  empirical tests from 141
    specification 141–142
    survey of research 142–153
squad 117
  composition of 181
standardized wages 140
Starting with Bloom 125
Staw, B. M. 78
strategic behavior 90, 92, 94, 95
  evidence of 95
  tests of 94
structural equation model 120
summary statistics 103

talent 77–78
  differences in 78
talent identification and development
  (TID) 47, 48, 65
  drop-out rates during 48–49
  expenses for clubs' investments in
    52
  investment of clubs in 56
  policies and investments 49
  processes 59–61
  soccer clubs regarding 50
Tannehill, Ryan 31
Tao, Yu-Li 128

team
  control group of 173
  data for 137
  managers 129
  owners 12
  production 9, 156
  quality 129
  'resource value' of 129
  salary standard deviation 155
  sports industry 168
teammates
  performances of 115
  pitching performance 114
  productivity of 115
  spillovers 113, 115
team payrolls 18–19, 130, 142
  graphs of 154
team performance 116, 125–131,
    170
  alternative measures of 121
  beneficial to 130
  negative effect on 128–129
  productivity spillovers on 113
tennis 143, 149
testable hypotheses
  fairness model 138–139
  from tournament model 137–138
Thaler, Richard H. 29–31, 34
TID *see* talent identification and
    development (TID)
tournament model 9, 136–140, 151,
    155
  predictions for 137
  tests of 142–143
tournament-style compensation
    scheme 137
tournament-style process 11
tournament theory
  aspect of 149
  extension of 128
traditional drivers, categorizing 76
traditional education 55
traditional life cycle model 48
training 5–7, 21–22
  compensation fees 53, 54
  types of 5, 6
training academy 47, 50, 52, 55, 56–59,
    65, 66
training and development (T&D) 5
transferability, lack of 12

Trax, Michaela 112
Turner, C. 99

UEFA
  Champions League 119
  rankings 122
unconditional negative relationship 150
United States Football League (USFL)
    11, 14
USFL *see* United States Football
    League (USFL)

Veblen, Thorstein 28
'vicious circle' explanation 179
vocational training 55

wage
  compression 138
  differentials 77
  dispersion 140
  effort hypothesis 136
  premium 80
  premiums 99–100
Walters, S. J. K. 100–101, 106
WAR *see* wins-above-replacement
    (WAR)
WARP *see* wins above replacement
    player (WARP)
Weimar, D. 81
WHA *see* World Hockey Association
    (WHA)
'white-collar' workers 140
Wicker, P. 81
Wiggins, Andrew 35–36, 38
windfall payoff 11
'winner-take-all' market characteristics
    55
wins-above-replacement (WAR) 77
  concept of 77
wins above replacement player
    (WARP) 100–106
  measures of performance 101
Winter-Ebmer, Rudolf 140
Winter, Eyal 113, 114
wisdom of crowds 82–83
within-team dispersion 155
Women's Tennis Association 149
workgroup, social cohesiveness of 6
work teams 9–10
World Hockey Association (WHA) 14

Yellen, Janet L. 138–140
youth academy, quality and reputation
    of 59
youth elite soccer education,
    differentiating factor in 54
youth group selection 66
youth recruitment
  implications for 49
  process 47–48
youth soccer
  academy, economics objectives of 57
  competitions in Europe 60

development 50
education, matching processes in 57
personnel economics of 57
youth teams, proportion of 61
youth/young players
  decision-making processes of 58
  development of 50
  financial compensation of 52
  performance of 59
  soccer, labor market for 55

Zweimüller, Josef 140